DD 522: Diary Of A Destroyer

*The action saga of the USS Luce from
the Aleutian and Philippine Campaigns
to her sinking off Okinawa*

DD 522 USS Luce (official photograph).

USS Luce enroute to Leyte Gulf mid-October 1944 in convoy to invade the Philippines. Taken from the conning tower of USS LST 1013 and probably the last picture of DD 522.

(Courtesy J.C. Phillips)

DD 522: Diary Of A Destroyer

*The action saga of the USS Luce from
the Aleutian and Philippine Campaigns
to her sinking off Okinawa*

By Ron Surels

A Valley Graphics, Inc. Book
Plymouth, New Hampshire
1•9•9•6

Second Edition
MARCH 1996

Copyright © 1994 by Ron Surels. All rights reserved. No part of this publication may be reproduced, transmitted, transcribed, or translated into any language in any form by any means including information storage and retrieval systems without the written permission of Ron Surels, except by a reviewer, who may quote brief passages in a review.

Published by:
Valley Graphics, Inc.
Route 25, Box 1950
Plymouth, NH 03264-1950
603-536-2020

Published and printed
in the
UNITED STATES OF AMERICA

Library of Congress Catalog Card Number: 94-61657
ISBN 0-9643403-0-5

First Edition printed November 1994

This book is dedicated to those who served in the U.S. Armed Forces in World War II. May what they sacrificed be an inspiration to youth today, who are awash in the darkness of our current history, and who desperately need to know of greatness past to emulate for their future.

The Ballad of the *Luce*
William R. Fotie

In 1943, at New York's Staten Island firth,
A man-o-war, called *Luce* was given birth.
She bristled with armament all up-to-date,
Luce! What is your destiny? What is your fate?

From North Atlantic to the dance in Port o'Spain
Thru Panama's passage to Pearl's harbor of pain.
Sailing and learning, aye, learning each day.
Prepare and make ready for the destined fray.

"Now hear this all hands. here's a fighting band!
We'll sail north. Yes north, to that icy cold land.
Dodging frothing mountains of water that be,
Tumulting down on us in that cold, cold sea.

The night of our baptism in the Kurile chain
Our guns did the job, then more of the same.
From Arctic thru Pacific islands we're found.
Guns firing often toward sky and the ground.

"Tween watch, sitting on deck or just around,
Talking about the sweet times that we'd found.
Listening to those tall liberty stories unfurl,
And hearing (or telling) lies 'bout that girl.

Entwining our lives with shipmates that care.
Remembering times bad, and good times so fair.
Battle thoughts shared, close friendships grew
And speaking of ports, where we lifted a few.

Given the job to help free the Philippine nation,
We did our job well and earned a citation.
But asking again, what's our destiny and fate?
Okinawa, we knew, was quite dangerous a date.

Among ships that have died battling at sea,
This gallant destroyer lives in ship's history.
Did any fight harder, braver? Odds with the foe?
They that were there wouldn't have believed so.

Each sailor performed, with all that he had.
Each doing his duty - and real fightin' mad.
But in final chapter, we just couldn't prevail.
Our *Luce* pointed skyward. End destiny's trail.

Dear shipmates, gone in the way of the sea,
You're not forgotten by country or we.
You responded well to your nation's crisis
And ultimately paid the highest prices.

One thing is certain. We paid liberty's debt.
Fought in most seven seas - better bet!
Spirits of sailors from ages gone by,
Must peer down, nod their heads and say "Aye".

Perhaps some late night, at rest by the sea.
A sleek shape drifts by, so well known to me.
I'll wave my arms and shout a greeting.
My heart will leap at the thought of meeting.
And I'll know, as the shape comes into view.
I see. Oh yes, I see! Look! On the Bow...522!

Eternal Father, strong to save,
Whose arms doth bind the restless wave,
Who bidst the mighty ocean deep
It's own appointed limits keep:
O hear us when we cry to thee
To those in peril on the sea.

O Trinity of love and power,
Our brethren shield in danger's hour;
From rock and tempest, fire and foe,
Protect them where-soe'er they go;
And ever let there rise to thee
Glad hymns of praise on land and sea.

(Old Navy hymn, verses 1 & 4)

CONTENTS

Foreword x
Author's Preface xiii
Contributors to this book xvi

Part One: *The Beginnings*
Chapter One: Commissioning and Shakedown 3
Chapter Two: Getting Underway 11

Part Two: *The Aleutians — First Blood*
Chapter Three: "A Most Depressing Experience" 20
Chapter Four: Battling the "Williwaws" 30
Chapter Five: The First Raid On Paramushiro 39
Chapter Six: More Raids-and Liberty! 50
Chapter Seven: "A Chance To See the Sun Again" 60

Part Three: *The Philippines-The Action Intensifies*
Chapter Eight: Supporting the Invasion 69
Chapter Nine: Leisure, Recreation-and Kamikazes 76

Part Four: *Okinawa-The Final Cruise*
Chapter Ten: Patrolling the Picket Line 94
Chapter Eleven: 4 May 1945-"Bogies Circling!" 107
Chapter Twelve: Kamikaze Attack 113
Chapter Thirteen: The Carnage 129
Chapter Fourteen: "Abandon Ship!" 139
Chapter Fifteen: In The Water 151
Chapter Sixteen: Rescue and Home 162
Epilogue 175
Aftermath 183
Glossary 190

Appendices
A. *Luce* Statistics 192
B. Telegrams and Letters 193
C. Destroyers Lost in World War II 197
D. USS *Luce* Casualty List 198
E. About the Author 204
Bibliography 205
Index 206

FOREWORD

When I was asked to write the foreword for a book about the *Luce* my thoughts went back to the first time I ever heard the word. It was at the Naval Academy in Annapolis where I had just become a Midshipman. One of the academic buildings was named for the scholarly naval officer, Rear Admiral Stephen B. Luce. In the four-story building of gray stone on the banks of the Severn River the Midshipmen were instructed in seamanship, navigation, leadership and the foreign languages of French and Spanish.

This book tells the story of a gallant World War II destroyer from her early days in the Atlantic. It is a comprehensive and authoritative narrative. It is told in the words of the men who manned her. It is vivid history packed with numerous acts of heroism.

Like other destroyers, she had a nucleus crew of experienced officers and petty officers. They arrived at the shipyard a few weeks before she was completed. Most of her crew, however, were new men fresh from recruit training or the Navy's schools. The officers and the nucleus crew trained the men in their duties. The ship's "shakedown" training in Guantanamo Bay, Cuba, and also in Casco Bay, Maine, was invaluable in getting her crew to work together as a team.

Some weeks after joining the fleet she escorted the new aircraft carrier *Intrepid* to Trinidad. A short time later she went through the Panama Canal to join the Pacific Fleet. The *Luce* proceeded to Bremerton, Washington. She was ordered to escort the veteran aircraft carrier *Enterprise* to Pearl Harbor where she reported to her new boss, Commander of the Destroyer's Pacific Fleet. He required new ships from the Atlantic to conduct a series of training exercises. While destroyers in the Atlantic were mainly engaged in anti-submarine warfare those in the Pacific also had to become proficient in anti-aircraft warfare and shore bombardment to support amphibious landings. Before going into the war zone destroyers had to hone their skills by firing at sleeves towed by aircraft and by firing both day and night at targets on a small island. Once she had completed the course satisfactorily the *Luce* was ordered to head north to the Aleutian Islands.

The *Luce* (DD 522) operated in the Adak area at first, mostly in anti-submarine patrol. Two days before New Year's eve she arrived in Dutch Harbor. Tradition has it that the log in ships of our Navy for the first four hours of the New Year shall be written in rhyme. Some of the crew of the *Luce* greeted 1944 in an untraditional manner that created havoc ashore.

During her operations in the Aleutians the *Luce* participated in bombardments of Japanese islands on three occasions. After nine months in that area she was ordered to San Francisco for ten days where she was painted with a new camouflage pattern.

The *Luce* then went on to the Philippines where she participated in the landing of our troops on Leyte Island when General MacArthur announced his return. The Japanese high command had now become so desperate it launched its kamikaze suicide attacks on our ships. The *Luce* was unharmed in the Philippines.

Ordered to Okinawa, she arrived in late March, 1945. She had taken aboard three fighter director officers and was immediately ordered onto the ring of fourteen pickets that surrounded the island to give early radar warning to ships present of the approach of enemy planes.

Each of the kamikazes carried a bomb. In addition to the exploding bomb there was always a flood of burning gasoline to fight. My own destroyer, the USS *Laffey*, had withstood a prolonged attack eighteen days earlier. In our ship there was anxiety within the crew, as there was aboard the *Luce*, as to when the kamikazes would strike. I had implicit faith in our gunners but I wondered if they would be good enough. Aboard the *Luce* there may have been similar questions. Her gunners had demonstrated their skill as late as 10 April in shooting down an enemy bomber. Certainly that performance should have reassured any doubters.

The interviews the author had with the men of the *Luce* indicated the degree of worry on the minds of some of the crew. As the ship was sinking it is sickening to read of the man paralyzed by fear and frozen onto the ship's rail. A shipmate stamped on his knuckles and pulled his hair to get him to let go but without success.

Although Japanese pilots strafed the men in the water, Marine Corsair pilots drove them off. They circled those in the water until they were rescued. I learned from another source that the men picked up by the light minelayer Henry A Wiley faced double jeopardy. They had no sooner arrived on board when a kamikaze came zooming in. Fortunately a Marine Corsair pilot saw him and shot him down. The pilot circled the ship twice to acknowledge the joyous shouts, the waving and boxer-like overhead handshakes.

At the time the *Luce* went down the devastating effects of the kamikaze crashes were withheld from the public. We did not want the Japanese to know how effective they were, although some leaked out in the press. Most books about kamikaze have been by prominent historians. Not so with this one. This book is an authentic firsthand account told by her crew. It is a worthy addition to those accounts that have revealed the hideous type of warfare to which the Japanese resorted in the final days of World War II.

Rear Admiral F. Julian Becton, USN, Ret.
Cherry Lane - Wynnewood, PA

AUTHOR'S PREFACE

This book is about a destroyer and its heroic crew which saw a brief twenty-three months of service in World War II before being sunk by a murderous kamikaze attack. Half the crew was lost. The material for this account was taken almost entirely from taped interviews of survivors of that attack. Other material came from family members of those who did not survive. In these pages the men of the USS *Luce*, DD 522, reveal their love for their ship as they relate in their own words the hardships and good times, life aboard ship, liberties, and the tragedy of the ship's demise. I have taken the liberty of some editing of their statements for the sake of clarity, but even then as little as possible so as to preserve individual expression and thought. My editing has also included anesthetizing some of the language so that youth, as well as adults, can enjoy this story without embarrassment. But even this was very minor as most reports were given with proper respect to propriety. I do not feel the need of "proving" my literary manhood by inclusion of foul language and immoral scenes. As I state in my dedication, I want this book to hopefully be an inspiration to our youth. There is plenty of the gruesome reality of life—and death—in this account. Anyone who may think they need a baser story can find reams of such material elsewhere in our corrupt society. But not here. I seek a higher plane of decency in which to present this epic of human courage and sacrifice. To do less would, for me, take away from and debase the tribute this book seeks to help bestow upon those who gave their all. The men of this book and all who served aboard DD 522 are genuine heroes. They represent the spirit of the greatness and sacrifice of all American fighting men. Hence it is that their story deserves to be told with decency and honor. However, the reader need not fear. The men portrayed here are seen as real people, with real fears, thoughts, enjoyments and difficulties. There is plenty of laughter, suspense, horror and tragedy. So enjoy—and be thankful for what they did for us as you read this sea story.

Almost to a man the people I interviewed for this narrative lament what has happened to their country since World War II. They fear that we have lost something precious in these intervening years. Some felt that we look too much to government today to solve our problems. Others feel that the decline of Godly Christian principles in society has spawned the aimlessness of the younger generation. Still others feel that we are losing our country today because we are swapping our freedoms for security—a false security promised by government. I heard somewhere that while the politicians often destroy our freedoms, it is the fighting men and women who actually gave them to us and continue to preserve them for us. The men of the USS *Luce*, like all their counterparts, have certainly helped to do that.

I first became interested in writing the story of the crew of the USS *Luce* upon meeting Freeman Phillips, S1/c, one of the survivors of the ship's sinking. After attending with him the 1992 *Luce* reunion in Philadelphia I came away knowing that I just had to write their story. The men and families at the reunion kept me busy day and night as they poured out their experiences into my tape recorder. I am deeply indebted to their cooperation not only at that reunion but in further contacts and research made over many following months. I was impressed to see that their common war experience had welded them together into a life-long commitment. I felt privileged to be able to tell their story, and it became like a "sacred honor" with me. Being a history buff, I also wanted to record a small piece of history that would not be told unless someone wrote about it. As veterans of World War II "take their liberty" of this world, what they have lived through and experienced in one of the most eventful times of our country—and of the world—will be lost to us forever unless it is set down and recorded. These veterans have many insightful anecdotes to enrich our understanding of a period of history which is becoming more remote with every passing year. We need to be about the business of capturing as much of their experience as possible in the short time left to do so.

I deeply appreciate Rear Admiral (Ret.) F. Julian Becton's writing of the foreword. I was privileged to meet him at the Philadelphia reunion. He was commander of a destroyer also at Okinawa at about the same time as the *Luce*. His ship, the USS *Laffey*, had the distinction of sustaining the most kamikaze hits without sinking. The story is aptly told in his book, "The Ship That Would Not Die."

I have followed the chronology of the Daily Deck Log Summary and the various battle reports and war diaries and have aligned the crew's testimonies in proximity with them as much as possible in order to present an accurate linear account of happenings. Every attempt has been made to contact all survivors and relatives of survivors of the ship. This has resulted in over sixty persons who have contributed information for the book. The contributors of this epistle have been most helpful and it goes without saying that this book could not have become a reality without them. It is their story in their words. I have come to know and appreciate these men—and their families—for who they are and what they represent.

A special thanks is due Freeman Phillips for his many hours of help. He has assisted me in the research and has reviewed the manuscript from the viewpoint of a crewman who was there. And I owe to my wife, Lynne, a debt of encouragement and love for the sacrifice of time allowed to do the work. She has been a loyal and stabilizing influence.

Great pains have been taken to insure the accuracy of the details and incidents. I offer my sincere apology for any errors which may be found. This book is a mosaic piece of our history, but more it is an attempt to memorialize the men of DD 522, especially those who are still at "General Quarters", as typical of American fighting men through the years. If the few accounts we have recorded here are able to shed some appreciation and insight onto a desperate time in our country's fighting history, that is good. But if we have been able to weave together a lasting memory as an example of sacrifice needed to preserve our liberty, then I think that we have accomplished something very worthwhile indeed.

Ron Surels
Hebron, NH

xvi DD 522: Diary Of A Destroyer

Contributors To This Book

Donald Allen, LT
Bert D. Alton, Jr., CRM
Joseph J. Bille, RT2/c
Thomas G. Blanck, Y1/c
Earl Blanton, GM3/c
Donald Brockhoff, TM3/c
William Burns, MoMM1/c
Ernest Carpenter, WT2/c
John A. Carpenter, WT2/c
Milton Cathey, BM2/c
Anthony DeFrank, Jr., WT3/c
Omer Emond, S1/c
Norman Foland, MoMM2/c
William Fotie, RM3/c
James M. Gory, WT3/c
George V. Graul, WT2/c
Leo Greco, SM1/c
Robert Harrison, RM2/c
Michael Heon, MoMM3/c
Orville Hiles, S1/c
Melvin Hubbard, TM1/c
Joseph Huss, Jr., QM3/c
John Hutchinson, LT
Waino Johnson, GM1/c
Cliff C. Jones, LT
William V. Lietz, TM2/c
Thomas Lynch, LT
Anthony Marchitelli, GM3/c
Thomas Matisak, RdM3/c
John McCormick, S1/c
Burr McFarland, WT1/c
Joseph McGuigan, RM3/c
Manuel Medeiros, F1/c
Derry O. Moll, LT
Robert F. Moyer, FC3/c
Martin J. Nyholt, FC2/c
Tom Parkerson, LT

Freeman Phillips, S1/c
James C. Phillips, SC1/c
Gerald Purdue, MoMM1/c
Arthur S. Replogle, LT
Clifford A. Roberts, CFC
Frank E. Scudder, ENS
Dr. Louis Shaffner, LT
Harry E. Snyder, LT
Robert E. Stanley, S1/c
Kenneth Sturm, TM2/c
Donald Sweeten, SoM2/c
LeGrand Van Uitert, CFC
Clarence J. Vanness, MM2/c
Paul Wallace, F1/c
John R. Welsh, LT
Art Whitney, MM1/c

Family members of deceased crew:
Val Appicelli
Robert Burns
Mrs. Vernon C. Downs
Mrs. Richard Flaum
Mrs. Hershel Freeman
Mrs. Walter C. Fischer
Anne Lavery
Elise Huss
Vincent Interlande
Francis A. Malinowski, Jr.
Joseph Powers

And the five sisters of Arthur Powers, S1/c:
Helen Brandt, Joan DeFlorio, Marilyn Delaney, Lorraine Gallipoli, Ethel Scanlon.

PART ONE: THE BEGINNINGS

1943 began the second full year of U.S. military involvement in World War II. The year began with President Roosevelt and Prime Minister Churchill meeting with military leaders at Casablanca to plan, among other things, relief for the Soviets from the pressure of the German invasion of Russia via military action in the Mediterranean. The Casablanca Conference also adopted a policy of "unconditional surrender" of the Axis powers. When the ten day conference ended on 24 January the two Allied powers had further agreed to concentrate fully on winning the European war. This policy of "Europe first" was to continue, at the expense of the Pacific theatre, until Germany was defeated. The result was that the U.S. forces in the Pacific had to wage their war with limited resources for quite some time.

On 30 January 1943 the first daylight bombing of Berlin was made by the British Air Force; and on 2 February the Battle of Stalingrad ended with the surrender of the decimated German troops around that city. In the Pacific, the six-months long battle for Guadalcanal ended with the dissipation of Japanese resistance on 7 February. Along with the devastation of the Japanese Task Force at Midway the previous June, this began the long and slow defeat of Japan. The Battle of the Bismark Sea, fought off the New Guinea coast on 24 March, further weakened Japanese naval strength with the destruction of a large portion of their task force. And almost simultaneously with the end of resistance in Tunisia half a world away on 12 May, thereby securing all of Africa for the Allies, U.S. Forces landed 11 May on Attu in the Aleutians. From that moment on and for the next year the U.S. Navy would conduct combat operations against the enemy from Aleutian waters to the northernmost islands of the Japanese home land. A few weeks after the landing on Attu, a small new ship which was to join with the task force operating in the cold Aleutian waters was commissioned at the Brooklyn Navy Yard. It was a destroyer of the Fletcher class, DD 522, named the USS *Luce*. After its outfitting and shakedown cruise through the Panama Canal, the USS *Luce* set out from Pearl Harbor to join the task force in the Aleutians—two days after U.S. Marines waded ashore at Tarawa on 20 November 1943.

CHAPTER 1

COMMISSIONING AND SHAKEDOWN

The USS *Luce* (DD 522) was named for Rear Admiral Stephen B. Luce, who was a leader in Navy affairs during his time. Born on 25 March 1827, Luce entered the Navy on 19 October 1841 as a midshipman. During the Civil War, he first served with the Atlantic Coast Blockaders, and then commanded the monitor Nantucket during the siege of Charleston, SC. Luce became supervisor of the Department of Seamanship at the Naval Academy, and wrote one of the first seamanship texts used by the Academy. After the war, Luce established a program for the training of seaman and was almost single-handedly responsible for the establishment of the Naval War College at Newport, RI on 6 October 1884.[1]

The USS *Luce*, which is the subject of this book, was the second destroyer to be so named. The first USS *Luce*, DD 99, was built in Quincy, Massachusetts, and was launched on 29 June 1918. The second, USS *Luce*, DD 522, was built by Bethlehem Steel Company at Staten Island, NY. The keel was laid down on 24 August 1942. At the launching on 6 March 1943, DD 522 was sponsored by a relative of Rear Admiral Luce—his grandson's wife, Mrs. Stephen B. Luce, Jr. Commander Donald C. Varian took charge of the ship at its commissioning on 21 June 1943.[2] Born on 7 March 1902, Varian was graduated from the Naval Academy in 1925. He

---

[1] Dictionary of American Naval Fighting Ships. Vol. IV, pp. 157-158.
[2] Op. Cit.

remained commander of the *Luce* until transferred on 22 November 1943[3]. Lt. John Welsh remembers Varian as a "flamboyant 'hell–for–leather' guy, very much beloved of the men. This was probably because he would reprimand officers in front of the men. But he was a very capable officer in many ways." J.C. Phillips, SC1/c, recalls Captain Varian as "a tough old boy–but he knew what we were going to face. He set the pace, and it rippled down through such officers as Nat Pierce and John Welsh and others who drilled the men into being first–rate sailors. (Lt. Alvah N. Pierce was the Executive Officer at that time.) And there was one chief, Armond Beausoliel, who was one of the few men who had some good battle experience. When he said something, the men listened. It was as good or better than the Captain saying it. The men also looked up to their divisional officers and the chiefs. Even though some men didn't particularly like them, they were respected. They had the most experience."

Throughout the country from various Navy bases and schools, men were receiving orders to report to the Navy base at Brooklyn, New York, for assignment on the *Luce*. Tom Matisak, RdM3/c, was sent from boot camp in Sampson, NY to Virginia Beach to radar school:

"We stayed at the Cavalier Hotel for the six weeks of training in radar. An elegant hotel. Top grade food, everything. We wanted to stay there for the duration. But the ship was being commissioned, and needed some radar men, so we were sent to the USS *Luce* in Brooklyn in June, 1943."

Lt. Clifford Jones, who had been a seamanship instructor in Chicago, was ordered to the USS *Luce* and also came aboard in early June:

"I reported to the executive officer who was Nat Pierce. He called in Don Allen and introduced us. Pierce said, 'First thing I want you to do is to count the number of pad–eyes'. This was a type of hook used for various things. I was ready to start out and Lt. Allen said, 'Let's go out on the fantail and have a cigarette'. I said, 'Don, don't you think we ought to get started?' He replied, 'Oh, forget it. Pierce doesn't know how many there are. We'll just make up a number and he'll be satisfied.' Don was a very smart lawyer from New York…We waited awhile and Don went back to

---
[3] Op. Cit.

Pierce and reported some number and the executive officer took that as being OK. The next day I was told I was to be in charge of the deck gang. So I said to the gang, 'Let's swab down this deck it's getting dirty.' Then to my utter chagrin, I said, 'Do you know where the mops are kept?' One of the men asked, 'What's a mop, Mr. Jones?' And I realized instantly that I had used the wrong term. So I didn't get off to a good start."

On 30 June a pilot came on board to guide the *Luce* to lower New York Bay in order to proceed with the rather dangerous chore of taking on ammunition. Begun before dawn the next day, the chore was completed in time for the ship to weigh anchor and sail on to Newport, RI. There the *Luce* took on torpedoes, and left for Guantanamo Bay, Cuba, to begin her shakedown cruise. While at Guantanamo the ship took on two more crew members. They were Bill Lietz and Russ Miller, both seaman second class. The *Luce* now had almost her full compliment of three hundred twenty-eight men and officers. The next several days until about 25 July the *Luce* conducted shakedown exercises out of Guantanamo. These exercises were not without some difficult adjustment for the men. An example is given by the ship's medical doctor, Lt. Louis Schaffner:

"The shakedown was difficult for everybody and some of us thought that in some ways it was due to the personality of the Captain and the executive officer. The Captain (Varian) was a full commander and rumor was that he had received his assignment somewhat against his will and, he thought, beneath his ability. It might have been because of some action that he had taken previously that did not set well with higher authorities. In any event, he had a temper and was not consistent in his orders or care of the crew. I realize now that he really had a job trying to train this civilian Navy crew. The executive officer whom he chose was also a civilian who had not had much experience. The exec was really caught in the middle. In any event, the matters which I now mention occurred during the shakedown period, which lasted until we got to Hawaii. I got the feeling that the Captain somewhat resented the fact that I could not stand watch and that he could not really give me any orders of a medical nature. Therefore, I was somewhat a guest along for the ride. He thought I was young and wet behind the ears, which I was, and he was not very hospitable.

"One time someone picked up a stray cat and brought it on board. This cat seemed to pick out two places on the ship to use as a litter box. One was under the sofa in the wardroom and the other was under the number one gun on the bow of the ship. It was a little unpleasant and difficult to clean up. And it didn't seem to be a very sanitary condition. I made the comment to one of the officers that I wondered if the Captain knew there was a cat aboard. I didn't think much about it until one evening, while I was sitting on the forecastle watching a movie, the mess boy came up and said the Captain wanted to see me in the wardroom. When I got there the Captain was sitting with his shirt off and his hair somewhat messed up. Obviously he had been over to the Officers Club. He looked up at me and said, 'I hear you don't like the cat being aboard ship.' I said, 'I didn't say that, Captain. I just wondered if you knew that there was a cat aboard.' He shot back, 'You're damn right I know there's a cat aboard and if I want it aboard I'll have it aboard and if you don't like it you can write a letter to the Bureau of Medicine and Surgery about it but you have to forward it through me!'

"Of course my only reply was, 'Aye, aye sir.' And that was it. I did learn later that one of the younger officers did stand up for me and explained that I was not complaining but just wanted to know if he knew that the cat was aboard. The Captain later acknowledged that difference to me."

As the months of shakedown passed by the men became more at ease with their ship. Somewhere along the way DD 522 picked up the name "*Lady Luce*" from her crew. Men and ship were being knit together in a bond that would prove its mettle in the months of action yet to come. As Bob Harrison, RM2/c, put it:

"We put the ship in commission, most of us did. And most of us put the ship out of commission the hard way. For just about two years we did it together. We trained together. I think that's the distinction between us and some of the other ships. I'm not saying we were the only ones, but this was a ship in which most of the crew was together during all of the *Luce*'s active life. They gave the ship life."

At a reunion years later, James C. Phillips, SC1/c would look back to these early days and echo what Bob Harrison felt:

"The crew gave the ship its life. When the commissioning crew went aboard the ship, it was just a hunk of steel, cold steel, in the Bethlehem Field Yards in New York. It had just been put together by the work crew. Now the crew coming aboard put life into the ship. They turned the first switch that started the first electric motor. They started the first steam generator down in the fire room... that generated the first electrical current that flowed through the wires. We generated the power that turned the screws that moved it the first inch and foot from the dock. We took it to sea. All this green crew, and most of us with little or no experience. Never seen an ocean, some of us. We took it into its initial baptism of fire. Not only the ship's initial baptism, but for most of us, it was our first action as well. There were very few in the crew who had seen action."

As the men put the ship through its paces and became familiar with its personality, the feeling grew that this was indeed a fine and sturdy ship, ready for whatever came its way. The crew was becoming highly trained and ready to fix anything that might malfunction. As Bob Harrison, RM2/c, recalls:

"From the day of the commissioning, I don't remember a major breakdown of any equipment on that ship. If anything happened, the crew had the expertise to fix it. A pump went out—it was fixed in no time. Same with the communication gear. We had excellent technicians."

Ken Sturm, TM2/c, and Freeman Phillips, S1/c, recall an interesting break in the daily routine off the shores of Cuba. As Ken relates:

"I remember catching sharks off the coast of Cuba... We had a very difficult time hooking them, but when we did, sometimes the hook would tear the side right out of their face, but they would come right back again... we finally hooked one and brought it up. We used big chunks of meat for bait."

Freeman continues:

"All the guys stabbed the shark... I never saw so many knives go into a fish in my life! They cut the head off, and threw the rest of the body overboard, and it was devoured just like that! Some of the guys kept the teeth of the shark."

Ken Sturm:

"I remember one of the men straddled the shark and drove the kitchen knife into it. All that meat... I don't know how much, but

I thought about meatless Tuesday back home, and here we were, putting big chunks of meat on a hook to catch sharks."

During this time of adjusting and getting used to each other and developing the ship's routine, the medical officer, Lt. Louis Schaffner, was still trying to figure out the relationship between himself and the Captain:

"In Guantanamo (Cuba) one night the mess boy came down and woke me up... and handed a paper to me and made a comment that the Captain wanted me to examine all fish caught aboard the ship for venereal disease. I asked the mess boy to repeat that and he did. Then I read the note which was really a routine harbormaster communique to all ships in the harbor that the harbor water was contaminated and that the fish caught aboard from the harbor were not to be used for food. The Captain was just being picayunish about it by waking me up with that statement about the disease."

Lt. Cliff Jones was also having his troubles:

"On one trial shakedown I had a large board with perhaps hundreds of keys on it. I was to pass out the keys to any who asked for one. When they brought the keys back I was to hang them on the proper hook. As a Princeton grad that seemed a simple enough task, but I hadn't realized that the board was not secured and also not realized what violent maneuvers the Captain was going to take the ship through to see what it could do. I sat there happily handing out keys to dozens of men. After we were out awhile, the ship took a violent turn port and that board went toppling and the keys scattered all over the deck in that room. I had not an idea where they all belonged on the board. I tried to put them back on the hooks where I thought they might belong. When the men came back with their keys, I put them on whatever hooks I had left. I thought this might get me a court–martial. As it turned out no one ever asked for keys again and the board was put back and I never heard another thing about it.

"I was also damage control officer. I knew where all the equipment was. During the shakedown we had several tests on damage. This took place off Long Island Sound and out in the Atlantic. The Captain would call down and say, 'We've taken a hit at locker so and so... ' The petty officer under me was a shipfitter called Napoli (Anthony, SF1/c), who by the way, did not survive our sinking. I liked him very much. Napoli and I and our crew would run to where the hit was announced and break out the axes, fire extinguishers, and so forth. Each time we did this our time improved, but the Captain would say, 'That's not good enough.' So the time came when we were to be tested by Naval officials who came on board. Napoli and I cooked up this little scheme and unbeknownst to anyone else we unsecured all the damage control equipment from their moorings and had them handily available in the various locations so we would not have to waste time doing them. Of course, we were in calm waters. If we hadn't been they would have been scattered all over the place, so we probably should not have done that. But we did. When the time came that we were notified we had taken a hit somewhere for the test, Napoli and our crew got there so quickly and our equipment ready in such good time that we earned a 'well done'."

Completing a series of training tests, the *Luce* set course for Portland, Maine. Gunnery practice was a priority in these early days, and Lt. Shaffner remembers one incident connected with an exercise off the coast of Maine:

"We were out having gunnery practice right after noon and it turned out that this one gun mount was individually shooting at the vessel that was towing the target rather than at the target. I was in the wardroom at the time and suddenly over the loudspeaker came 'Doctor—lay up to the bridge!' When I got up there the Captain said that the head of that gun crew must be drunk, and he must be drinking on board ship because liberty was over at 0100 last night and here it was past noon and he couldn't be drunk for over twelve hours. He must be taught a lesson. I asked the Captain what he wanted me to do and he stated that he wanted me to give the gunner a tumbler full of castor oil. I said, 'Captain, that's a mighty big dose.' He asked, 'What will it do to him?' I said that I didn't know, but it might kill him. Then I screwed up my courage and said, 'Captain, generally speaking I don't like to use medicine as a disciplinary measure.' There was silence for a minute. Then the Captain scoured at me and said, 'Well, what do you think I ought to do?' I replied that I could give him some aspirin and pump out his stomach, but that we really couldn't do anything but let him sober up, which would take some time. The Captain then said, 'Well, you handle it. You handle it.'

"So there I was, and that's what we did. We let him sober up. I think the Captain realized that I had the upper hand on that decision, because he couldn't force me to give the man castor oil against my medical judgment. The policy for using medicine for disciplinary measures was not good and I had the guts to say so, though I did it with some apprehension at the time. I really feel that after that he respected me more, but he still was not overly friendly. I always got the feeling that the fact that I was the only one aboard who had control of the brandy which was in the medical supplies upset him—also that I could give that out but nobody else aboard could legally have liquor without my permission."

As the men continued through their shakedown period, they began to develop a deeper appreciation for the ship's agility and firepower. For most of the crew now aboard, the USS *Luce* would be their 'home' for the almost two years of the ship's service. And for almost half of the men their destiny would forever be entwined with the destroyer known as DD 522. But the foreboding clouds of that time were not yet on the horizon as confident crew and proud ship raced through warm and bright sunny days of eager preparation and practice.

CHAPTER 2

GETTING UNDERWAY

From Casco Bay (Portland), Maine, the ship sailed for Boston, where she escorted the Queen Mary to Halifax, Nova Scotia. Then it was back to Maine and the familiar waters of Casco Bay on 12 August '43 where the crew gratefully received on board some 300 pounds of fresh fish from local fishermen.[1] During this time, inspection parties came aboard on 13 and 16 August, and favorably commented on the condition of the ship. Then it was on to Brooklyn Navy Yard on 17 August '43 for several more days of outfitting and preparation. While in Brooklyn, shore leave was granted two consecutive times for about 100 men each. Several additional crew members were also added. And once again, the waters of lower New York Bay lapped against the sides of the *Luce* as she took on additional ammunition supplies.

From New York, the *Luce* departed for Norfolk, VA, stopping off at Newport, RI for two days before arriving at Norfolk on 7 September. During the next month, the *Luce* conducted various exercises off the Virginia coast. Again, several men were added to the ship's roster to pretty much complete the crew before setting course for Trinidad. On the way to this British West Indies port, the *Luce* escorted the aircraft carrier, USS *Intrepid*. The *Luce* anchored in Trinidad just long enough for Bill Fotie, RM2/c, to join the crew. It was during the layover in Trinidad that one of the ship's cooks, James C. Phillips, finally learned to make bread, but

---
[1] Daily Log Summary

not without some difficulty:

"I was the ship's cook, second class, when I went aboard. My battle station was 20 millimeter #5 Gun on the fantail. I was assigned to duties as a gun captain back there. It requires the services of ten men to operate the three 20 millimeters, three on each gun, and one to tork up the spare magazines. The tork man was Urstle Keck, S1/c. We tied up to the docks in Trinidad. We had bought commercial bread in Norfolk to supply bread for the crew until it ran out. Well, it ran out when we got to Trinidad. There were about twelve men assigned to the Commissary, cooking and preparing the meals, and serving them, and all. I was the second in command. I didn't like to bake, and chief cook didn't like to bake, so he told me I was the baker. He out ranked me by one rate. So I had to bake. I never baked before in my life. We got the book out, the old navy blue cookbook. I read up on how to do it, and set my dough. We didn't have any mixing machine. We mixed the thirty–pound dough—I was trying to make fifteen two–pound loaves. I mixed it by hand in the sink where we washed pots and pans. I set it and added the yeast and all the ingredients, like the book said I was supposed to. Then I was supposed to cover it up and let it rise, punch it down, and let it rise again. Well, my bread never did rise the first time. So, after about an hour, I decided it wasn't going to rise, and that I had made a mistake, so I gathered that thirty pounds of dough up in my arms, and went out to the starboard side of the ship, and just dropped it. I never waited to see if it hit the water or not. I went right back in. It was night, and the ship was all darkened and everything. I set another dough, and it did the same thing. So I dropped it over the side. Then I decided I'm really not doing this right. We ain't gonna have no bread tomorrow if I don't find out how to make bread. So I went over to the ship that was nested up with us. I don't remember which one it was—it might have been the USS *Badger*, or one of the other ones. There was a baker there, so I asked him to help me. He came over, and we got a dough set. It came up like it was supposed to. He showed me where I was making my mistake—I was mixing salt at the wrong time, which was killing the yeast. Anyway, I got enough bread baked for the next day, but it wasn't real good bread. It was only about three inches high, and it was right heavy.

"When the cooks came to make breakfast, I went to bed in the compartment. This was probably 4:30–5:00 in the morning. About 9:00 the chief boatswain's mate came down and woke me up. He was very angry, and told me to come up to the quarterdeck immediately. He told this to me in sailor terms. In sailor talk. (If you've been a sailor, you know what I'm referring to). So, I immediately got up and apologized to the chief. His name was Abie. He was a senior chief, and I feared him more than I did the Captain. He had so many hash marks on his arm, I thought that he was one of the original navy people. I was just a kid. He had a voice that got right down to where it was supposed to go. He showed me what was over the side of the ship, between the *Luce* and the other ship. It was my dough that I had thrown over the side. It didn't go in the water—it landed on the fenders that separate the ships from rubbing together. It looked like it was the size of a bed. The tropical sun had hit that dough, and it had raised up between those ships. The ships had rocked a little bit, and it rolled up and down the side, sticking to both ships. He put me over the side in a boatswain's chair. I spent the rest of the day getting the dough off the sides of both ships. And you can rest assured that if I ever threw anything over the side after that, I waited until I heard it hit the water, and not onto something else."

From about 13 October to 18 October 1943, the *Luce* wound her way through the Panama Canal. Bob Harrison, RM3/c, remembers a little trouble he got into during this time:

"In the course of passage through the Panama Canal, I made up a box that I was going to send to my mother. I happened to come across a wardroom teaspoon that I put in that package. They censored it, and opened it up, caught me, and I went to Captain's mast, and I was restricted to the ship. I think our next port of call was San Diego, and I didn't get to go ashore. I didn't miss anything because I had never been to San Diego before."

Before leaving the Canal area, James C. Phillips, SC1/c, recalls a couple of incidents which caused a bit of trouble for the crew and officers—one which involved an "unauthorized visitor":

"We went ashore at Panama City. Although I was legally ashore, many were not. There's a very high tide on the Pacific side. When we got off the ship, it was even with the dock. About midnight when we came back, the ship was about 30 feet down. The tide had gone out. All of us guys that had legal passes to go ashore just showed our passes and went aboard. But those guys who had just stepped off the ship and gone ashore without proper documents were forced to present themselves to the officers of the deck, and were restricted. We stayed there a couple of days.

"Then somebody brought a little spider monkey aboard, about half the size of an alley cat. But it was illegal to bring those animals aboard. Some guy put him in his clothes (to get him on the ship). They put this monkey back in the peacoat locker. Everybody put his peacoat in there, because it had an expanded metal cage, so if that compartment flooded, they could pump it out, and the coats wouldn't get sucked up into the pump. Then somebody approached me about some bananas. We had taken on quite a few bananas in Panama—enough to last two or three meals. So I shared with the monkey. He got special treatment. In the meantime, the monkey was bedded down in the peacoats. Well, sooner or later, somebody took that monkey out of the peacoat locker, and was playing with him and petting him, and the monkey got away from him. He was looking for the highest place on the ship, and that's the mast, where the radar is at the top. That's where he went, right to the top. Clarence Vanness, MM2/c, remembers that one day a couple of the boys greased up the pole, and the monkey kept falling off. Captain Varian saw him, and this upset the Captain immensely, because we were already at sea for two days, headed for San Diego. Then the big investigation went on—who brought the monkey aboard? Got to punish somebody, but nobody would admit bringing the monkey on the ship. So, we're out to sea for two days, and the big investigation goes on. To my knowledge, nobody ever admitted to bringing it on. Somebody thought maybe the monkey just jumped aboard off the tropical docks, but the Captain didn't believe that. The monkey again went up on the radar antennae. They had to shut the radar down and send someone up there to get that monkey. I think it was Leo Greco, SM1/c. The Captain thought that Greco had the monkey in the flag bags, because the Captain saw the monkey jump off the flag bags. Greco can't remember this monkey thing, but I believe that Greco was the one that the Captain directed to go up to the mast and get the monkey, and the monkey just chewed up the man's hand on the way down. We took that monkey to San Diego with us, and we gave him to the zoo there."

Leaving the Canal Zone, the USS *Luce* headed for San Diego, arriving there on 25 October 1943. Four crew members were transferred to the Naval hospital, and the ship took on some 108, 146 gallons of fuel oil. Departing San Diego for Bremerton, WA, James (J.C.) Phillips, SC1/c, recalls that the sonar dome was ripped off from the bottom of the ship by "some kind of underwater object, maybe a whale." This necessitated a dry dock repair at Bremerton. As they entered Puget Sound, Freeman Phillips, S1/c, caused a little excitement for the whole ship:

"We were just standing in, what they call standing in port, and I was lookout on the port side. There were these phosphorous fish darting everywhere. The first one that I saw was heading right for the ship, and it looked to me like a torpedo, so I shouted, 'Torpedo on the port quarter, torpedo on the port side!' They swerved the ship to starboard to get away from it. They really gave me the business for that when they found out it was just a fish!"

The ship's sonar dome was repaired in no time, and the *Luce* was on her way around 31 October, escorting the USS *Enterprise* to Pearl Harbor.

J.C. also recalled another humorous, although perhaps a bit more dangerous, incident that occurred on the voyage to Hawaii:

"We were technically still training how to make all the equipment perform and how to shoot guns, and how to aim them, and all that. We had an anti–submarine screen position off the starboard side of the *Enterprise*. We were supposed to be out there half a mile to a mile, to make sure no submarines fired any torpedoes into her. Bob Moyer, from Buffalo, NY, was a fire control striker third class, at that time. They fired those K Guns that launched the depth charges, about a 45 degree angle from the ship, and they were positioned along the side of the ship. They would fire them from the bridge with a button. Every day they had to check that circuit to make sure that it was in working order. That was the fire control chief's orders. Bob had been sent to the K Gun on the main deck with a test lamp or a screwdriver or something, to disengage it for the test purposes. Bob was sort of a high strung, nervous type, young man. All of a sudden, Bob didn't get his test lamp on the right wire, and the thing fired. The depth charge was thrown right out in front of the *Enterprise*. All the ships had a mad scramble to change course. The *Enterprise* got out of the way. (But the thing never did go off, so evidently it was on safety, and went to the bottom of the ocean.) As soon as the depth charge fired, the officer of the deck hit the general quarters button, and everybody ran to general quarters, because we knew we were in trouble, and we didn't know what that depth charge was going to do. Bob was standing up, a young kid just 17 or 18 years old, with this test lamp in his hand, just as white as a sheet. He didn't know what he'd done or how he'd done it, but he knew he did something wrong. Then the P.A. system came on immediately: "Bob Moyer, report to the bridge." I don't know what they did to Bob for doing that. I think they took him off the depth charge detail. The admiral didn't look favorable toward us. He gave us a new job right away, which was the rear–end job, the last of the lot. If we hurt anybody, it would only be ourselves. So he put us behind, screening in the rear. When we got to Honolulu, He assigned us to be the last one to get in. We screened out there for half a day, and the rest went in port on liberty. So we had to hunt for submarines that weren't even out there for half a day, to make sure we knew how to handle those depth charges and practice up on that."

As the USS *Luce* sailed into Pearl Harbor the crew stared silently at the residue of the carnage wrought there by the Japanese attack almost two years previous. William Burns, MoMM1/c, was one of the sailors surveying the damage:

"The Japs sure made a mess of this place. It is almost two years since they struck here and there are still plenty of signs of the terrific bombing this place took. I'm glad we were not anchored in the harbor on that famous day. If we were I'm quite sure I would... be in the great beyond. Some of the ships that were hit and burned are still sitting where they were as a grim reminder of Pearl Harbor Day... But the more I look at the land bases the better satisfied I am that I took sea duty. I can't imagine anything any worse than to be tied down on one of these islands."

And like many who viewed the destruction, Burns had thoughts of retaliation and expressed them in a letter to his wife:

"Very soon and most likely before you even read this we will be giving them a dose of their own medicine. I think the first places we will hit will be the Marshalls and some other islands near it, such as the Gilberts."

In the period between 7 November and 23 November 1943, the

Luce operated out of Pearl Harbor, conducting various exercises, and generally honing up on battle situation skills. During this time William Burns noted that "our crew had increased to way over three hundred. The men are sleeping under the guns topside, in the aft steering room, in the machine shop, the magazines on the decks, and the engine and fire rooms. Some are even sleeping in the boatswain's locker and the whaleboat—and even in the heads! Pretty crowded, but I just work here..."

One of Burns' jobs was to keep a close watch and repair on the captain's gig. While berthed in Pearl Harbor he observed a humorous incident concerning the gig:

"The comedy for the day was the crew of the Captain's gig. (They were all fairly new at manning a boat.) The engineer didn't know the bells (signals), the hookman was scared to death, and Clark (Harry, S1/c), was the coxswain (steersman). Well, the captain and the exec wanted to go ashore, so they told the crew to man the gig and pull up alongside. The engineer put on too much speed and Clark didn't dare pull in close so they zoomed right by the ship. This happened twice. On the third try in a desperate attempt they smashed the side of the ship. By then all officers including the captain were pulling their hair out... They managed to get aboard and went over to another ship. The crew was to call for them later. For the return trip they were determined not to make any mistakes. But the engineer got mixed up again and for the stop signal he put on full speed ahead. Of course they shot by the ship again, this time splashing all hands with water and oil. Once more they circled around and missed by just a few feet. After a third attempt, they were ordered back to our ship to put on a new crew. This was done, and everyone finally got safely back. The captain wasn't any too pleased with his engineers in general for a while."

On 22 November 1943 there was a change of command. Commander Hinton A. Owens relieved Commander Varian as captain of the *Luce*. Owens was born in Augusta, Georgia, on 12 March 1909. He graduated from the Naval Academy on 2 June 1932 and subsequently served on several ships until war broke out in 1941. Owens was then assigned to a staff position with COMDESRON (Commander Destroyer Squadron) 31 until he was given command of the *Luce*.[2] Lt. John Welsh became good friends with

Captain Owens and remembers him to be a very gentle person, even self–effacing. "He was the antithesis of Captain Varian; quiet and unassuming. He was not very well known by the men and therefore not so well liked. He didn't appear to be a very military person."

Excitement was in the air. With a change of command and the taking on of several torpedoes it was obvious something big was in the offing. As the destroyer, along with a fleet of other ships, prepared for its cruise everybody, recalls J.C. Phillips, "was speculating about where we were going to go when we left Honolulu. Some hoped we would go to Australia, or the South Pacific. Some scuttlebutt! After gunnery practice for a few days, we went north!"

And north it was—deep north, into the teeth of extreme cold, ice, and vicious storms—and their first contact with the enemy. On 23 November 1943, the USS *Luce* set course for the Aleutian Islands.

---

[2] Bureau of Naval Personnel, Naval Department, Washington, DC

PART TWO
THE ALEUTIANS:
FIRST BLOOD

CHAPTER 3
"A Most Depressing Experience"

The last days of November, 1943, saw the USS *Luce* steaming into Adak Harbor in the Aleutian Islands under the watchful eyes of Bert D. Alton Jr., Radio Technician, Second Class. For a year Bert had been attending Navy electronic schools, and, in a roundabout way, had been shipped to the Aleutians. For what, he didn't yet know. Because of a surplus of electronics technicians around Adak at that time, Bert found himself assigned KP (kitchen police) duty on the USS *Markab*, a destroyer tender converted from a Victory type cargo vessel. Lounging on the deck one day, the LORAN (Long Range Radio Aid to Navigation) technician thought about the ships entering the bay:

"As I leaned on the railing, staring out to sea and pondering my fate, I saw a beautiful sight: Two destroyers, obviously brand new, handsome in gray and black camouflage, were steaming into Adak Harbor. My next move was clear, I didn't hesitate an instant.

"I literally ran down to the repair shop in search of the Electronics Repair Officer. Not there. I hurried on to his stateroom, knocked at the door and heard 'come in.' He was seated at the desk doing paper work and seemed surpised to see me, as I was not one of his regular tech's. Mr. Parker was a young man, but heavy; a reservist LTJG. He constantly smoked a big, smelly pipe which, when it wasn't in his mouth, he carried in a leather holster in his belt. He was a gentle and quiet man, out of place, I think, in the often crude military environment. His men told me they liked him because he left them strictly alone.

"I explained my mission: 'There are two destroyers out there and I want to be on one of them.' The officer stared at me, took the pipe out of his mouth, paused and said, 'One of them is the USS *Luce*, the other the USS *Picking*. Which do you want?' I casually told him it didn't matter, but my heart was jumping. I was about to join the world of useful people.

"He explained to me later: He had already known about the two 'tin–cans' in the harbor and, when I knocked on his door, was agonizing to find a fair way to select two people out of our ten to transfer to those ships. He must have had a perception that to send a soul from the luxurious and comfortable *Markab* to a dangerous destroyer was equivalent to sending him down a one–way street to certain death. Nice thought, but I was glad to save him from some of that agony. Soon I saw a signal man on the bridge semaphoring to one of the destroyers and, before the day was out, my seabag was packed and I was on one of *Markab's* boats heading for the combat ship–of–the–line, USS *Luce*, (DD 522). On the boat I looked back and said a silent goodbye to the hulking repair ship—now looking strangely attractive when compared to the sleek but tiny destroyer bobbing in front of me. I confess to a fleeting misgiving over whether I was doing the right thing. An important bridge had been crossed and was burning behind me."

The highly trained radio technician had his ship and felt he was going where the action was. Bert had all the excitement and confidence that a red–blooded young man yearning for adventure could have. His idealism dimmed a bit, however, during the first several hours of a rather trying adjustment to his new home:

"My check–in on the USS *Luce* didn't go all that well. I didn't really expect a red carpet reception, but I was now informed that the ship was full–up with people. There wasn't one single bunk available for the new technician. I cooled my heels on the quarter-deck while the officer–of–the–deck made numerous phone calls about what to do with me. In the end, a decision was made for me to sling my hammock in a passageway in the aft crew's compartment. Good grief, back to the hammock! I had thought my hammock days were over after leaving Bremerton. But I knew enough to keep my mouth shut and not complain. Things would probably get better.

"That night, doubled up in the hammock, I tried to get some sleep, but it was difficult. The aft crew quarters was a crowded and dimly lit cave, stinking with cigarette smoke, ventilation fans making a hellish racket and even noisier sailors. This wasn't the environment that I had expected. Did I make the mistake of my life when I brashly confronted the *Markab's* electronics repair officer in his stateroom and demanded a transfer? My brain whirled with these doubts, but I finally dozed off. Then something really unexpected happened. Loud noises rudely awakened me to witness a nightmarish scene of human conflict. A few feet up the passageway a brawny, screaming sailor was being wrestled by the Master–at–Arms force toward the brig, adjacent to my hammock. The man was a raging bull. Clubs, fists and elbows were flying in a noisy melee moving in my direction. As the milling knot of people went under my hammock, I was upended and had to hang on for dear life to avoid crashing to the deck myself. They herded the guy into the brig, slammed the barred door, and, after a couple more bellows, he subsided into a drunken stupor. I climbed out and inquired of my neighbors: 'What in the world is going on?' They explained that he was a cook, called Beaver. He'd gotten crazy drunk on torpedo fuel (a mixture of alcohol and other toxic aromatics), had somehow located a .45 cal. automatic pistol and had been wildly shooting at imagined enemies in the deserted ship's galley. The MAA's had waited until they were fairly certain that he was out of ammunition and then gone in and collared him. What kind of hell ship was I on? My new acquaintances assured me that this was an unusual incident. Besides, to the denizens of the aft crew's quarters, the whole episode was pure joy and entertainment."

Burr McFarland, WT1/c, recalls Beaver had the rank of Ships Cook 1/c. McFarland credits Derry Moll, who was later awarded the Bronze Star for heroism off Okinawa, for defusing the situation:

"Beaver... had a .45 and was going to kill Lt. Pierce, the executive officer. Derry faced off with Beaver and told him, 'Beaver, you can shoot me if you want and they'll hang you; I can shoot you and I'll get a medal; or you can put the gun down, go to jail for awhile and get treatment.' Beaver handed over the .45 to Derry."

J.C. Phillips, SC1/c, remembers patching up the holes made by the .45 with dough to keep light from shining out the door at night. But Bert Alton's initiation to his first night aboard the *Luce* was not yet over:

"I was to be disturbed once more that night. Beaver had awakened and thrown a lighted match into a refuse can which was now burning merrily away. More sailors bumped under me, this time with fire hoses. It was a long night. The next morning, Ship's Cook Beaver was transferred, in chains, to the beach to await a court-martial and undoubtedly a bad conduct discharge. I inherited his bunk. Good ol' Beaver, he was my red carpet reception!"

RM3/c Bill Fotie's introduction to the Aleutians also caused several questions to run through his mind:

"Rumor had it that we were to go to the invasion of Tarawa, but we didn't. We had sailed into Adak in the Aleutians and relieved the Little Beaver Squadron of old destroyers. That squadron had a big reputation and I wondered if we were going into battle right away. The old four stacker cruisers also made me wonder how well equipped we were to fight anybody. I understand these cruisers (one was the *Richmond*), were turned over to Russia later on."

The next several days men and ship fine-tuned their preparations for their cold Aleutian sea duty. Ammo and powder were taken on board from the USS *Sproston*; the *Luce's* gig rescued a drifting Higgins boat and secured it to the fantail, and the fuel tanks were topped off. A few short patrols helped to hone up the skills of the crew. Bert Alton was also busy continuing to find his niche on the ship:

"The morning after the Beaver incident, I made my first trip to the bridge and met the Navigation Officer, Lt. Thomas Lynch, USN. He was polished, smart, every inch a gentleman, and greeted me with open arms—a nice change. He had already experienced the impracticality of trying to navigate by the stars in the Aleutian Islands. He showed me the Loran set, installed in Pearl Harbor on their way north. Together, we checked out equipment, twiddled the controls, and pored over the charts. At that moment I knew that I had finally come full circle and would fit okay in my first job and my first ship. Lt. Lynch and Radio Technician Alton were now the navigators of the USS *Luce*.

"Off into the Bering Sea on patrol that afternoon and my next problem: seasickness. Never did I think that a 370 foot ship could heave around like this. I didn't leave Beaver's old bunk for four days, except to drink water and relieve myself. If I stood on my feet I immediately became dizzy and then sick—it was that simple. Was it a chronic problem? I hoped not. I knew of sailors who had to leave the Navy for this very reason. On the fifth day—weak, pale and several pounds lighter, I was finally able to hold down food. Lt. Lynch was understanding. He operated the Loran himself, night and day, although he preferred that I ran the thing.

"The other crewmen were friendly, too. Mostly Irish and Poles from the Boston area. The radio tech in charge, however, was from Kansas City. Chief Radio Technician, Wayne Lawton, was jolly and full of stories. He looked, talked and acted like Santa Claus without the beard. He was courteous and insisted on briefing me on all of the other electronic systems on the ship. I was soon assisting him in maintenance on the most failure prone devices. I now believe that he looked upon me as his potential replacement. I know he wanted to leave the ship. Maybe he had a premonition... In a locked vault, adjacent to the radio room, was the ship's Electrical Coding Machine (ECM). All incoming classified radio meassages to the ship were decrypted there in codes that changed daily. The ECM was a glorified teletypewriter, classified secret, and only officers knew how to type and they universally hated the gadget. Teletypes were an enjoyable toy for me, having operated them for a year in the San Bernardino Western Union telegraph office. So I volunteered to help out on the message decoding chore. The Communications Officer passed this tidbit on to the captain, who agreed. Now, against the rules, I was 'breaking' classified messages on a daily basis. It was just for fun for me, but I know the gold braids appreciated it."

Bob Harrison also had the privilege of decoding five letter code groups using the ECM. This could be a real challenge especially when dealing with a garbled portion of the message. Harry Snyder, who came aboard the USS *Luce* in September 1943, was first an ensign and then made Lt. junior grade. He was sent to school after the ship arrived in the Aleutians to also learn how to operate LORAN.

"It seems they had a school there on Adak which teaches you how to operate the LORAN. So they arranged for me, this little ensign, to go ashore and learn how to operate the LORAN. One cold winter night, in a small open boat, I was put ashore in a snowbank on this little island off the Alaskan chain. I walked down the snowy street and found a hut to report in and so I was there for two weeks. While I was there, the ship went out to sea and back. I finished the course. There happened to be a couple of Air Force officers in class with me. They asked me if I wanted to go for a ride in their B–24. I said sure, and off we went. They let me go back in the waist of the ship. We flew around the islands. They said, 'If you want to use a machine gun, go ahead.' I shot it at some mountains. Then the fog started rolling in, and they just barely got us back down on the ground before the thick fog came in. Then I went back to my ship."

Marty Nyholt, FC2/c, reflects the feelings of most of the servicemen on ship and shore in the Aleutians:

"Duty in the Aleutians was a most depressing experience because of the weather and because there was simply nothing to do for entertainment. The soldiers and sailors on the beach were committing suicide at record rates–the highest of any theater in the world."

The best remedy was to dwell on something other than where they were and concentrate on their duty and hope for the best.

The *Luce* cruised up along the Aleutian Island chain to Dutch Harbor, where she arrived just two days before New Year's. On the way, however, it was discovered that the ship was short on food supplies. As James Phillips, SC1/c, recalls:

"We really had creative cooks in the galley—lots of spaghetti, I think; whatever we had left. Mostly dry storage, actually. There were no apple pies. I can remember we had run completely out of shortening and several other items. We were supposed to get supplies, but we went to sea without them. That's when I experimented. We had an abundance of elbow macaroni and dried kidney beans. I don't know if the guys remember, but I cooked that up for breakfast, dinner, and supper. I tried to make it up in different forms, so they wouldn't know exactly what they had. One day, I attempted to make a meatloaf out of red kidney beans. You know, you can cook red kidney beans, if you cook them a long time real slow, into a gel substance like jello. And if you keep on cooking them, they fall down like scrapple. You can put them into a bread pan, and they'll actually form into a loaf like a loaf of scrapple or some pimento loaf. So I cooked these elbow macaronis and red kidney beans, and one afternoon I was trying to figure out something for breakfast. I put them in these bread pans, and when they gelled and set up, it was a good firm loaf, and you could slice it. The next morning, I sliced that up, and we had red kidney beans and elbow macaroni scrapple. But the crew didn't like it. They just didn't like it. It didn't taste right. It doesn't even sound right. These guys had some real high protein, though. Kidney bean loaf for breakfast. And I made gravy out of cornstarch and drippings from what little bacon we had. I cooked that all together and made up what I call a sawmill gravy to go over that red kidney bean and elbow macaroni loaf. But they just did'nt go for it. No way could you disguise it. That's another case where you begin to have doubts about who you could trust being the cook, you know. You didn't have no bravery medals, but when it got dark and you didn't know if they were going to hit you and put you over the side, you walked around and put up a brave front. If you was tough, and you had to be tough, you could overcome those hard times."

Upon docking at Dutch Harbor, the ship's crew was given liberty. It was New Year's—the night of the infamous "New Year's Party"—which disturbed the entire Dutch Harbor area so much that the USS *Luce* was forced to weigh anchor and leave. Bob Harrison, RM3/c, and James Phillips, SC1/c, remember some of the details. Bob relates:

"That was the New Year's Eve of 1943. I guess some part of the crew concocted some really good torpedo alcohol, either raisin jack or torpedo juice. It was a joint effort. Quite a few members of the crew formed what we called the congo line going around the ship, up to the bridge. When midnight came, someone hit the ship's whistle, and tied the whistle down. I'm telling you, the senior officer present afloat on the cruiser USS *Richmond* was mad and ordered us out of port. 'Get under way out of here!' I remember that."

J.C. Phillips:

"I can go into a little detail of how we acquired all the cocktail makings. I wasn't a drinking man in those days. We made up, that is, anticipated this party, several weeks before. My job was to make all of the wine. So I had several vinegar jugs setting up in the issuing room. Of course the inspecting officer always thought it was vinegar. But really it was raisin wine. Raisin Jack. I had made about four jugs, I believe, of Raisin Jack. Murgatroyd, Wm. C., the pharmacist mate, had acquired from either the Destroyer Tender Blackhawk, or some other ship, some additional medical alchohol that we had stashed. We had a little still back in the machine shop that we would run off mash and make regular corn whiskey out of it. I'd make up the mash, the corn meal mash, and I would let it ferment in different parts of the ship, maybe down in the store room underneath the ice boxes, in order to keep the officers from finding it. We had wooden water kegs on rafts– five gallon kegs. We would pour out the water and put the wine in that we had made up. This way the officers wouldn't discover it."

Bob Harrison, RM3/c:

"One of them was stored in the sonar dome. I think that was the one that exploded."

J.C. Phillips:

"The one that exploded was in the forward part of the whaleboat which was pulled up right next to the bridge. When it exploded, it shot that putrid booze we was trying to make out on the officer's deck on the bridge. Somebody had put the bung too tight, and it built up pressure in the keg, and it blew the bung out of the keg and squirted out over the bridge area. It saturated the officer's deck or whoever was up on the bridge. Our secret was lost. But getting back to the Dutch Harbor Party—we had set up the bar in the machine shop. They were serving cocktails out of the machine shop. The cocktails consisted of a mixture of Raisin Jack, medical alcohol, torpedo juice, and grapefruit juice. I broke out the grapefruit juice. We had about ten gallons back there in the machine shop. As the New Year's Party got going, somebody dared somebody to go up and gag the whistle, tie it down, with the steam on down in the fire room. He was to go up and tie the whistle down, and at exactly midnight, turn the steam on that whistle, so it would sound off."

Bob Harrison:

"There was silence in Dutch Harbor. There wasn't much going on. All the lights were out. Most of the portholes and hatches were closed. And minimum lighting."

J.C. Phillips:

"When that thing went off—Whew! Most of the officers were ashore with the admiral, having a New Year's Eve party. We just had a minimum amount of officers on the ship, that stayed there long enough to get under way to get out of the harbor if we got under attack. I guess our whistle and our New Year's Eve party really broke up the party on the beach, because everybody started rushing back to their own respective ships. The whole task group was anchored in Dutch Harbor. All of the officers were madly rushing to get back to their ship because that type of a whistle was signifying an air raid. They thought that the Japs had jumped down on us from the air, and everybody made a mad rush, broke up the admiral's party, and then some of the ships got underway, dropping their anchor, cutting their lines from the dock. It just really created an emergency situation. But there was no emergency. It was the *Luce* having a New Year's party. The admiral didn't appreciate that. He made us leave."

Marty "Moose" Nyholt, FC2/c speaks of the bad reputation the *Luce* developed bacause of the incident:

"The ship's whistles began to blow and people aboard came out on deck to dance and yell 'Happy New Year'... while the lights from the passageways shone out over the sea... because someone disconnected all the darken ship switches at the hatches. The next day, the shorebased Navy and Army brass conducted an investigation. The result: the *Luce* was barred from ever entering Dutch Harbor. When our Squadron was in there, the *Luce* had to load ammo, supplies and fuel and leave immediately to patrol outside the nets to the harbor during the Squadron's stay."

And so the USS *Luce* bid fond farewell to Dutch Harbor and headed back to Adak. Being New Year's Day, J.C. Phillips was busy cooking turkeys for the ship's crew:

"The water was rough out there. That ship started doing everything that you could think of, jumping up and down. The turkeys were jumping out of the oven. The ship was dodging so bad out there in the rough seas that some of those turkeys would fall out on deck, and I would put them back in the pan, and shove them back in the oven. The guys didn't know how much traveling those turkeys had done before they got cooked. I was holding on with one hand, and trying to cook turkeys with the other."

And Donald Brockhoff, TM3/c, typical of so many others, was also trying to hold on with one hand, and then eat what he could of the turkey. Don remembered it being so cold that at gunnery practice he noticed ice forming on the edge of the gun barrels from moisture created between firings.

But the men of DD 522 were yet to have their first real initiation to sea duty in the Aleutians. They were sailing in one of the stormiest sea areas in the world.

CHAPTER 4

BATTLING THE "WILLIWAWS"

It came suddenly, dangerously, and without warning on 13 December 1943. So quickly did it descend upon them that the ship was forced to leave port stranding a liberty party of 71 men on shore. It was called "Williwaw" and as Bill Fotie, RM3/c, recalls:

"It didn't take long to be introduced to the 'Williwaw', the sudden unpredictable storms that were unbelievably violent. Adak's harbor wasn't too well built at the time we arrived (if it was built at all) and when a storm came up, we had to go to sea and ride it out or there was a danger we would go aground."

(The name "Williwaw" was adopted from the term given to the violent squalls that blow through the Strait of Magellan in the southern tip of South America).

"'Williwaws' were to be an all–too–common event in the lives of this crew and those of other ships. These storms would be remembered for the rest of their lives for all who experienced their ferocity. James C. Phillips, SC1/c, remembers that these storms would sometimes "really batter the ship, putting it in bad shape." He was usually in the galley, trying to carry on normally in serving meals. Often, however, the storm would make mealtime almost impossible:

"A lot of times in the Navy it was customary on smaller ships, if the weather got rough (to where they couldn't sit at the mess deck) to just serve the crew sandwiches out of the round stuff, like hardtack."

Bert Alton, RT1/c, felt that during these stormy times a destroyer was no place to be:

"The *Luce* was a 2100-ton flush-decker of the Fletcher-class. Three hundred seventy-six feet in length, these ships were the most modern destroyers in existence. They were efficient fighting machines but crew comfort was not a priority to the designers of the Fletchers. An example was the lack of a fore-and-aft inside passageway. This meant that when a sailor from the aft crew quarters needed to go forward on duty (say to the bridge), he was forced to go outside to make the journey. In the Aleutians, this meant, at the minimum, to dress in foul-weather gear just to walk 200 feet. At worst, on a stormy night, the only safe route (to prevent being washed overboard off the main deck) was to climb to the torpedo deck and inch your way in blackness and rain past an obstacle course of guns, torpedo tubes, searchlights and radars. I ran this gauntlet on a thousand occasions—each time audibly cursing the team of draftsmen who perpetrated this horror. Somebody surely did get to them. The Fletchers were the last destroyers to have this kind of crew arrangement."

Marty Nyholt, FC2/c, especially remembers the extreme cold:

"The weather in the Aleutians and the North Pacific was unbelievably bad. Perpetual fog, cold, snow, freezing temperatures and stormy seas. I think that the sun came out nine times in seven months. The water temperatures were below freezing and a man would die in something like five minutes should he have to go into it. We had a fellow fall overboard in Attu and fished him out in about three minutes. Too late, he suffered so much from exposure that he was transferred to the hospital in Dutch Harbor and was subsequently discharged. We located several downed aircraft during our tour, but the crews were always dead from exposure, even though they were in their life rafts. We did locate and facilitate recovery of a Russian freighter which had broken in half in a storm in the Bering Sea. It was the *Valery Checkhov*, a U.S. built liberty ship. It took us almost six hours to get a cable hooked on her because of the heavy seas, but we got her towed back to Alaska and saved her crew."

William Burns, MoMM1/c, will never forget the first williwaw they encountered on the way to Adak. He was with Gerald Perdue, MoMM1/c:

"The poor old *Luce* was bending and lurching heavily, to say nothing of it's occupants. Several times we were tipped forty-seven degrees. That's as much as anyone saw—after that no one dared look. Depth charges broke loose from their racks and rolled and banged across the decks. Oxygen and acetylene tanks broke loose and smashed around for awhile. Our life rafts ripped off their moorings. The ladder and ammunition in back of my bunk thrashed and clanged all night—no sleep at all. How could you sleep with 5-inch shells rolling around like ping-pong balls within six feet of your bunk and kegs of TNT tossing around above you? At 0330 Perdue and I started for the forward engine room. Perdue made it. I got as far as the torpedo rack when a wave got me. It was very cold with about a seventy mile gale blowing. The cable I was hanging onto let loose so I got a hold on a rail on number four gun mount and hung on for a few minutes. I made it back to the aft section and found some protection. It was pitch black with rain and sleet and cold. I wished I had a light. When Perdue made the forward engine room he told them I was on the way. When I didn't show up after fifteen minutes they figured I went overboard. The call came over the speaking system that no more hands were to venture on deck until daylight. I stayed near the aft crew quarters and hung on until daylight."

Freeman Phillips, S1/c, also remembered the first storm they encountered on their way to Adak from Pearl Harbor as being one of the worst:

"The storm bent our lifeline stanchions over and broke the stops on our guns plus other damage. The storm was so rough that it took paint right off our bow. I remember standing just outside the hatch going down to our mess hall, and seeing water at about a 50 degree angle above us. And then as we would come up out of the trough, the water would start pouring off both sides of the ship. The weight of the water caused the ship to shudder. The ship would just sit there and shudder as it came up from under the tons and tons of water. And then we'd go on the tip of a wave and then slide off again right into the ocean at a very steep angle. When you get down into it, it would just seem like you're a submarine. And then it would just start the process over again—shuddering and coming up out of the ocean. It happened for five or six days like that, day and night. It was a very scary situation. I was right up on the bridge as a lookout. All the men who were below in their bunks, had to stay there, and all the men who were on duty had to stay on duty. We ate very little. They brought around sandwiches when they could, but we had buckets to vomit in right beside us, because the whole crew was seasick. You know what seasickness is. You would just as soon die. Every time we left port, I would be seasick—for the first (maybe) 24 hours. Once my stomach got with the roll of the ship and so on, I wouldn't be seasick. The only way that I found relief from seasickness was to lay on my bunk and close my eyes, and eventually I would go to sleep. And that would take care of it. I saw a lot of rough water on the *Luce*, especially in the Aleutians and in the Bering Sea. Chief Boatswain's Mate (we called him 'Abie') was from Berlin, NH. He used to get great amusement out of everybody's being seasick. He would just kind of laugh and say, 'You'll be alright, Lad, You'll be alright,Lad.' He was quite a lot older than the rest of us and had been in the navy for many years. During this storm on the way to Adak, I saw him standing under the whaleboat, vomiting over the side, and I said to him, 'You'll be alright, Abie, you'll be alright.'"

The "Williwaws" caused any duty to be at the most an almost impossible task, and at best an exceedingly difficult one, as Bob Harrison, RM2/c, recalls:

"Somewhere along the way, while we were operating up there, we got word that a Kaiser Liberty ship had broken in two. I think it was the *Sprosten* and the *Luce* that were dispatched. We were assigned the bow section. The sea was so rough up there in the Bering Sea, we spent four or five days just trying to get a line over so we could take it in tow. (It was difficult to do because there were no crew members on that bow section—B. McFarland). The *Sprosten* got the stern and towed it in. We were successful on the bow. That was quite an experience. You can't get too close or with the high seas you would ram the Liberty ship."

Freeman Phillips adds:

"One minute the Liberty ship would be down here, and we would be up there. The next minute, we would be down here, and the Liberty ship would be up there. All the time we are trying to get a line across. You are worrying about whether it was going to come down on top of us. The seas were running so heavy. We used a Very pistol to put the line across. Shot it across. And like Bob says, I don't know, three or four days we were on that. It took us a long time."

(This was that same Russian ship—the *Valery Checkhov* given to Russia by the U.S.—which was towed to Sand Bay, Alaska.)

Meanwhile, being the dedicated cook that he was, James Phillips, SC1/c, was doing his best to keep the crew fed:

"All those rough seas up there. I always had a meal of something, though. In other words, whatever I was cooking might be jumping out of the pot, but we had a meal of something. If the guys could get to the mess deck, they had something to eat. But we always tried to serve the crew a meal. We did have sandwiches a few times. That was when the watches were froze, and everybody would stay where they were. One man could come and get the sandwiches for everybody. Only the cooks were allowed topside."

Meals were available, but the trick was, according to Freeman Phillips, S1/c, to eat them:

"I can remember standing in the mess hall with my arm around a stanchion, holding on to the tray trying to eat because we were rolling and pitching so bad that you couldn't sit down at the table. Our trays would slide all over, spilling the food. In fact, it was tough even just to stay on the ship. As the ship would roll to port, we'll say, we'd run up the starboard side to get to wherever we had to go. When it would roll up the other way, we'd run up the port side. The low deck generally had water on it, on the main deck. We would be rolled over far enough so that the wave would come down on the deck on the low side, and whatever was on the deck, it would take it back to sea. So you would go on the high side and you would run just as hard as you could before the ship rolled back over to get you. And if you got the roll in the middle, and you were halfway up the deck, you would find something to hold onto until it went back up again. Then you scramble all over again."

J.C. Phillips:

"But normally, in real high seas like that, we had a cable that ran from the mount three from where you come out of the escape hatch at the head, and there was a safety cable run up to near the radio shack somewhere hooked on to the 0–2 level up there. And we had some life rings on that you could put a belt around. That's what we did at 4:00 in the morning. And I put on that belt, with three or four feet of line on it, and hooked this belt into the O ring on that cable. I walked up to the spud locker, which was an escape hatch coming out of the galley, and went down into the galley. I took that harness off when I went into the galley to make spuds, to start the meal. Whatever meal. If I got to the spud–peeling room, that's the preparation room, the hatch went into the galley from there. So that's the way I got from back at my berth end."

Bob Harrison, RM2/c:

"The ships out there in those conditions were like corks, bobbing around. When we'd get in a trough or go to port or starboard, you'd think it was gonna tip over, but she'd come right back."

Freeman Phillips:

"When she would go under a wave, when she'd dive, she'd take on a lot of seawater, and then when she'd come up, she'd just shudder. The tons of water would pour off the decks and the sides of the ship. The screws would come right out of the water."

Bob Harrison:

"Sometimes when that bow would come down again, 'Boom', it's just like hitting a brick wall. It would sometimes knock you down to your knees. A tremendous concussion would be created from the bottom of the ship after it dropped 20–30 feet. If you weren't paying attention and you weren't aware of what the ship was doing, it would go right out from under your feet sometimes, too."

Again, the watch would be frozen. For a man to go from the fantail, or back, of the ship to the bow he would have to travel the distance above deck. There was no way to make the trip below decks. It was extremely dangerous for anyone to do anything except to stay put, as Joe McGuigan, RM3/c, relates:

"To go from forward to aft or aft to forward you had to go topside. Today's destroyers, they found out, have to have a way to go below deck and get from fantail to bow without going to topside, because up there it was so bad that they would freeze the watch again and again. If you didn't, there would be a very good chance of getting washed over the side or falling over. Let's say your watch was 12 to 8, and they froze the watch. So, if you were in your sack, you stayed there, and if you were on watch, you stayed there, whether it be 8, 12, 16 hours—whatever it might be till that sea lets up a little bit. Thank God I was in my sack most times."

Freeman Phillips:

"I remember, I was on watch and I was port lookout. But, it was so bad, if the ship rolled that way you could be thrown over, no problem. As a young sailor, I was scared to death. I came up out of the mess hall, the day one storm started, and I happened to step onto one of these expansion plates. At that particular time, I didn't know that the ships had these expansion plates, and they overlap each other. It's so that the ship can bend. As you understand, a 376 foot long ship would have to be able to bend or it would simply break in half—which some ships did. But these plates that were right in the deck would move back and forth over each other. I happened to step on one of them and felt it give way under my feet. It scared me half to death. I thought, 'Is this ship breaking in half or something?' I wasn't aware of the fact that it is supposed to give, you know. Much the same as tall buildings give in a storm. We continued on to Adak, and if I remember correctly, the other ships didn't enter port all together. We had gotten split up in the storm."

For Bill Lietz, TM2/c, and his companion one storm was especially difficult:

"I was a third class torpedoman and part of our ordinance was the four stern smoke–screen generators. During the storm one of the generator bottles broke a holding cable. Joe Wisniewski, TM3/c, from Philadelphia was in charge and I was working under him. We crawled back to the stern from the after hatch. The waves were breaking over us. Had it not been for the lifelines, we would've been washed over the side. We secured the bottle and on the way back to the after compartment hatch, a large wave hit us and rolled us up against the metal three foot hitch ring and the after 20 mm guns. The wave broke Ski's (Wisniewski's) leg. I went back and dragged him to the safety of the hatch. Doc Shaffner fixed him up temporarily. Back in Dutch Harbor he was transferred to the hospital and that was the last time I saw him."

The ship's log reported that Joe Wisniewski fractured his right femur bone.

The results of such storms was something the crew would always remember. Freeman Phillips, states that at times "every wave that came over (the ship) froze. The saltwater would freeze on the ship, and we had to chip the ice. We also used steam guns and fire axes to clear the ice away from the guns."

James Phillips adds:

"There are certain times of the year up there that this would happen. At night, if we were going into the wind, and the water spray was coming from a certain angle, that spray would freeze on the superstructure. The next morning, if you let it go and didn't chip it off, in a few hours you would have a list. Your ship would lean because of so much weight on that side. That would cause an imbalance, and you would lose the trim of the ship. So that's the reason we had to chip. Every morning, there was a detail for chipping ice. Everybody had a place to chip."

Freeman continues:

"Then as we would run south, getting close to Japan, it would thaw out. Then we would make our return trip, and going back we had the same thing again. I know, because I was one of the ones out there with a steam gun, cleaning the guns."

Clarence Vanness, MM2/c, will never forget that one storm "was so bad it ripped the gun mount up off the deck and turned the gun around and broke the stops on the number–two 5–inch gun."

For the times when the storms might not be quite as fierce, Bill Fotie, RM3/c, had a plan to traverse above decks:

"You could look straight up and see the waves towering over you—it was scary. The Fletchers class destroyers didn't have through passage and many times the watches were frozen because the relieving crewmen could not get from the aft part of the ship to forward. On any night getting from aft to forward was a 'dangerous mission':

1. Let the ship roll until you were on the high side. Quickly unlock the hatch (your hand was already on the wheel), dash out and climb halfway up the ladder to the torpedo deck. Wait for the next roll, climb up the rest of the ladder.

2. Run (in pitch black) along the torpedo deck until the next roll, then dash to the center of the ship at the torpedo tubes. If you were lucky, you could make the radio shack on the next roll. Then you tied yourself into your seat and began your watch. I couldn't remember how we handled the 'boiled' coffee. We probably called it and it walked over to us.

"When we sailed west (or east at that point), we would be

loaded with ice hanging from all over the ship. Within a few hours after entering the Japanese current, the ice would melt."

The men never really got used to the 'williwaws.' At best these storms were just another kind of war to be fought—a defensive war, in which you just 'held on' until it was over. And when it was over there was, of course, relief—until the next one. It was this kind of weather, along with the cold and the isolation, that caused the men on these ships to grow to hate Aleutian duty. No farewell tears were shed when, their duty completed, they sailed away for warmer climes. But before that could happen, they had to execute some offensive action against the enemy's northern frontiers.

CHAPTER 5

THE FIRST RAID ON PARAMUSHIRO

The USS *Luce* departed Massacre Bay, Attu, Alaska on 1 February 1944 to help make up Task Force 94.6 along with several other Fletcher–class destroyers. With the destroyers were the light cruisers *Richmond* and *Raleigh*, completing the small group. The Task Force had been formed to provide a diversionary attack on the Japanese owned Kurile Islands, in order to draw the attention of the enemy away from the on–going invasions in the Marshall Island atolls of Kwajlein and Enewetok. As Bert Alton, RT, recalls:

"We were soon joined by the other destroyers to make up Destroyer Squadron 49, among them the *Sproston*, *Wickes*, *Badger* and *Wm. D. Porter*.[1] But why were we all there? Who were we going to fight? And then, amazingly, four ancient 4–stacker cruisers, two of them ghostly in white paint, also steamed into Attu. What were they doing here? The rumors started, and proved to be accurate. All of us, cruisers and destroyers, were going to conduct the first–ever land bombardment of the Japanese home land."

The news of their mission electrified the men. Their first real test was coming up. All that they had been trained to do was about to be put into operation. The USS *Luce* was going to war. Many of the men had conflicting emotions. There was excitement, fear, and expectation. Bill Fotie, RM3/c, was one of them:

"I suppose one of the scariest times of my life was when we

---

[1] The *Luce* was one of nine destroyers making up DESRON (destroyer squadron) 49. The others were: *Isherwood* DD 520; *Kimberly* DD 521; *Sproston* DD 577; *Wickes* DD 578; *Young* DD 580; *C.J. Badger* DD 657; *Wm. D. Porter* DD 579; and the flagship, *Picking* DD 685.

40 DD 522: Diary Of A Destroyer

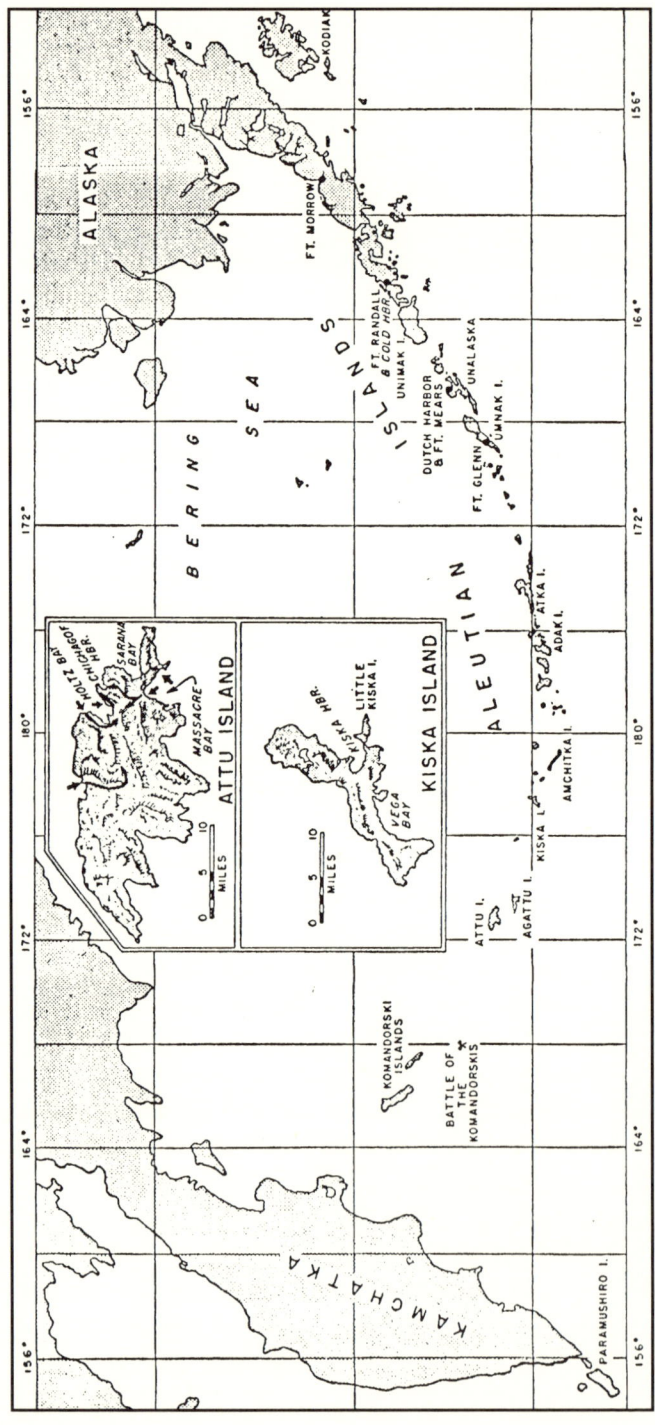

The Aleutian Theater Of Operations

From *The Great Sea War* by Admiral Chester W. Nimitz and E.B. Potter. Copyright© 1960. By permission of Prentice-Hall, Inc.

were told we were going on a raid to Paramushiro. Rumor had it that we were going in under the noses of huge coastal guns. In addition, that we were looking for the Jap 9th Fleet with their huge guns... 18" I think... they were larger than the Geneva Convention allowed. Of course none of this happened but at the time we didn't know it... and considering this was our baptism, we were ready to believe anything."

Paramushiro Island is one of the northernmost islands in the Kurile Island chain and as such was part of the Japanese home land, as Marty Nyholt, FC2/c, relates:

"The Kuriles included the home base of a powerful Japanese surface force of cruisers and destroyers. Paramushiro had a fine airfield which was the home base of a Japanese naval air squadron and protected against U.S. Army and Navy aircraft which raided the Kuriles from Alaska. It also housed Japanese combat troops and had a large fish cannery. The Jap Fleet, based in the Kuriles, sortied out for operations throughout the Pacific and posed a constant threat to the Aleutians and Alaska.

"The distance between Attu and Paramushiro was approximately 500 miles. The Task Force left Attu covered by a dense fog with temperatures well below freezing. All ships were encrusted in a thick coat of ice."

An interesting part of the *Luce's* training for her officers concerning Paramushiro was developed by Lt. Thomas Lynch, as noted in the Action Report for 9 February 1944:

"The CIC (Combat Information Center) evaluator, Lt. Lynch, was in charge of collecting and evaluating all intelligence information and photographs. A folder was made containing all this information.

"Just prior to departure on the mission a conference of all officers, CIC personnel, director personnel and leading chief petty officers was held and all details of the mission were explained. A chart showing movements and function of each task unit, targets, illumination, etc., was explained.

"Lieutenant Lynch prepared the following day a model of Kurabu Zaki, made of flour, water and salt on a large piece of plexiglass. Since the point of land is predominantly low, contours presented no problem. The most important possible targets and gun implacements were cut from cardboard and properly located.

The model was almost entirely white, so painting was not necessary. The Director pointer and trainer and gun captains studied the model and learned the relative location of good targets. It was stated that the model enabled them to recognize targets much more quickly than they would have otherwise. The model required about three hours to make and was based on the excellent photographs distributed by the Advanced Intelligence Center."[2]

The men of the *Luce* were ready to prove themselves, as James Phillips, SC1/c, relates:

"We were anxious to get over there and exhibit our abilities to the rest of the ships. We had come a long way since the depth–charge incident. I'm sure that the whole navy learned about that. We were sort of treated like a red–headed step–young–un until such time as we could prove ourselves. And we were anxious to get on with that. So we eagerly went on this raid with that task group."

While cruising to their destination the Task Force weaved their way successfully through a mine field. This did cause some consternation among the crew, and Bob Harrison's thoughts were probably typical of many:

"We all of a sudden were in a mine field. I don't remember how many, but I know there must have been, particularly on the port side, five or six, and we slowed to almost a snail's pace near Attu, on the way. They were Japanese mines. We just slowed. They didn't make an announcement. They didn't go to general quarters. They just weaved through those mines, and I'll tell you, that was more scary up in those waters that are cold. They didn't announce it because you're dead when you hit that water. We had some men with rifles on the port side firing at the mines presumably to disable or explode them to prevent our hitting them. I thought the mines were so close that it was just as well they didn't hit a vital part so as to explode them."

James Phillips had some thoughts on the probable reasons why the crews were not told they were going through a mine field:

"The laundry list would have been terrible. The guys would have jumped up off the deck. When you get in a mine field, everybody walks about two feet off the main deck to lighten the ship so you get it up off the water. The laundrymen would have

---

[2] Action Report of USS *Luce*, DD 522; 9 February 1944.

been terribly overworked. Everybody would have taken a bath and that would use up all the fresh water too. So I guess that's why he didn't tell us regular peons that we were in a mine field."

The threat to Paramushiro was designed to draw attention away from another naval operation, as Freeman Phillips, S1/c, relates:

"We crossed the Bering Sea, almost to Russia. Then we ran south from Russia to Japan. That way they didn't know where we were coming from. They were supposed to think that we were coming from Midway Island. This ties in with the invasion of the Marshall Islands. The reason we were up there was to draw the Japanese away from the South Pacific… "

The seas were calm as the Task Force approached the southern coast of Paramushiro. The *Luce*, along with the *Badger* and *Kimberly*, were in the lead. The Battle Report records that the temperature was 22 F., the moon was bright with a few clouds, and the ship's speed was 20 knots. All was silent as the fleet maneuvered into position to fire upon the unsuspecting enemy's shore installations. As the Action Report written by the *Luce*'s commander, Hinten A. Owens continues:

"Approach—The approach was made on course 335 degrees T at 20 knots using S.C. radar to check position. At 0130 'blanket' was executed which was the signal for minus 60 minutes. At this time… Paramushiro could be plainly observed in the radar scope. No enemy forces were observed. At minus 30 minutes Task units 94.6.1 and 94.6.2 came right to 020 degrees T, speed 20 knots. At this time, land could be seen from the bridge since it was snow covered and reflected the moonlight. The top of Kurabu Zaki could then be seen in radar scope and off–lying rocks at first appeared to be three ships in column. From tracking it was found that the objects were stationary and several minutes later it was evident that the targets were rocks. At about minus 15 minutes slight radar interference was received from the general direction of Kurabu Zaki. The interference was not strong nor was it consistent, and was possibly caused by the RDF station located on the point. At minus 5 minutes buildings and installations could be seen clearly and it was decided that CIC would relinquish gun control to the director immediately after the first starshell salvo. The entire approach to within 3 miles of the land was apparently undetected." [3]

Marty Nyholt, FC2/c, continues:

"As we approached the target, we broke out of the fog and approached under a cold, crisp, star–filled sky with full moon. The target was snow covered and sparkled... looking like an incredibly beautiful Christmas scene. I felt a sense of guilt as I viewed this scene with the small columns of smoke spiraling slowly up from the chimneys. It was a marked contrast to the hell the Task Force was about to unleash upon it.

"When the Task Force was about 4,000 yards from the shore, it changed course and proceeded in column to the right and paralleled the beach to unmask all main battery guns for a broadside on targets. My job, as the Main Battery Rangefinder Operator and Spotter, was to range on the target and send these to the computer in Fire Control Plot and then correct/spot the errors in range by observing outbursts. Dick Flaum, FC3/c, who subsequently married my sister, Maryann, was the operator of the Fire Control Radar in the Main Battery. Bob Moyer, FC3/c, was the Trainer, White (Cracus J., S1/c) was the Pointer and Lt. Lynch was the Gunnery Officer.

"At approximately 0230 (2:30 A.M.) we commenced firing on our first target... a hanger, which housed combat aircraft, with a 'Zero' fighter plane warming up on an apron in front of it. This was one of a number of hangers and buildings along the airstrip. Our first salvo exploded the aircraft and the hanger, which burst into flames and heavy black smoke poured out obscuring the target. We continued firing, in rapid fire, and then quickly ceased fire as it was difficult to see the target. A gun emplacement at the north end of the airstrip opened up on us, and the *Luce* was the second ship in column as we switched target to the base of where the tracers were originating. After one salvo it ceased firing. Our next target was a large building near the fish cannery. We opened fire and blasted away for several minutes and the building was burning briskly with heavy smoke pouring out of it. I could observe many people running from the building and in its vicinity. As it became difficult to see the target, we ceased fire and looked for a new target. In the meantime, the other ships had been concentrating their fire on the cannery. As we trained right, I got

---

[3] Action Report, OP. CIT.

a good look at the buildings and they looked like a scene from Dante's Inferno: collapsed buildings, flames and smoke shooting high into the sky and groups of people running around near the burning structures."

Cliff Roberts, CFC, was on the computer:

"I went to the gunnery officers meeting before we went because the accuracy of the fire had to be perfect or we would not return. We had to hit them by surprise. It was the only raid made where there was a clear moonlit night. The first two things we had to take out was the communications shack and tower on the first salvo. Otherwise, fifty-five miles north the Japs had a huge airbase that could send out planes. The second target was a small airfield. If those planes got in the air we would be in trouble. Our first salvo took out its target okay, then we immediately turned toward the airfield. Our first salvo on that took out the hanger. One plane got on the runway, and a shell landed right under that plane and blew it up. I saw it clearly. They never got the plane in the air and never got word out on that communications tower. If that had not happened, we would have never gotten back from that first raid. Then the Japs opened up skyward, thinking it was an air raid. By the time they corrected, we were well on our way out of their range."

Then the guns of the *Luce* turned to another target opportunity, as Marty Nyholt recalls:

"Our next target was a small freighter moored alongside a dock. We fired two salvos and she seemed to blow up from stem to stern with great balls of flame shooting skyward. I advised the Gunnery officer that she was through and sinking so we ceased fire and looked for another target. After firing a few salvos at a gun emplacement, the word for the Task Force to cease fire came. As we trained slowly to observe the results of the bombardment, we noticed that the freighter, which we thought that we'd left sinking, was now underway and seemed to be heading straight toward us. She suddenly stopped, swung rapidly around and rolled on her beam toward the beach. She had beached herself, much to our great relief and, I might say, my personal embarrassment."

Although the battle report states that there was no return fire, Bill Lietz, TM2/c, believes that this was not the situation:

"I was in charge of the stern depth charges and smoke–screen generators. We were first in line of seven destroyers. We had made our first run with our number three 5 inch guns firing starshells. The other destroyers were doing the same. When the Japs saw the starshells they thought it was an air attack and began firing in the sky. Finally they realized they had been hit from the sea and leveled their fire at us. I could hear the schrapnel hit the port side of the ship's stern. I was flattened out on the deck waiting for the word over our JU phone circuit to activate the smoke–screen generator. In about 30 seconds we were concealed in good white smoke. Great protection, I thought."

Marty Nyholt describes the feeling of the men after their first taste of action:

"This whole operation lasted about 45 minutes and the Task Force swung around on a retiring course and increased speed. This was our first taste of combat and we felt that it was most successful. In addition to reducing all of our assigned targets, we got credit for sinking a small freighter. Needless to say, we were all very proud of ourselves. We had just completed the first surface bombardment of the Japanese home islands and came away with no damage to any of the ships and no casualties."

There were some slight "casualties," however, as noted in the official Action Report's documentation of the mission:

"Bombardment—At plus 001/2 minutes the first salvo of starshells was fired, and seemed to be well placed relative to the first target which was the lower group of hangers. The bombardment was continued with the director in control of the guns. No shipping could be seen in the radar, but after a ship which was observed visually was taken under fire, a 'pip' separated from the land. This was reported by CIC to the bridge. This 'pip' later merged with the land again. At about plus 10 minutes the Director was instructed to shift bombardment gradually to the north according to plan. When smoke obscured most points of aim, CIC furnished control to locate targets. At plus 14 minutes Task Group 94.6.2 was directed to carry out phase 2, which was the bombardment of the Otomaye Wan area. Otomaye Wan had not been photographically covered and exact location of installations or even their presence had not been established. At plus 19 minutes, bombardment of Kurabu Zaki was ended. At plus 22, changed course to 070 degrees T for Otomaye Wan bombardment—at plus 25 fired first starshell salvo with CIC in control. The stars illuminated the beach, but no targets could be seen. CIC remained in control throughout bombarding general area of reported installation. No return fire was encountered, nor was any damage observed. It is thought that there were no installations in this area. This emphasized the value of photo coverage. At plus 35 minutes fire was ceased and Task Unit 94.6.2 rejoined Task Unit 94.6.1 at 30 knots. Task Unit 94.6.3 rejoined about 10 minutes later.

"Retirement—The retirement course was 110 degrees T, speed 25 knots with DD's in anti–submarine screen and cruisers in column. At about plus 45 minutes the *Richmond* reported a 'bogey' to the north about 25 miles and closing. The S.C. radar was energized. At first the antenna was stuck due to ice, but after about five minutes it was freed and tracking commenced. The 'bogey' appeared to be 3 or 4 planes and closed to 5 miles. The formation was maneuvered radically to avoid the 'bogey,' but the 'bogey' was headed for Kuabu Zaki about the time the planes merged with the land. The 'bogey' was undoubtedly our own ventures, but identity could not be definitely established. No future incident occurred during retirement.

"Four personnel casualties occurred among 5 inch gun mount crews, and were due to powder fumes. The gun captain and hot shellman in #5 mount became unconscious, and the others were partially affected, so that firing was stopped. The unconscious were treated in the dressing station, and were not able to return to action. They exhibited signs similar to those produced by nitrous oxide 'laughing gas' anesthesia. Two others, one in #1 mount, were momentarily unconscious, but returned to duty after a few minutes of fresh air." [4]

Bill Fotie, RM3/c, was one of the men afflicted:

"My own battle station at that time was the handling room of number three—five inch cannon. I was on the platform and was manually handling up the powder cases into the mount. After a little while of firing, and before I knew what had happened, I passed out and fell off the platform. It seems that the exhaust system failed and the mount filled with smoke and knocked everybody out or at least they couldn't stay there. I believe the

---

[4] Action Report, OP. CIT.

mount personnel went out on deck but I'm not sure of this. After the raid, we were ravenously hungry. Someone produced a (stolen) ham and we gobbled it up."

Another "casualty" related to the mission is described by the ship's medical officer, Lt. Louis Shaffner:

"On the way back from that run the executive officer got the darndest case of hives I ever saw. He just had pink welts all over him and was just miserable, scratching everywhere. He came to me for relief, and I had to eventually give him injections of adrenaline in oil to give him some relief. It would help him for maybe an hour and a half or two hours and it would wear off and he would have to have another shot again. Seemed to me that this fellow had just gotten to where he was under so much pressure and stress that this was his response to it. I really hadn't had much sympathy for him up until that time, because his personality wasn't very good and he was working with a crew that didn't have much respect for him. After that run to Paramushiro when he had so much responsibility, he just cracked. Of course everybody that was up there was just raring to get off the ship or get back to the States or get to warmer weather and here this executive officer had hives that I couldn't control. He certainly wasn't fit for duty in that condition, so I put him ashore at the hospital in one of those Aleutian Islands, and they eventually transferred him back to the States."

The first attack by American sea forces on the Japanese home land was an unqualified success, and the USS *Luce* had certainly "proved" herself on this early morning raid. The enemy freighter she had fired on was a 2,000 ton ship and the hits scored by the destroyer forced its beaching. Their mission completed, the Task Force began the return trip back to Attu. Along the way they formed a scouting line to search for missing P–38's, but did not find the planes nor their pilots. On 5 February at 1655 DD 522 anchored briefly in Massacre Bay, Attu, and at 1931 got underway for Adak. Rough seas met the *Luce* as she steamed out of the harbor, and soon the ship was in the middle of another "williwaw", which she safely sailed through. The ship was on its way to rejoin with the Task Force for another mission.

After arriving at Sweeper's Cove in Adak on 7 February, Joe Wisniewski, TM3/c, was transferred ashore for treatment of his injured leg. At the same time Waino Johnson, GM2/c, reported aboard for duty. Operating out of Kuluk Bay, Adak and Sand Bay, with a trip to Great Sitkin Island, the *Luce* sailed back to Massacre Bay in Attu where Lt. Thomas G. Lynch, according to ship's log, was transferred from the ship on 25 February.

And it was about this time that a sailor on the *Luce* had his own "rough seas." Arthur Powers, S1/c, was notified that his mother had died on 29 January. It was not possible for 'Arty,' as his family called him, to go home so he wrote a letter to his father, and one to his brothers and sisters. He told his siblings to "be good and stick together. This is what our mother would want. Always stick together." And since that time his family has been especially close.

CHAPTER 6

MORE RAIDS—AND LIBERTY!

On 1 March 1944 the *Luce* again departed Massacre Bay, Attu, in the company of Task Force 94 to inflict another raid on Paramushiro. Two days later while enroute, the Task Force was alerted to search for a Japanese convoy suspected of being in the area. Marty Nyholt, FC2/c, recalls that on 4 March, contact was made:

"Our Task Force, on the basis of reports from U.S. Navy submarines and aircraft, had made a fast run to the Kuriles and entered through a narrow strait to the Okhotsk Sea in pursuit of a large Japanese convoy. After several hours of searching, we found an 18–ship convoy of transports which turned out to be Russian. After boarding and searching to verify and identity contents, we let the convoy proceed. At this time, the Russians were not at war with Japan. These ships had apparently loaded up with cargo in Japan and were proceeding back to Russia. We proceeded back through the narrow eight mile strait to the Pacific and returned to base. I understand that Admiral Baker, the Task Force Commander, was relieved of his command shortly after our return. Taking the Task Force into the Okhotsk Sea, which was a 'Japanese lake' and home base of major naval warships, was too great a risk relative to the results that could have been expected. All I can say is that the sailors aboard the *Luce*, especially me, were 'shaking in our boots' during this whole trip and were darn glad to get back."

The ship's log notes that this same day, 4 March, the convoy again changed course "to go through the Kurile Island chain, into the Okhotsk Sea." Several hours after the change, the convoy was again in position off the shores of Paramushiro, but the scheduled bombardment of the island's military facilities was cancelled because of poor visibility. The ships remained in position waiting for conditions to clear, and at 1847 hours, when it appeared this was happening, general quarters was sounded. But the fog again thickened, and for the second and last time, the bombardment was cancelled at 1937 hours. All ships secured from GQ and the Task Force headed back toward Adak by way of Attu.[1]

Lt. Cliff Jones had quite an unusual experience during this time:
"A Kansas City man was a Vice–Admiral there in the Aleutians. His name was Admiral Frank J. Fletcher, and he was a good friend of my mother and father in Kansas City all his Naval career. Somehow he learned that I was on the *Luce* and that we were being selected for a 'suicide' run into the Sea of Okhotsk, west of the Kurile Islands and the Japanese Islands. There was only one way to get in or out. The reason it was a suicide run, so called, was because the Japanese could have bottled up the narrow passage and we would not have been able to break through without being destroyed. We were on a search party to find an important convoy and destroy it. A huge storm came up, we never found the convoy, and the enemy never knew we were there. We got back in good shape. But before this took place, Admiral Fletcher sent a message to our Captain requesting that I report to him at his quarters on Adak. I, of course, knew Admiral Fletcher—I don't think I ever met him before—but he knew my parents. I went there, and here he was with his chief of staff sitting before a warm fire in easy chairs. He asked me to pull up a chair, and asked me about family things. He mentioned that we were going to go on a rather dangerous mission. After a nice visit, when I got back to my ship, the Captain (H.A. Owens) wanted to see me and wanted to know what Admiral Fletcher had told me. I had enough sense to act a little mysteriously about this. I said, 'Oh, nothing much, Captain.' I don't think I told him that Admiral Fletcher was a friend of my parents. The Captain was puzzled by this, and therefore, when he got the word of the suicide mission, he did something very

---
[1] Deck Log Summary, p.5.

unusual. He invited me to his cabin on our ship. He and his executive officer were seated, and they asked me to pull up a chair. He gave me a cup of coffee and commenced to tell me we were going on a suicide mission. Now, this was an extraordinary thing for him to do to me, and I was a very junior officer. The fact that I had had this very mysterious summons to Vice Admiral Fletcher, who was in charge of all the Aleutian area, made him treat me with more respect, for which I was grateful."

As the *Luce* visited the various ports in the Aleutians, Bill Fotie, RM3/c, had a certain duty which he performed, but not always to perfection:

"It fell to my lot that whenever we came into some ports, I had to go ashore to the joint Army–Navy com centers and pick up codes and anything else the radio shack needed. When I came back from the center at Adak, some bad weather came up, and as I started to climb the ladder back onto the ship, I slipped and went into the water—this was real death–threatening in the Aleutians, and doubly so, because I was between the ship and the whaleboat. The coxswain grabbed me with his hook and hauled me back to the ladder where I scrambled up and was rushed to sickbay. That day I was the envy of the ship. Doc Shaffner broke out a little bottle of brandy for me. The sad part was that I lost the codes and spare parts but saved the box of Hershey bars I had managed to obtain. On another occasion, I went ashore to pick up codes and the *Luce* took off without me, and I was stranded on a destroyer tender or machine shop ship for about a week or so."

And J.C. Phillips, SC1/c, was still doing his best to provide the crew with bread. But he, too, was having some difficulty:

"In Adak Harbor I was gonna get some bread from the USS *Richmond*. So Virgil Degner, BKR2/c, and I commandeered the Captain's gig and we went over to the *Richmond*. The officer on the deck that was standing watch on the *Richmond* gave us such a hard time, that I told the Coxswain, 'Let's just forget the bread and go back to the ship.' We had either come up on the wrong side of the ship or made the wrong turn. That was the Admiral's flagship. 'Let's go back to the *Luce*. I don't feel at home here. Those people are making me unwelcome.' So we went back without the bread, and I baked the foolish bread. That settled that."

Fueling up in Adak, the *Luce* received orders to proceed to Attu for conducting various exercises. These maneuvers took place during the days and nights of March, 1944, in company with the destroyer USS *Badger* and at times, the log relates, with the destroyers *Sproston* and *Young*. While on one of the exercises, an emergency message went out to the destroyers to begin a search for downed flyers in a life raft. Speed was of essence as the chances of survival in those frigid waters were minimal. On 1 April the *Luce*, in company with the USS C.J. *Badger* and the USS *Doherty*, began a search exercise of expanding squares and fired a starshell every half hour through the night. The next day, 2 April, the USS *Austin* joined the search, but it wasn't until 3 April at 1614 that the life raft was finally sighted. Bert Alton, RT, remembers reading an article in a magazine sometime later that a search plane "had tried to land, but the people in the raft waved them off because the seas were too rough." The search plane had radioed the downed flyers position to the destroyers before having to leave the area to refuel, but when the destroyers arrived there was no sign of the life raft. Bert felt that had they arrived on the scene earlier, the situation might have turned out better:

"The planes came out again in daybreak, found them, dropped smoke bombs, and we went out and got them, but all three of them were dead before we could rescue them. We tried as hard as we could. We did everything we could, but if we only had had an airplane orbiting them when we first were there, we could have gotten them out alive."

Bob Harrison, RM2/c, recalls:

"They were frozen stiff and we picked them up and put them right into the freezer... I'll always remember that. That was an example of if you hit the water up there, you don't last long. You're even afraid to drop the bodies on the steel deck for fear they will crack. They're just that frozen."

A similar incident which occurred near Adak which also testified to the severe temperature of the water was witnessed by Freeman Phillips, S1/c:

"We lost a man overboard... and the deck officer was right there. The deck officer always had another man with him, and I happened to be the man that day. We fished him out with a boathook immediately. He almost didn't make it. I know he wasn't in the water for more than three or four minutes. He just almost didn't make it. It was extremely cold. That's the scary part about operating on those cold waters. If something happens—we get hit and end up in the water, that's it for you."

The *Luce* arrived in Massacre Bay, Attu late in the day of 4 April and the bodies were transferred the next day under an honor guard to the naval dispensary. On 6 April the exercises were continued with the USS *Badger*. A few days liberty ashore was given to much of the crew upon mooring at Sweeper's Cove, Adak on 17 April. It was during this liberty that some of the men, among them Art Whitney, MM1/c, and Freeman Phillips, S1/c, were witness to a rather serious accident. Some 16 men got hold of a truck and drove up a steep mountain road. One of the truck sides fell off, and many of the men went with it into a canyon. Freeman hung on for dear life. "I was in the back of the truck, right up next to the cab on the high side. I didn't fall off." The log summary lists only four men as being injured—Roger Bernier, Dick Burlingame, John Day, and Jim Gory—but the War Diary states that a total of eight men were injured and "one man, Hagan, G.T., BM2/c, died the next day at Naval Dispensary Adak, Alaska, as a result of injuries received in the accident." [2] Art Whitney remembers the accident taking place in the evening after the beer party. The truck was stolen from the Army motor pool, and Freeman recalls that Captain Owens had a lot of explaining to do to the Army general.

Much of the time, life aboard the ship was a tedious routine for most of the crew. Leo Greco, SM1/c, remembers that the men went ashore to a play and heard a song which was an instant hit with the sailors. The words are as follows:

SQUAWS ALONG THE YUKON

1st verse–There's a salmon–colored girl
Who sets my heart awhirl
Who lives along the Yukon far away
With the Northern Lights that shine
She rubs her nose to mine
She cuddles close and I can hear her say

---

[2] USS *Luce* (DD 522) war Diary, April, 1944.

2nd verse –OOGAH OOGAH MOOSHKA
Which means that I love you
If you will be my baby
I'll OOGAH OOGAH MOOSHKA you
Then I take her hand in mine
And set her on my knee
The Squaws along the Yukon
Are good enough for me

3rd verse–She has the Air Corps down
The Sourdoughs hand around
Chechackos try to date her night and day
With a landing gear that's fine
And a fuselage divine
And a smile that you can see a mile away

Ending–Carry me back to Old Alaska
The squaws along the Yukon
Are good enough for me

When liberty was granted in the various ports, there was not much for the men to do. Contrary to what one might assume from the song, women were almost nonexistent in Aleutian military ports of call. Orville Hiles, S1/c, who was in one of these ports for two months before being assigned to the *Luce*, discovered for himself the scarcity of feminine companionship:

"They said there was a woman behind every tree, but they didn't tell us that there weren't any trees! A woman by the name of Kiska Pat was the only woman in the Aleutians, but I never saw her."

Bill Fotie, RM3/c, had a few thoughts on the subject of liberty:

"On both Adak and Kiska we were warned about boobie-trapped souvenirs and shells. I understand a lot of servicemen were killed and injured with these. On Kiska there were many caves and we were warned not to go into them due to unexploded shells and boobie traps. On one occasion, we went to Dutch Harbor and had liberty. I was one of the wildest. There were three or four makeshift bars and you stood in line for a drink. You stood at the bar with a line of sailors in back of you and drank all you could drink, then moved or was carried out of the way for the next sailor to step up."

The officer's club on Attu offered slot machines as entertainment. Named "Hammerhead Hank's," the club's operations were suspect in the gambling procedures, and Lt. Don Allen echoed the feelings of several officers:

"Hammerhead Hank had some slot machines that were rigged to pay off about once every thousand years. We got revenge one day when I was coming back (to the ship) in a whaleboat, and one of the slot machines came along with us and went to the bottom of the sea."

Lt. John Welch also had opportunity for revenge against the machines, but it caused him a little trouble:

"There was a 'williwaw' one night when we were ashore, and unfortunately, I was a senior officer present at the time. I didn't know it, but it turned out later I was. Well, we all played the slot machines. We had to sleep there in the club that night, because there were no boats going back to the ship. We played the slot machines, until we ran out of money. Then, we didn't have anything to do. We upset a couple of the slot machines, and shook the money out, and we sat around on deck, and everyone took a quarter, and then everyone took another one, until we all wound up with a couple of handfuls of change. Well, the 'williwaw' blew out that night, and we got back to the ship the next morning. I brought my handkerchief full of change and into the wardroom for breakfast, and began telling everyone the stories of what happened. Then the old man called me up and said, 'John, what happened over at the club? I have a message from the Admiral ashore who wanted to know about wrecking the club last night.' I said, ' Oh, no!' Pretty soon, we got a letter from the Commodore, and I was, as senior officer present that night, supposed to go over and see to it. I got over there and called a board of inquiry, and asked to see the chief of staff. The chief of staff said, 'Was so and so over there with you last night?' And I said, 'Yeah, I think he was,' and he said, 'He's my brother–in–law. You know I'm gonna try and squash this one.' And I said, 'Well, that certainly would be nice!' So, it got squashed. Nothing ever came of it."

Completing various battle exercises with the destroyer Squadron (DESRON 49), the *Luce* sailed into Dutch Harbor on 23 May

1944. After resupplying and continuing exercises, DD 522 again joined up with Task Force 94 for a raid on Matsua, Kurile Islands. Early in the morning of 13 June, according to the log summary, the Task Force performed their "hit–and–run" raid on Matsua for a total of 31 minutes before setting course back to their home base. Marty Nyholt, FC2/c, believes the raid actually took place on 14 June with the following details:

"This raid was conducted in dense fog and the fire control of the main battery was conducted by CIC, using their radars and their direct input to Fire Control Plot. The guns can be most accurately directed, when the target is visible, visually by a Trainer, a Pointer and Optical Range Finder in the Main Battery Director. The second most effective method is by Main Battery Director using the Fire Control Radar involving night targets when they are not visibly trackable such as in very heavy fog or at night on land–based targets. At 0514 (5:14 A.M.) we commenced fire by salvo fire in 10 second intervals. After 15 minutes, two targets appeared on the S.G. Radar at 6,000 yards, target angle 'Zero,' speed 35 knots."

Bob Harrison, RM2/c:

"I remember I was on the phone in the Combat Information Center (CIC) looking at a radar scope. Coming up from the rear was one blip, and all of a sudden, they spread, and there was about three or four Japanese torpedo boats. That's scary also. In water that is only 20 degrees, you last about five minutes or less. Apparently, we did everything undetected, until we started firing... "

Cliff Roberts, CFC:

"Don Sweeten, SoM3/c, was on the stern on a 20 mm. I heard over my phones from the Director that PT boats were on our stern. They were getting so close that they were becoming dangerous. I reached over and pulled the fuse–setting knob like we were shooting airplanes so it would send shrapnel out. Nobody knew I did that, and nobody ever asked me what happened, because by the second or third shell there were no more PT boats. Someone on the phone yelled that we had been hit. There was blood and guts all over the deck; but what had happened was the concussion of the five–inch guns over the garbage cans had spilled garbage over everyone who was on the fantail. It was at night, and they couldn't see, and thought it was blood and guts."

J.C. Phillips, SC1/c:

"We fired the 5-inch number four and five. The torpedo boats were coming in our wake. They thought they were slipping up on us, but we had them on the scope. The orders came to the 20 millimeters, which was my gun crew, to stand by because torpedo boats were approaching from dead astern. It was dark. We couldn't see nothing. We all trained our guns back there. Without telling us, they put mount five and mount four on the Fire Control system, and they gave rapid fire for about five minutes or so. The boats disappeared so we assumed that they were sunk by the five-inch, or we ran them off. They retired or they were sunk, one of the two."

J.C. also remembers the fog being used to advantage for the raid:

"After the shooting and we escaped from the PT boats, we then hid in the fog. At this time Japanese aircraft came. There was several of them. They were searching for us. The people who were doing the weather had it figured that we could do the bombardment without air support. We could do this bombardment, and then get back out into the fog and hide, because the Japanese didn't have radar on their planes. They would come out and search for us, but they couldn't see through the fog."

For Freeman Phillips, S1/c, the aircraft provided a somewhat humorous finale:

"At this time, a plane jettisoned a wing tank that came down and landed on top of number five, 5-inch gun, and dented in the top of the gun mount. At that point, all of the men in number five mount came bouncing out of the gun, and they just hopped around in a circle and when they realized they hadn't been bombed, they went right back into the gun."

A few days of organization and the Task Force was again off and running, this time to raid Karabu Zaki off the tip of Paramushiro. General Quarters was sounded at 0145 on 26 June and firing commenced at 0400, as again described by Nyholt:

"The Task Force left Attu, Alaska at 0730 (7:30 A.M.) on June 24. We arrived at the target, Karabu Zaki, at 0300 hours (3:00 A.M.) on June 26 in heavy fog. Fire Control was handled by CIC, because target was not visible. On our approach, we could see gun flashes ahead, but couldn't determine if they were shore batteries or aircraft bomb bursts.

We commenced fire at 0400 on assigned targets and fired about 500 rounds of 5–inch 38. Before and during bombardment, we kept hearing reports of torpedo wakes around the ship, and could hear other ships on TBS (Talk Between Ship) circuit reporting attacks by PT Boats. At 0417 we ceased fire and began to cover the retirement of the Main Task Force units, with special attention to torpedo attack by small surface craft."

Bert Alton, RT, remembers seeing Karabu Zaki "all a fire" as the ships broke away for Great Sitkin Island. The raids were planned to keep the Japanese off–guard and keep them guessing as to our intentions. And although there is little or no documentation in the log or battle reports, some of the men aboard the *Luce*, along with Marty Nyholt, seem to remember that during this raid the Japanese attempted to retaliate by again sending out several PT type boats against the Task Force. Lt. Tom Parkerson recalls that "one of the ships in the screen called our attention to some bogies on our tail. We were the last ship in the screen, and we requested permission to maneuver to fire at them, because only one gun could bear, and they said POSIT (Take Proper Station) and so there we were."

Lt. Don Allen adds:

"I remember that because we fired on them. We sank them. Well, what happened was, we fired and nothing was happening, and then the bogey disappeared, so they were figuring it must have been a PT boat or something."

Lt. John Welch "distinctly remembers firing on radar pips, and they were doing something like 40 knots. They were going too fast for a service ship. The airbursts seemed to stop them." There seemed to be no harm done, however, and the ships continued their way back to port. Their time in the Aleutians was fast coming to an end.

Chapter 7
"A Chance to See the Sun Again"

The Task Force made their way back to Great Sitkin Island through a very heavy fog. Because of the fog, navigation was often difficult in the Aleutians, and now when alerted to try and find a disabled ship, it gave Lt. John Welsh some anxious moments:

"I was the navigator. We were up there for nine months, and I did not take one celestial sight, except a couple of sunlines on the days the sun came, and that was all. LORAN in those days wasn't all that good, but it was the best we had. The old man, Captain Owens, was really ticked off with me when we couldn't find the disabled ship. He said, 'You don't know where you are!' And I replied, 'I know where I am, or I think I know where I am—within reason.' He said, 'I don't think you know or have a ghost of an idea where we are.' He was getting mad. We couldn't find this big ship we were supposed to be on. I said, 'We should raise the peak of Great Sitkin tomorrow morning. We should be able to see it come daylight.' I was never more glad to see anything in all my life, and as it turned out, the disabled ship was on the other side of the Aleutian chains from where they said it was. We were just searching in the wrong place, and I was about to get fired as a navigator!"

Arriving at Sand Bay, Great Sitkin Island, the *Luce* moored portside to the USS *Wm. D. Porter* at the oil docks. The next day, 29 June, was when Orville Hiles, S2/c, who couldn't find women or the trees that were supposed to hide them in the Aleutians, reported aboard the *Luce* at 1115 hours for duty. The log for the next few days revealed ship inspection and a trip to Adak to provide transportation for Rear Admiral E.G. Small USN Commander Task Force 94 back to Sand Bay and then return to Adak. The inspection was somewhat distressing for the ship's doctor, Lt. Louis Shaffner:

"We were to meet out on the dock at 0900 for a formal inspection. Most of us thought this was unnecessary at that time, but that's what he had ordered, so everybody was out there all lined up waiting for the commodore coming around inspecting everybody. Finally he came, and it was obvious he was late because he had been at the officer's club—had spent the night there—his uniform was all messed up and he needed a shave. He wasn't in good shape. He came walking by inspecting the various crews, and he got to our ship's company and stopped right in front of me. He looked right at me and said, 'What's that?' I said, 'What do you mean, sir?' And he said, 'The thing on your upper lip.' He was talking about a mustache which I had been growing and twirling with beeswax (all of us were 'Asiatic' at that time). I said, 'That's a mustache.' He replied, 'That's the most disgusting thing I ever saw. I want it cut off and I'll have an inspection aboard your ship at 1300.' Well, that sort of shook me up a little bit. When inspection was over and we were aboard ship and I asked the Captain, 'What shall I do? Do I have to shave this off?' He said, 'Well, I don't believe I'd shave it off. I think I'd just trim it a little bit.' I trimmed the handlebars off—I didn't cut the mustache off all the way. We waited with trepidation until 1300, expecting this commodore to come aboard to inspect me among other things. He never did come, but at least that was part of the situation up in the Aleutians when everybody was anxious to get back to warmer weather."

Safely moored so the crew thought, again in Sand Bay, a submarine coming alongside hit the *Luce* and caused some damage to the port propeller. This necessitated a trip to the dry dock in Finger Bay, Adak for repairs. The delay was only about a day and 0814 hours on 14 July saw DD 522 underway conducting exercises again with DESRON 49. During these exercises, the destroyers responded to an emergency message concerning a downed plane. Fortunately, the search succeeded in rescuing the pilot who was picked up by the USS *Isherwood*.

It was while in port (Sitkin Bay) on 22 July that an event known as "The Spitting Incident" was discovered to have taken place and, according to the log, three men were indicted at "Captain's Mast." Being one of the cooks, J.C. Phillips was witness to the incident:

"The officers didn't have a baker, so we baked all of their cakes. None of the officer's steward cooks knew how to bake. Helping Virgil Degner, the baker that night, was a Frenchman, S1/c, Joe LeBlond—a big Frenchman. Joe had been assigned to the galley because nobody else could handle him. He was a big kid, and he had a short temper. You had to know how to handle him. He had had some run–ins with some of the officers. He was bitter. But he would do anything that we asked him to do. So Degner asked him to make the icing, and he was pretty gifted. We used him to peel potatoes and cut up celery and peel the onions. But Joe really wanted to be a cook. So he was helping Virgil that night. Degner was a second class baker from Ashland, Oregon. He was the man who would also load my gun (He died when the ship was sunk). I had left the galley, and I wasn't there when this incident took place. Otherwise, it would have never taken place. But they had had a few drinks. They had gotten into my 'Raisin Jack.' Degner had assigned Joe to the job of making that cream icing for the cake, and it amounted to mixing the powdered sugar and a little bit of cream and some granulated sugar together, and making a cream–type icing. So Joe got to thinking about the misfortune he'd had with a court-martial with the officers. He knew that this cake was going to the officer's mess. So he spit in it to get a little revenge. A few of the guys saw it. Virgil knew it happened. But Virgil didn't want to make up another batch of icing. So he just put it on the cake, and sent it on its way. Nobody knew about it for a couple of weeks. Then somehow or another, the word got out on the ship that Joe had done this thing, and they had an investigation. I guess Joe admitted it, and they court-martialed him. After we got down to the Philippines, they sent Joe down to the Army brig for two or three days over in Leyte. That was the last any of us saw of Joe. It probably saved Joe's life, because he was in one of the magazines, and I know he would have never got out."

Lt. Tom Parkerson recalls another incident while the USS *Luce* was moored alongside Commodore Gearing's flagship, the USS *Picking*:

"We had a seawatch on, which means that we had a couple of boilers lit off, so that if we had to get under way because of weather, we could do so quickly. So, the captain was in the Sea-Cabin—a little place to sleep up on the bridge. When it came time, M.L. Rogers, the first class Boatswain's Mate (we always called him 'M.L.'), called up from the mid-ship passageway on the phone and requested permission to pipe reveille. I looked at the time and said 'permission granted'. About that time the Captain happened to get up. He walked out, then I began to hear this sound over the P.A. system, and it was the old song, 'Mose kicked the Bucket—Old Man Mose is Dead.' And the Captain said, 'Sparky, what's that?' I says, 'Captain, I think I know—just a minute.' I went down in the mid-ship passageway, and there was Rogers with a record player, playing 'Old Man Mose is Dead!' He says, 'You gave me permission to pipe reveille, and I can pipe it any way I want!' And I said, 'The heck you can!' And I turned the switch off, but you would have to know Rogers. Rogers (I believe his first name was Merle) was an old-peace time Navy guy, and there's an expression in the Navy, and that expression is 'Asiatic.' If you say he's 'Asiatic,' you mean he's a little crazy from being at sea too long. This comes back from the old China station, way back, and Rogers came from way back! They were a little different than the rest of the folk! Just a little bit different, and so, I believe it was a little later in the morning, and the Commodore saw our Captain, he says, 'What've you got? A night club going on the *Luce*, over there?' So, at least the Captain knew what it was, and was able to explain. Roger sure had his own ideas."

On 8 August 1944, after a full nine months in the Aleutians, the USS *Luce* sailed from Sweeper's Cove, Adak, enroute to San Francisco. Most of DESRON 49 went with her. Marty Nyholt, FC2/c, had some thoughts concerning their Aleutian tour:

"The Karabu Zaki, Paramushiro Raid was our last operation as the Northern Pacific Force. We headed for the States—San Francisco and shore leave. Man, we were really looking forward to it... During our nine months in the Aleutians, the *Luce* and other units of the Task Force drew individual and group assignments such as searching for downed aircraft to rescue their crew and patrolling the Bering Sea on Submarine Patrol. We had lots of alleged Jap sub contacts but never actually located one. We did sideswipe an

American sub once and badly damaged one of our screws. That was the time we were hoping to go back to the States to get it repaired but they towed a floating dry dock up to Adak instead and repaired the propeller.

"Needless to say we were glad to be leaving the Aleutians and, as the sailors said, getting a chance to get into 'the Real War,' and equally enjoyable a chance to see the sun again."

Passing under the Golden Gate Bridge on 15 August, the *Luce* was moored port side to the Bethlehem dockyards. In port some changes in personnel occurred. While on the *Luce*, Bert Alton, was promoted to the rank of Warrant Radio Electrician. He was dismayed, however, to find out that he was one of those changes, and he reflected back on the cause of his being transferred:

"I had set up and taught an electronics course for the radar operators. Their jobs were boring and tiring—staring at mostly blank radar screens for four out of every twelve hours. I thought the class might keep their interest up. It apparently worked, and I received good response from the students. Largely as a result of that class, I was recommended for a promotion to officer status. A couple of months later, the recommendation was approved in Washington D.C., and I was now a commissioned warrant officer. But there was a problem. The destroyer did not have an allotment for a warrant officer in the ship's personnel complement. My new officer friends thought that this fact might be overlooked in D.C., and that I could slip by and stay with the ship. No such luck. Orders for my departure came in the next mail. The USS *Luce*, having completed her assignment in the Aleutians, sailed for Hunter's Point, San Francisco and there I bade a sad farewell to my destroyer friends. I had orders to report to the USS *Mindanao*, ARG-3 (a repair ship) and the *Luce* was to have new radar equipment installed and then proceed to the Central Pacific."

An attack of appendicitis put Lt. J.R. Welsh in the Naval Hospital at Treasure Island on 18 August for a time; and on 23 August, Joe Bille RT2/c, reported aboard to replace Bert Alton. Bill Fotie, RM3/c, had an interesting experience as well as a slight problem while in San Francisco:

"After leaving the Aleutians and returning to San Francisco, my commanding officer told me to draw a .45 and boots and accompany him to pick up the new codes at the super–duper secret underground command center. It was just like a James Bond movie, being checked in and out, underground elevators and steel doors banging. A little time later, I was called to the bridge because Captain Owens wanted to see me. This was traumatic. The Captain just doesn't see a seaman first class. He looked at me and said, 'Why in the heck didn't you tell someone you were an Italian citizen?' To understand this, the radio shack is a top secret place and because most officers couldn't type, they had sailors like myself (secretly) run the ECM coding machine. I was born in Italy and told him that when my parents were divorced, I would be an American citizen because my mother was a natural born citizen... well, it seems that the immigration people take a dim view of divorce judges making immigration decisions. Owens turned to the communications officer and chaplain, told him to get a Bible and preceded to give me a temporary oath as an American citizen and get back to work. I received my official citizenship after the war."

The workers who came aboard the ship to do the necessary work were rather amazed at its condition, as Burr McFarland, WT1/c, relates:

"All of the yard workers who came on our ship wouldn't believe that we had been on active duty for over a year with nine months in the Aleutians. The reason for the disbelief was that while underway from Adak to San Francisco, the deck divisions gave the ship a complete paint job (North Pacific deep blue) all the way to the waterline. The engineering spaces were spruced up and in the fire rooms we cleaned and polished tubes in all four boilers. No wonder the workers didn't believe us—we looked brand new. So what happened? They brought paint hoses aboard and gave us this camouflage job. How ironic!"

J.C. Phillips, SC1/c, recalled that personnel who lived on the West Coast obtained leave while others were granted liberty. Finally, on 26 August, the USS *Luce*, in company with DESRON 49 pointed her bow west and headed out under the Golden Gate Bridge. If anyone had taken a real close look at the *Luce* then, however, they would have seen a rather unusual sight. Waino Johnson, GM1/c, was over the side of the bow in a Boatswain's chair:

"I believe that it was Parkerson who asked me if I'd paint over the numbers (of the ship). So there I was, looking down at the water rolling by like a running river—over the side, painting over the numbers while heading out, and I enjoyed it! But then I enjoyed everything like that. And that's the way we started that trip for me."

Thus the USS *Luce*, with a happy sailor dangling off her bow erasing DD 522 to complete the camouflage, entered the wide blue Pacific and sailed onto further exploits. Her destination and purpose: the Philippines, to assist in the invasion.

PART THREE
THE PHILIPPINES:
THE ACTION INTENSIFIES

On 25 August 1944 while the USS *Luce* was in San Francisco Bay preparing to get underway the next day for Pearl Harbor and points west, the crew received the happy news of the liberation of Paris. The year 1944 had seen great progress in the Allied push to free conquered territories from the Axis powers. In April MacArthur's forces had landed at Hollandia in New Guinea, while in May the Allies began their Anzio, Italy, offensive and on 4 June took Rome unopposed. Then came the greatest invasion in all history—the long-awaited D-Day on 6 June at Normandy, France.

That summer while the USS *Luce* was completing her last few sweeps of the cold Aleutian waters, the Americans continued to hammer back the Japanese forces in the central and south Pacific areas. On 15 June the U.S. made their first air raids against Japan with the new giant aircraft, the B-29 Super-fortress. On the heels of this event came the Battle of the Philippine Sea where the 19th of June saw hundreds of Japanese aircraft shot down by U.S. carrier pilots with very minimal losses. Known as the "Great Marianas Turkey Shoot", it helped greatly to permanently cripple the Japanese air forces.

Saipan, in the Marianas, was finally taken after twenty-five bloody days on 9 July. Guam fell to the American forces after three weeks struggle on 10 August. The "Rising Sun" of the Japanese Empire was sinking fast. Meanwhile, details for the planned October invasion of the Philippines were being worked out—an event which found the USS *Luce* in the thick of the action.

Chapter 8

Supporting the Invasion

The USS *Luce* arrived in Pearl Harbor on 31 August 1944. The next day saw the commander of LST Flotilla #3, Commander (CDR) Arthur A. Ageton, come aboard to establish the *Luce* as his flagship. He brought with him a staff of five officers and nine enlisted men. That same day, the *Luce* got under way to join up with LST Flotilla #3, and for the next few days CDR Ageton led the ships in his directing of rehearsal landings in the Hawaiian Islands. Lt. John Welsh, who studied CDR Ageton's book on navigation at the Naval Academy, recalls what life was like with the commodore on board:

"I remember he had a million radios up on our bridge—just loaded with radios. He would really start talking to his chief, Melaney… and berate him… Melaney would hold the talk button down, and that would cut off the bridge. When he let it up and heard silence, he would say, 'Commodore, you're over–modulating. You're talking too loud. Would you repeat your last message?' And again the Commodore would start to unmercifully ride Melaney. This went on until his chief got him to speak normally."

Lt. Tom Parkerson had the job of decoding the Commodore's messages that he received:

"His communication officer wanted us to decode… I told him that there weren't enough hours in the day to decode all of the messages that he wanted us to decode. We took the ones that were addressed to our group or our overall group and that sort of thing, and it just took time, and there was a lot of traffic. So when I tried to explain to him the practical limitations that we couldn't decode it all, he told me there's no such thing as can't in the Commodore's vocabulary, but reality prevailed.

"I also remember John Welsh helped us out by letting us get our sleep through all the activity of being a flagship."

LST Flotilla #3 with flagship USS *Luce* rendezvoused on 11 September, and set course for Manus in the Admiralty Islands via way of Eniwetok. Along the way, various exercises were conducted, preparatory to support of upcoming amphibious landings in the Philippines. The ships were designated "Task Group 33.6 OTC CDR LST Flotilla 3 in USS *Luce*." The International Date Line was crossed, then the equator, and Orville Hiles, S1/c, took part in a ceremony marking the event on 2 October:

"This was my first experience with the 'polliwogs' and the 'shellbacks'. I never had heard of either of those two terms until I was confronted with that experience. The 'polliwogs' were the people who haven't been below the equator, and the 'shellbacks' were the ones who had been across. Two days before this, the 'polliwogs' were doing everything they could to the 'shellbacks'. Then it reverses when you go across (the equator). I remember one of the officers—I don't recall his name—that some of the guys didn't like too well. They put him on the focsle in barrel of hot water… going across the equator. They were getting a little even on that, everybody becomes equal at that ceremony. They said that from his waist down he was just peach tree red from the heat of the water. And then they have these slop chutes to keep garbage in for three or four days and they get you sliding through these chutes—almost the length of the ship."

Freeman Phillips, S1/c, remembers that this officer in the barrel was given a pair of binoculars to look for the equator—and he looked for it.

The *Luce* sighted Eniwetok Atoll tower at 0835 on 25 September. After refueling, taking on mail and exchanging movies with LST 270, course was again set for Manus Island in the Admiralty group. Here in Seadler Harbor, the ships refueled and set out on 11 October for the Philippines in company with Task Group 79.6. Their destination was Leyte Gulf to cover the first landings of the

Philippine invasion.

Freeman Phillips, who was "striking" (in the process of learning) for the rank of torpedoman from seaman first class, was awed by the collection of ships in the fleet:

"The day before the invasion, when we got up and it got daylight, I remember walking out on the deck and seeing ships as far as the horizon, in all directions from us. We were traveling with the invasion ships and other destroyers screening us that were going to be the invasion force. It spanned out all over the sea. There were just hundreds of ships—hundreds."

Tongues of orange flame accompanied by a thunderous vibrating roar and drifting clouds of smoke signaled the start of the Philippine invasion on 20 October 1944. One of the men overwhelmed by the spectacle on the *Luce* was J.C. Phillips, SC1/c:

"It makes you right nervous. You don't know where the next shell is coming in. Before the army started landing, the first hour or so, they were firing those 16th shells right over us. They sounded like a freight train coming over you. You were hoping and praying that the guy doing the aiming out there on the battleships didn't fall short, 'cause it would have been terribly embarrassing if he had blowed us away. That made me nervous. Coming from one side was the battleship shots, and coming from the beach side were the mortars. You were stuck between the devil and the deep blue sea. I was standing back there on the fantail with nothing between me and them but the wind. We were firing that 20 millimeter and it got hot and we got to sweating. Your mouth would get so dry you couldn't spit. When you fire the corks on the end of those five–inch powder containers, they go all over the ship. It gets in your mouth and in your ears, and when you breathe, it gives you a funny taste in your mouth. I'm standing back there, and the wind's blowing the cork right on me from the number five 5–inch. I thought we had gotten ourselves in a life–threatening situation. But I saw those boats go by with the soldiers in them, and I thought, well, we are lucky. Those guys are the ones that are really gonna get it."

Bill Fotie, RM3/c, also had some thoughts concerning the bombardment:

"I remember the bombardments– watching the big shells from the *New Jersey*, *Iowa* and *Missouri* arching thru the air. I heard over the radio the pilots telling the shore command that the Japs had tied Filipino women and children to their tanks and trucks as they came up to the landing because our big guns were knocking out tanks 50 miles inland. The Piper Cubs were spotting for the guns. The small 'rocket boats' were going in close and releasing their barrage. It seemed to me that we were very close to shore on a number of occasions and most of all, I remember the landing boats carrying the troops into the landing. I was also glad I wasn't on those boats."

The Daily Deck Log Summary records that the first assault wave from the LST's departed at 0850. Lt. John Welsh and Lt. Tom Parkerson assisted the Commodore in lining up the LST's for their run to the beach.

Lt. Welsh:

"Arthur Ageton, as the Commodore, was the one who formed them up. Then he talked to them on his radios, and then when they got to a reasonable line, he would dispatch them to the beach. Fortunately, there was very little resistance. We bombarded the beach first."

Lt. Parkerson:

"Radar made this possible, but keeping all those ships, smaller vessels in a formation, keeping track of them all–this could never have happened without radar, because you could see them all on the screen, and somehow you could get a message to one of them, any of them that got out of line. And they did tend to get out of line."

Lt. Welsh:

"Arthur A. was very intolerant. He would say, ' LST in line number 6, why are you lagging? Close up, close up!' It was very difficult to keep the formation military. There wasn't much resistance on the beach, and all the LCVP's got in there, and then we went somewhere else. There were a lot of LST's, and he kept having a tough time keeping those guys straight, but he did a great job."

Bill Fotie and some other crew members took the opportunity to promote a little capitalistic venture:

"We were selling the LCVP crews breakfast for five bucks on the fantail, because they had been on C-rations for I don't know how long. We would empty our stuff into a tray and run up the fantail, and they'd pull up alongside the fantail. Well, I don't think we were the only ones doing that, and we'd sell them our breakfast for five bucks, because we figured they didn't need any money where they were going anyway! All of them trooping merrily to the beach. We waved to them."

And while some of the troops in the assault craft reached the beach with full stomachs, others came riding back on the receding tide to the ships with lethal wounds, as witnessed by J.C. Phillips, SC1/c:

"The bodies from the first landing were the soldiers that we had seen go by at 6:00 A.M. That was high tide. When the tide started coming back out, it started bringing the bodies back out. That was right sobering. You saw them going in at 6:00, and when the tide started coming out a couple of hours later, the bodies came floating back out, still in the full battle pack. That was very sobering, indeed."

Freeman Phillips saw a column of Japanese tanks going along the top of the hill:

"Our fire was directed to them. We knocked out some of those tanks—how many, I can't remember. But there were at least four or five tanks on top of that hill, silhouetted against the sky. Made real good targets."

It was during this invasion that the Japanese introduced a terrorist form of warfare for the first time—the kamikaze suicide planes. Kamikaze means "divine wind", and was the name given to a storm which wrecked an enemy flotilla intent on invading Japan in the Middle Ages. Through the use of these suicide tactics, as the more radical Japs later hoped, such fierce damage would be inflicted on the American fleet by this means that the U.S.A. would lose its desire to continue and sue for peace. The Philippine campaign saw only a few of these kamikaze attacks—basically an introduction, as previously noted. But this was a grim foreshadowing of the carnage to come in the months ahead around islands closer to the Jap home land. Orville Hiles, S1/c, echoed the thoughts of the average seaman when it began to dawn on them what they were up against:

"At that point I was still very patriotic, you know—flag-waving, but when we got into Leyte and we started seeing the kamikaze planes starting to come, self-preservation took over pretty darn quick, and you're there to protect your own backside rather than fight for that glory or whatever the cause might be that you are in."

The men of the *Luce* would be very thankful for their limited contact with kamikazes in the Philippines. They dared hope that perhaps they might be as lucky in the future...

At 1120 hours Red and Blue beaches were reported secure. At 1603 spotters aboard the *Luce* reported that the USS *Honolulu* had hoisted a signal that she had been torpedoed. A noticeable list was observed on that ship. As the *Luce* proceeded to her night patrol station just outside the transport and LST areas, she received a report that enemy planes were reported to be in the vicinity. At 1844 hours a Japanese bomber was seen coming directly for DD 522 from the beach. The *Luce* soon joined with the other ships nearer the beach, in opening fire at the elusive bomber. No hits were scored as the plane flew over and disappeared, and the enemy likewise did no damage. The twilight and low clouds had concealed the plane most of the time.[1]

On 23 October, after two days of supporting the invasion, the *Luce* was released from her duty to help provide escort for ships heading back to Seadler Harbor. Before getting underway, Commodore Arthur Ageton transferred his pennant to LST 483.[2]

The destroyer left just in time to miss the sea battles fought around the Philippines in the areas of Leyte, Surigao Strait, and off the coast of Samar from 24 to 25 October. The situation had become so critical in these battles, however, that some ships, including the *Luce*, turned back to assist, as recalled by Freeman Phillips, S1/c:

"We had been escorting these ships, which had been damaged in battle at Leyte, for maybe a day or so, and we got the report that the Japanese Fleet was in the arena and was ready to attack. At that time, they turned two destroyers, the USS *Badger* and us, around and we headed back toward where the Japanese were. At some point, they turned us around again and sent us back to continue screening the damaged ships—probably because the Japanese had already left the area after the battle. That was the first battle of the Philippines for us."

---

[1] Action Report on the Assault of Leyte Island, Philippines; Period 20–23 October 1944; Serial 025, 4 November 1944.
[2] Ibid.

But the crew of the USS *Luce* could hear the sounds of the battle that they had barely missed over the intercom. This made quite an impression on the men, as voiced by Orville Hiles, S1/c:

"Then the big Battle of Leyte took place. Thank God we were sent into New Guinea to pick up paratroopers that were going up to Luzon for that invasion! We listened on the intercom to all those battles that were taking place up there. I remember hearing the destroyers getting lined up to go in to shoot. You would hear them talking, and you would hear a boom, and then hear them no more. They were just clicking the guns like crazy."

The *Luce* found it necessary to refuel at sea and received 85,409 gallons of oil from the USS *Thurban*, which was one of the ships with the *Luce* making up CTU 79.14. Other ships, according to the log report, were the USS *Cavalier, Alshain, President Hayes, Stembel, Preble, Long* and *Palmer*. Her escort duty to Manus completed, the DD 522 joined up with CTU 79.15 to guide the USS *Cavalier* to Oro Bay, New Guinea where she stayed for several days.

The crew of the *Luce* was about to gain a little breather from her rigorous duty before heading back to the Philippines.

Chapter 9

Leisure, Recreation-and Kamikazes!

While berthed in New Guinea the men of DD 522 had time to go ashore and participate in some recreation, such as football as Freeman Phillips, S1/c, describes:

"Talk about a game getting rough! It was only touch football, but, boy, you fall down on that coral and you were cut to pieces! They would take so many coconut trees and tie a line around them, and each ship kept to their own group inside of these boundaries. And you're not supposed to go into another group because it would start fights, so we all stayed within those ropes. I remember that the battlewagon *Tennessee* had a group not too far from us. Of course they had a lot bigger group than we had, and they were getting real boisterous over there, having a real party, and I remember us worrying for fear they were gonna swamp us! Whereas we only had about 150 men ashore, they had a couple of thousand. They were right near us, but each ship's crew stayed within those ropes. And then I remember other places where we'd run up and down the beach, and collect seashells."

It was during the lay over in Oro Bay that Bill Fotie RM3/c, was left behind and received quite a scare:

"I went ashore to the joint Army–Navy Com Center to pick up new codes. When I came back to the dock, the *Luce* had taken off. I stayed on the Army base for about two weeks before the *Luce* came back. While stranded there, I got lost in the jungle and had the heck scared out of me when I met up with Aborigines all painted with ships' chromate."

Safely aboard ship again, Bill sailed with her back to Leyte Gulf on 11 November 1944. Spending a few days around Leyte Gulf on patrol duty, the *Luce* again sailed with the task unit to Manus. Some personnel changes were made at Manus before leaving for Borgen Bay, New Britain on 27 November. Operating out of Borgen Bay through 10 December, DD 522 participated in anti-submarine patrol. Then it was back to Manus again. This was an opportunity for the ship to receive provisions from the Australians. But as J.C. Phillips, SC1/c relates, the conditions were not the best for handling all that food:

"Once while anchored in Seadler Harbor in New Guinea, we took provisions from the Australian supply ships. We took an LCVP from one of the transports and went over to get these groceries. We got alongside and they asked us how many units we wanted. None of us knew what a unit was, I asked the chief how many units he wanted. He didn't know what a unit was either, and told us to tell them to give us five units. We then said to the Australians, 'Give us five units'. They swung over so many nets loaded with goods that it almost sank the boat. Here we were at the other end of the harbor, about twenty miles from where our ship was, making only three or four knots because of the load of the food—which was frozen—and the temperature was about 110°. We got back just before dark. By this time all the meat was thawed out—big half sides of oxen and all, ox tails, some six feet long—and the thawed meat leaked out fat from the netting sacks the meat was in, and it stank! We finally got it all stored aboard our ship. And then when came time to serve and eat the stuff, the crew just threw it over the side, it was so bad. Soon the harbor was full of floating meat, and the commander of the fleet wanted to know what ship was doing this. Of course we never owned up to it. The meat finally just floated out to sea. We had also received hundred-pound bags of flour, but bugs, or weevils, had got into it. We put this flour on deck at first while we stored the meat. It was so hot that a lot of the weevils came out of the flour to seek shade, and a lot of the crew saw that. A few days later when I started baking the bread I noticed that some weevil parts went through the sifter. I put raisins in the bread so the crew couldn't tell the difference.

"Then there was the dehydrated food. At that time they were

just coming out with the stuff, and we were the guinea pigs they experimented on. They shipped us dehydrated eggs, cabbage, and potatoes. They gave us directions on how to soak them for so long, and so forth. If you reconstituted the eggs and ate them right then, they were tolerable. But if you held them for ten minutes then they would turn green. So before I could get enough cooked and down to the mess deck the last guys in line would get green eggs. And the cabbage had to be soaked in cold water, which we didn't have down there on the equator. So we would soak it in water at room temperature—which would be about one hundred degrees. It would make it barely palatable. But the kool–aid, when mixed up, was just rancid! It would curl your shoe soles right up! So we had our food supply problems... "

Arrangements were made to have the *Luce* take part in the landing maneuvers at Huon Gulf, New Guinea during 17–19 December. Plans were made for the destroyer to accompany DESRON 49, which was escort for the task force which would invade another area in the Philippines—Lingayen Gulf. To help round out the crew, Ensign Art Replogle reported for duty at Seadler Harbor the day after Christmas. And sometime while DD 522 was doing all this sailing from port to port before setting out for the Philippines again, another crew member was added who knew Burr McFarland. He was John B. (Jack) Rechkemmer, F1/c, from Oelwein, Iowa, and how he came to meet Burr half a world away is quite a story, as McFarland relates:

"I'm from Independence, Iowa, which is only fifteen miles away from Oelwein. One day I was down in the forward fire room, which I was in charge of, and this young fellow came down the ladder and said, 'I'm looking for Burr McFarland'. I said that I was he and what did he want. He replied, 'I'm Jack Rechkemmer. Your dad sent me here'. Well, here we are in the Philippines, and Jack shows up. I asked him, 'What do you mean, my dad sent you here?' 'Well,' he said, 'You know your dad is on the draft board... I got in a little trouble down there in Independence, and Sheriff Hart picked me up and took me to jail. And he said to me, 'Now Jack, you got two choices. Either go to jail, or go into the service.' I was only seventeen at the time and I didn't want to go to jail and get a record, so I told him I would go into the service. The sheriff took me to the draft board, and your dad was there. He asked me what branch of service I would prefer and I said that I didn't know and what would he suggest? And your dad replied, 'Well, I got a son in the Army Aircorps, but with Sheriff Hart picking you up there's no way you could get in the Aircorps. I got another son in the Navy." So that's what I picked– the Navy. Your dad sent me here.' And that's how I met up with someone from home."

John Rechkemmer, like so many others aboard the USS *Luce*, never made it back to his home in Oelwein, Iowa.

On 27 December 1944 at 1237 the USS *Luce*, DD 522, sailed with DESRON 49 and sortied with Task Units 79.5 and 79.6. Their destination was the Lingayen Gulf to support the second invasion of the Philippines. 7 January, Bill Lietz, TM2/c, recalls, "was the start of the kamikazes for us. We did a lot of bombarding and escorting of troops, plus anti–submarine patrol. That was the start of the *Luce* being called 'The *Lucky Luce*' from the survival of the morning and evening attacks."

In an article written several months later, the action of the destroyer DD 522 was chronicled:

"On the way to Lingayen, in the Surigao Straits, the *Luce* began her combat life against the Japanese planes. Only one other destroyer was in the convoy with the *Luce*, and both were targets of the red–balled planes. As two Zekes came in from the port bow of the convoy, the hail of fire was too thick for them to fly through. They dropped their bombs aimlessly and started to hightail for home. One Zeke, however, was blotted out before it could pull up out of its dive.[1]

The log credits the *Luce* for the destruction of the Zeke. Freeman Phillips, S1/c, believes that one of the ship's first salvos hit the plane "because we commenced firing at five miles... as soon as they came into range of our 5–inch guns. She went down at four miles, so that says we had been shooting at her while she was traveling one mile."

The gunners of DD 522 were beginning to build a reputation of being excellent marksmen. Freeman recalls that "whatever we aimed at, we got. We were known to be among the best shooters in the fleet."

Then on 9 January 1945 things began to heat up as the kamikazes came out in greater force. Several ships were hit by the

---

[1] Pinkowski, "The *Lady Luce*." Our Navy, Mid–December, 1946, pp. 60–61.

suicides. Later in the day the *Luce* helped to even the score when she downed a 'snooper' plane. The action report states that the 'snooper a twin–engine bomber, "crossed our bow at close range (3000 yards). His exhaust flame was clearly visible and (the) engine could be heard. (At 2006) Plane was seen to catch fire and crash to north of transport area. Just before the plane caught fire, it was fired on with 40 mm by a ship near the transport area. We fired 26 rounds 5"/38 with a good fire control solution, and it is believed this fire shot down the plane."[2]

Cliff Roberts, CFC, was directing the firing sequences:

"They tried to use automatic ammunition on me and I wouldn't accept it. I said every fourth shell is going to be a tracer so I could know whether we were hitting above, below, or behind or what. And I said 'When you see the first burst, tell me whether it's lagging, leading, up or down, so I can correct the computer.' That Jap plane was going almost parallel with us and our computer couldn't even meet the speed that the plane would hit. We just didn't have the capability. They yelled, 'You're lagging, you're lagging!' I just reached down and turned the target speed knob up about one hundred knots over what they had as the speed, and the plane ran right into those shells."

Bob Moyer, FC3/c, was also helping to aim the guns on the speeding plane:

"I saw the exhausts in the dark and thought the plane was strafing us. I heard Lt. Cliff Roberts screaming that we had a perfect solution except that he's closing and the computer is going into the stops. Then Jones gave the order to fire at the same time Captain Owens did. With the computer going into the stops (which meant the guns could no longer fire on target) we had to get the plane or we might have been sunk. We got it."

Marty Nyholt, FC2/c, explains the difficulty of this type of encounter at night:

"We picked up this 'Betty' bomber at night, first by fire control radar. Our radar had a problem of being off at about ten degrees in elevation, so we liked to get the target visually. If you fire at night and miss, your gun flashes destroy the night vision of your crew. If you miss, your flashes give the pilot a pin–point location,

---

[2] Action Report on the Assault On Luzon From Lingayen Gulf. 9 January 1945; serial GI–45; No. 106124.

and he comes in and wastes you. At night we tried to locate the plane's exhaust flare, which is very visible, and then tracked him to a 'perfect solution' in quick order. At 3,000 yards (mostly straight up) we opened fire and blew the sucker away with the first salvo and (then) ceased fire. When the guns flashed, I could see a very visible pilot in that cockpit, and I could see a torpedo. It was 20 to 30 feet below the Betty, having already been dropped. I reported to the gunnery officer that I saw a 'Baka', and that I don't think we got him. He must have been blinded by the gun flashes, and he crashed into our wake."

The Japanese one–way suicide attacks were not confined to aircraft, however. Individual Japs would swim out to the ships from land to try and sink them, as J.C. Phillips and Freeman Phillips (not related) remember.

J.C.:

"The swimmers came out...with a pack of explosives on their backs to blow a hole (in the ship). So orders came down from the bridge to shoot anything that comes by. Don't let anything get in close enough to where it can do damage to the ship. So we're shooting anything that comes by—empty boxes, full boxes, anything that floated by."

Freeman:

"They (Jap swimmers) did this several times while we were in the Philippines. All during the invasion, we would shoot with small arms fire anything that floated by—a tree stump, boxes—because we knew that the Japs were attaching explosives to swimmers and trying to hit our ships. (In one case) a suicide boat came out with a white flag on it, coming very slowly toward our sister ship, the USS *Charles J. Badger*, and when just a few yards from the ship, she opened up her engines at top speed and fired a depth charge that exploded under the *Badger* killing several men. They were using desperate, desperate measures—any way they could hurt us, in any way they were up to it."

And J.C., firing at the threat posed in the water, knew that it was either them or him, as the Japs kept coming out with those bodies, underneath those boxes that had been emptied from various supplies.

"I didn't have nothing for them but some 20 millimeter cannon bullets. I didn't have any sobering thoughts about them. I knew for sure if somebody's got to die, if you don't make the other guy die first, then you are going to die. That's the way it has to be. Whenever I got strapped up in my 20 millimeter cannon, and there was a target in view, and I got my sights on that target, most of the time I was so conditioned in my mind and my reactions that the only thing on my mind was making sure that other guy died first. You could have stuck a bayonet through my belly, I believe, and I would not have felt it, because I was so emotionally involved with that target. And I knew that if I didn't kill him, he was gonna kill me. I was the gunner on number five 20 millimeter, and when a target approached my ship, and I was his target, (then) it was between me and the other man—either in the aircraft or in the boat or swimming. One of us had to die. That was all that was on my mind. No thoughts passed through my mind other than you've got to get him on the first shot, because if he fires first, he might get you. And he stands a good chance of getting you; so you make sure that the first salvo or burst got home. That was all that was on my mind. And we were forever shooting—day and night…

"Up until then, I felt like I might have a chance to get home. But after the Philippines, when they started the suicide tactics, then I never expected that I would be home, ever. I thought I would die in the Pacific. I never had any feeling that I would ever return. It's the adrenalin that focused your mind, as it did me. I had no fear, I wasn't shaking. But when the battle was over, and I looked around and thought of what happened, that's when I got shook up."

Another time, the gunners of 522 ceased their fire on a lone bandit when it flew out of range. As the plane flew on, all guns secured except for the one Milton Cathey, BM2/c, was manning. It had one shell still in it—as Milton relates:

"They told me to shoot the shell (to clear the gun). I shot it, and it hit the plane, way over there, and we saw the explosion, so we were pretty sure it hit the plane."

Freeman Phillips witnessed the episode and thought that "where it was so far away, you don't know whether it hit the plane or not, but we just assumed it did because we saw the flash."

The men of the *Luce* could see the effects of the action in the Philippines invasions on both land and sea. Much of the time they were either eyewitnesses of, or in the center of, the fighting. Bill

Fotie, RM3/c, remembers this and a rather grim scene:

"We covered a number of the invasions of Leyte and Mindanao, and many times we battled Jap planes and watched dogfights in the sky. At night there was always a fireworks display going on and, of course, we had Nighttime Charlie flying just out of gun range with his motors off key, keeping us awake and at general quarters.

"At that point, war was daily routine. In one incident, an LST came by towing a rope behind it, and there were dead bodies tied to the rope... it was the tropics and bodies didn't last long. Someone standing next to me said, 'If their mothers could see them now...' "

The action report for 12 January credits Waino Johnson, GM1/c, with spotting three enemy planes with his naked eye coming in to do their worst.[3] As he recalls:

"It was breakfast time. I had just finished my breakfast and I went topside. It was a real sunny morning. I laid down on deck to rest.... and all of a sudden I spotted this plane. It was pretty high and looked small. I jumped into the gun mount and put on the phones and reported the plane to the bridge."

The *Luce* at this time was leading the other ships in defense tactics. The destroyer fired so fast other enemy planes now coming upon the scene circled just out of range for a time. To Lt. John R. Welsh, the *Luce's* 26 year old executive officer, it seemed that the planes were afraid to close in:

"Finally one of the planes made a suicide dive on a large transport which had already been damaged. It... overshot it's mark... and dropped into the water... By this time our CAP (Combat Air Patrol) arrived and got into the fight.... a Nip started to smoke and dive toward us. All ships opened up on it... on our port side and... it dived through a hail of antiaircraft fire to the water."[4]

The action report of 12 January states that the transport was the USS *War Hawk*.

The next day at 0758 an enemy plane crashed into LST 700. Lt. Tom Parkerson remembers this incident very clearly:

"A Jap kamikaze had attacked one of the LST's, and one of the

---
[3] AA Action Report of 12 January; Serial 02-45, No. 105998.
[4] Edward Pinkowski, Op. Cit.

young men on board was knocked overboard, and we picked him up. Our doctor, Lt. Louis Shaffner, amputated his leg. As it turned out he was a young guy that was too young to be in the Navy, and had lied about his age, and here he is, losing a leg, but the Doc saved him. It was a near miss by the kamikaze, and it just ticked, grazed him, but knocked him off."

The wounded sailor was transferred to the USS *Appalachian* on 17 January. Destroyer and crew obtained a few days of respite when DD 522 put in at San Pedro Bay, Leyte, on 16 January for refueling and provisions. During this as at other times, while docked in the Philippines, some of the crew would be able to get ashore for some relaxation. Liberty in the Philippines was a bit different than in the States. Strange sights and different experiences from a native culture would be remembered years afterwards by these young sailor boys. Lt. Art Replogle, Supply Dispersing Officer:

"Bananas! The bananas were so tiny! About five inches long. Once when ashore, we went to huts which were stilted, with the animals underneath, and they had Singer sewing machines in those huts. You could have gotten anything in the world if you had a needle. They had broken needles, and they needed sewing machine needles badly. It seemed incongruous—a very primitive way of living, and they had sewing machines!"

Burr McFarland, WT1/c:

"During the invasion of Leyte, the Filipinos came out in dugout canoes from way down the beach, away from the invasion forces, and came up to fantails of the destroyers, the very ships that were in close, and they had coconuts and bananas, and Japanese invasion money, all this kind of stuff they wanted to trade for our mattress covers, and our skivvy shirts and shorts, and any white goods we had, so they could make clothes out of them."

Orville Hiles, S1/c:

"There were flat beds in the huts, and the old man or the father would sleep on that, and the family would all sleep on the floor, and they would have the cooking baths outside. I tried to explain to this guy what a bed was, and in spite of all the language I could come up with, I could not convince him what a bed was. He had no reason for it. He was perfectly happy on that mat. All these little kids were naked, diving into the water when you threw money, and so forth. There were ten or fifteen kids all in one little neck of the woods and if you had money or cigarettes that you wanted to trade, they would dive down to get them and so forth, and that was very interesting."

Bill Fotie, RM3/c:

"I went ashore a number of times, don't remember if it was liberty or duty, but I met some girls and drank raisin wine. They sure did live dirty in their thatch huts. I remember giving someone one of my T–shirts and some socks, as I always carried spares. They were starving and almost without clothes."

Omer Emond, S1/c:

"They had this place outside where they cooked. They used to have big vats with rice in it. The rice was on a pad-like, and the whole village used that area to cook their rice. They put it in four or five large pans. They would put the new rice in the center, with the old rice around the edges, and eat from it. I remember going up a big hill where they had their rice field away from the village, and I went so far, that I thought I had better turn around because there could be some Japs there. They looked the same (as the natives), you know..."

Freeman Phillips, S1/c:

"I was at one of these houses on stilts, and the family was showing me how they lived. There were chickens and pigs and other fowl running around, right underneath the house. And at night, the family would roll out a bamboo mat, and the whole family would just lay down and sleep on that mat in that one-room shack. And I remember they would dive for money. We would throw a dime into the water, and they would dive out of the dugout canoes after that dime, and they would always get it before it even hit the bottom. We got 'cat's eyes' out of there, too. Cat's eyes were little shells."

Lt. Art Replogle:

"Cat's eyes were orange, and they had lines through them. We collected them, and made bracelets or necklaces. It was sort of something to take back...if we got back."

Lt. John Welsh:

"At Tacloban on Leyte' we probably had the biggest bar I've ever seen, and the fastest dispensing of booze that I have ever witnessed. Oh, it went fast. And it was all free. No one had any money. There was raisin wine and tube juice. Made me sick as a dog! We tried to get Philippine beer. One time I had to go ashore at Tacloban to pick up the communication publications for our ship. They used to call them the 'skids'."

Bob Harrison, RM2/c:

"We anchored off a small island called Samar, one of the thousands of the Philippine Islands there. I went ashore. I took two socks full of rice. I was going to parlay something, I don't know for what, maybe I'd marry one, I didn't know. Most of the people in that village on that island were refugees from the city of Manila when the Japanese invaded the Philippines. I got talking to a family... They really accepted me, and I stayed overnight on a mat. I was supposed to be back probably six o'clock that night before dark, because there were Japanese snipers on that island and there was a curfew for us. I guess they came looking for me. I came back the next day anyway. I went to the Captain's Mast, and they gave me ten hours in the forward boiler room...but the water tenders and firemen didn't put me to work, for which I was thankful. They said to get in the back of the tubes and take a nap."

There were other activities designed to give the crew some diversion from their routine. Freeman Phillips was involved in an activity with M.L. Rogers, BM1/c, (the man who, according to Lt. Tom Parkerson, had earlier played a record for reveille):

"It was early in our service in the Philippines that the executive officer would have as many of the crew as possible to participate in boxing. It was one of the few activities you could do aboard ship as space was limited. A lot of us did participate in boxing, which was done on the fantail where there was room. There was a man on board called M.L. Rogers. We all called him M.L. He was a first class boatswain's mate. He had been the light-heavyweight champion in the Asiatic Fleet before the war. He was kind of a character. A lot of us in the crew called him 'Asiatic' because he had been out there in China for a long time. He would go for hours and days without speaking to anyone and then one day he would corner you and talk real fast—talk you to death! Then he might not talk to you again for several weeks or months. I was on the deck force under M.L. and our job was to keep the topside clean. Because I was right there with him all the time I got to know him about as well as anybody. He was almost always in on the boxing bouts but didn't fight much at all because there was no one up to his speed. When working Rogers would give his orders in a very curt way. He didn't mince his words. He gave an order and expected it to be followed. That was just his way. No one dared cross him.

"We had another fellow in the crew who was a pretty good boxer. I went up against him a couple of times but he just massacred me as I wasn't in his category at all. I was young and cocky and didn't mind taking the punishment. One day Rogers said to me on the deck, 'Phillips, I'm going to teach you to box.' We had a set of boxing gloves hanging over number five 5 inch gun and any two people that were having problems with each other were invited back there to put on the gloves and settle things right then and there. Rogers would take me back there and show me what I was doing wrong and teach me the correct methods. A lot of it had to do with footwork. He would spar lightly to train me but he wouldn't hurt me. About the time when I was better and knew more of what I was doing, another bunch of men transferred aboard. Among those was a man by the name of Pren Son, coxswain. He was tall and a golden gloves boxer from St. Louis. He seemed quite a bit more cocky than I was and most of the guys. Pren was assigned to work with us. Soon one day Rogers came down the deck and gave us one of his curt orders and walked on by. Pren Son didn't like the way he said it and muttered, 'One of these days I'm going to teach that guy a lesson.' At this particular time he hadn't said anything about being a golden gloves boxer. Pren went on to say that he would get him on the fantail. We all knew what he was talking about. I said, 'You will?' He replied, 'You bet I will!' I kind of laughed. He said, 'What's the matter?' I said, 'You won't teach that guy no lesson on the fantail—he'll teach you a lesson!' He came back with a sharp reply, 'We'll see who will teach who!'

"Pren had taken it that I was a smart alec and the next time we were on the fantail he decided he was going to teach me a lesson. He asked me to put on the gloves with him and I did. About two minutes later I was in the head and a couple of my buddies were trying to get my nose to stop bleeding. He had broken it. I didn't even know where it came from. Then I learned that he was a golden gloves boxer. Well, M.L. Rogers had witnessed the whole thing. Later he took me aside and said 'I'm going to teach that guy a lesson. You got yours, now I'm going to get mine.' He meant that he was going to take care of Pren because of what he did to me. Rogers liked me as well as he did anybody.

"Soon he asked Pren to put the gloves on with him, and Pren jumped at the chance. Well, Rogers just played with him like a cat with a mouse. He didn't hit him to knock him out or break his nose or anything like that. He just played with him. He would come in and smother him with flurries and then just back away and let Pren come to him. Pren couldn't even land a punch on him. Remember, Rogers was the champion of the fleet before the war. He just kept playing with Pren and finally Pren just turned and walked away. That kind of ended the episode. Pren found out that he was out-matched. After that Pren just accepted Rogers for what he was."

The *Luce* sailed from San Pedro Bay on 25 January 1945 and took up her screening station off Zambales, just north of Subic Bay, Luzon. The invasion there was unopposed as Filipino guerrillas had already taken control of the area. DD 522 didn't have to fire a shot. The landing of U.S. troops was to prevent the Japanese from retreating to the Bataan Peninsula. On 31 January the *Luce*, in company with another destroyer, the USS *Badger*, steamed into Mangarin Bay, Mindoro. Because Commander Hinton A. Owens' expertise was needed in COMDESPAC (Commander Destroyers, Pacific), a change of command was effected as Commander Jacob. W. Waterhouse relieved Owens as skipper of the *Luce*.[5]

Born on 3 August 1906 in Wheeling, West Virginia, Commander Waterhouse graduated from the U.S. Naval Academy on 8 June 1929. He had successive service on battleships and destroyers until June 1936 when he returned to the Naval Academy and did postgraduate work in Naval Engineering, finishing in June 1938. Assigned to the destroyer USS *Case* he served first as her Engineer Officer and then, from April 1941 to about the time he assumed command of the *Luce*, he served as the *Case's* Executive Officer. The *Case* was undergoing normal overhaul at Pearl Harbor when the Japanese struck on 7 December 1941. The destroyer managed to get underway with the skipper and Waterhouse shouting frantic commands lest the Japanese should return and deal them the same fate as so many other ships in the harbor. For

---

[5] Deck Log Summary; entry for 25 January. 1 February, 1945.

the next six months the USS *Case* was engaged in escort duty between Pearl Harbor and the United States. Remaining with the *Case* as Executive Officer, Waterhouse saw the destroyer through the Marshall Islands campaign, the Hollandia and Marianas campaigns, and various Pacific raids before taking command of the *Luce* on 1 February 1945. According to Lt. John Welsh, Captain Waterhouse was well accepted by the men. He was the studious type, academic, and very capable.

For the next several weeks, well into March, the *Luce* performed various routine duty as she traveled into and out of ports such as Subic and San Pedro Bays in Leyte. Then it was farewell to the Philippines as DD 522 sailed away on 24 March 1945 with Task Unit 51.7.9. As they left, Joe McGuigan, RM3/c, and Freeman Phillips, S1/c, counted three Japanese planes downed by the *Luce* during their stay in the Philippines. Now they were headed closer to the Japanese home land, to be stationed around Okinawa, where the opportunities to down enemy planes would be greater—and so would the risks. But while they were getting underway, Lt. Don Allen, who thought that he was going to continue serving on the destroyer, was transferred:

"I started out as first lieutenant when we put the ship in commission, and then somewhere along the way I became gunnery officer. But I missed the exciting part to come, because I got off the ship a few weeks before it went down. I had my orders in the Philippines, and the Captain said, 'I'd like to have an experienced man just for the Okinawa landing, so stay around, will you?' And I was dumb enough to say, 'Yeah, I'll stay around'. But as soon as things quieted down, he let me off and I was transferred at sea. So I missed the exciting parts sure enough..."

And as he was being transferred from the *Luce* by breechers buoy, the men of the *Luce* dunked him in the water between the ships. They saw him turn around after arriving on the deck of the other ship and shake his fist at them.

Lt. Allen and the men he left on the *Luce* might have had an inkling of the excitement that awaited them, but they had very little idea of just how exciting—and terrible—their part would be as their ship ploughed through the sea swells toward Okinawa.

PART FOUR
OKINAWA:
THE FINAL CRUISE

On 3 February 1945 U.S. troops entered and secured Manila. The battle for the Philippines was winding down, and the U.S. Command turned its attention to the islands closer to the Japanese mainland. U.S. Marines invaded Iwo Jima, only 750 miles from Japan, on 19 February, finally securing the tiny island after severe casualties on both sides on 26 March. In Europe the Allies were pushing against the last of the Nazi's resistance, to finally end the European war with Germany's unconditional surrender on 8 May. Everywhere the decimated Axis forces were reeling under the relentless surge of the Allied war machine.

But even though the Japanese were being rapidly hurled back toward their home land, suffering huge losses from which they could not recover, the pugnacious enemy seemed to resist with growing ferocity. The invasion of Okinawa on 1 April saw a significant increase in the enemy's use of that horrific weapon, the kamikaze suicide plane. And although these suicide missions to crash their planes into Allied warships had made their debut in the Philippines, it was at Okinawa that the full fury of their intent was to be felt. The Japanese hoped that perhaps these missions would cause the Allies to stop hostilities and sue for peace. But the Americans had no thought of this. They were out for total victory.

From the start of the invasion (called "Operation Iceberg") the U.S. fleet began to feel the heat of the kamikaze attacks. To counter this threat, Vice Admiral Richard K. Turner, commanding all Naval forces around Okinawa, except the fast carriers, had established a radar picket system surrounding the island:

"Admiral Turner's screening plan for protecting the expeditionary force in and around Okinawa was unusually comprehensive. He set up two anti-submarine destroyer screen, an inner and an outer, a destroyer screen to cover possible approaches of surface raids, 'flycatcher screen' to catch suicide motorboats, and most important, the radar picket screen, composed primarily of destroyer types but supported by LCI(G)s and other small craft. These radar picket stations were the posts of greatest danger. They were disposed around Okinawa at distances of between fifteen and one hundred miles from land, so as to pick up flights of approaching enemy planes and, with the aid of CAP,[1] to intercept them. From 26 March on, each station was kept by a

---

[1] Combat Air Patrol

destroyer type with a fighter–director team on board. This controlled the CAP, maintained all day by Admiral Durgin's escort carrier planes. The picket vessel patrolled night and day within 5000 yards of her station, and when bogies appeared on her radar screen, the fighter–director officer vectored out CAP to intercept. By this means a large proportion of enemy planes approaching Okinawa was shot down before they reached the island, and our forces engaged in landing, unloading or fire support were given timely warning of an air raid. Hundreds of sailors lost their lives and about a score of ships and craft were sunk rendering this service."[2]

The USS *Luce* was to be one of those ships sunk, with half of her crew being lost. As they sailed toward Okinawa, the crew did not realize what awaited them. They had encountered some kamikazes in the Philippines but had successfully warded them off. They felt confident and secure in their marksmanship, and only a little uneasy at the unknown. Their ship was the *"Lucky Luce"* and, as some hoped and prayed, their luck might still hold true. Their's was a fighting ship in excellent condition and ready for whatever awaited them. Only when they were on picket duty around Okinawa and saw the terrible damage being wrought by the enemy did they begin to wonder how long it might be before disaster struck them...

---

[2] From THE TWO–OCEAN WAR by Samuel Eliot Morison. Copyright (c) 1963 by Samuel Eliot Morison. By permission of Little Brown and Company. pp. 542-544.

DD 522: Diary Of A Destroyer 93

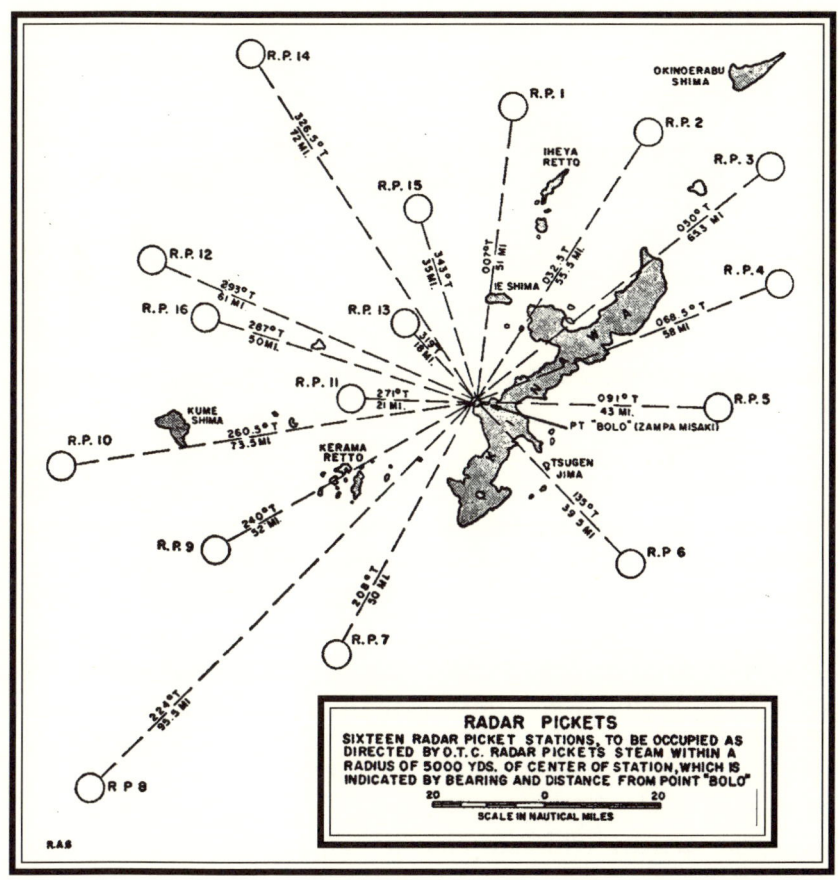

From THE TWO-OCEAN WAR by Samuel Eliot Morison. Copyright (c) 1963 by Samuel Eliot Morison. By permission of Little Brown and Company.

Chapter 10

Patrolling The Picket Line

Leaving Leyte on 24 March 1945 at 0900, DD 522 sortied with Task Unit 51.7.9. Arriving off Keise Shima (a small island just off Okinawa) on 31 March, the *Luce* began screening the landing area in preparation for the invasion of Okinawa, which was scheduled to take place the next day, 1 April.

But before the *Luce* had sailed out towards the dangerous seas around that island, the ship's capabilities had been beefed up by adding some key personnel. One of these was Ensign Frank Scudder:

"I was a former pilot, and I had some engineering background. That was the reason they selected me to become a fighter-director. Trained for carrier duty, I was assigned to flagships. The first one was the USS *Estes*, and then I was aboard the USS *El Dorado*, and then aboard the USS *Biscayne* for the Iwo Jima operation. I was the specialist assigned to these different ships to direct the fighter planes from the carriers. The USS *Luce* was in the Philippines, and they assigned me to that destroyer for the next operation. I came aboard in early March, 1945, after being in the Iwo Jima operation in February. LTJG Bob Murray and Ensign Bob Pierce came aboard with me. Bob and I were together in the Iwo Jima operation as fighter-directors. We control our aircraft in pursuit of the enemy planes which, of course, were the Japanese kamikazes. We tried to intercept them and knock them down before they did damage to our ships."

The addition of these men gave the *Luce* a complement of five radar operators and three communications men. Lt. Cliff Jones was selected to be the new gunnery officer:

"Although very inexperienced in gunnery, having never fired any of the *Luce's* guns, nevertheless I was confident. After all, I had been three months in gunnery school in Honolulu. Lt. Don Allen had left me a well trained crew, and I had formulated my own training program, which I did begin the very next day after he left. That day that Allen was transferred off the ship, we steamed out at twilight from Buckner Bay, Okinawa, to take up radar picket duty fifty miles offshore. There I was, as darkness settled, up in the Director now for the first time with full responsibility for every offensive weapon on the ship—the five 5-inch guns, the 40 mm and 20 mm guns, and the depth charges. It was a lonely feeling."

Tom Matisak, RdM3/c, remembers that it was Easter morning when they were screening the landing area. It was "a bright vibrant morning. Our destroyer squadron, DESRON 49, was doing some shelling on the island when one of the destroyers became stuck in a sandbar. The Japs, in spite of all the bombardment, were firing on the immobile destroyer. So we naturally turned our guns on the Japs, being careful not to hit our invading troops. When you go through bombardment technique in training, the spotter on land will tell you whether you are short or long, and will say to go up two or three, or down two, whatever it may be, in order to zero in on target. But we had no spotter. We were trying to figure out by sense of direction where the flashes were coming from. In the midst of all this, we could see our own troops going ashore, and could see them use the flamethrowers. That's how close we were. Those Japs were so entrenched in their caves that they were peppering that destroyer. But soon the ship got loose from the sandbar."

Within hours DD 522 was assigned to radar picket duty, as the battle report relates:

"On April 1st, the *Luce* was transferred to the Commander Screen at the objective area, CTG 51.5. We acted as fighter direction ship on various radar picket stations for the remainder of the period; being supported at times by another destroyer and various small craft. Our mission was to detect and report the approach of enemy aircraft and to intercept and destroy such aircraft with fighters under our control, and by anti aircraft fire."[1]

Almost immediately after arriving on her picket station, the crew of the *Luce* spotted three downed Japanese aviators in the water, as noted by the Action Report:

"About 1000 hours on 1 April 1945, two bodies were sighted in the water northwest of Okinawa. The medical officer accompanied the Executive Officer and a volunteer in the whaleboat which was lowered to investigate. The men were Japanese aviators, floating in lifejackets side by side face up; still breathing but unconscious. They were pulled aboard, searched for weapons and guarded. A third survivor sighted from the ship was also rescued. He was wearing a lifejacket and was conscious and swimming. As the rescue boat approached, however, he ducked his head beneath the water and apparently tried to drown himself. When pulled aboard about a minute later, a large quantity of water drained from his mouth and nose. He was already unconscious, but breathing well. He was an enlisted man. The first two were officers all had been in the water approximately eight hours. One of the officers regained consciousness in the rescue boat, grimaced and became tense with fear upon first realizing he was in enemy hands. In a few minutes, however, he relaxed and dozed until taken aboard ship."[2]

Several of the men took particular note of the details connected with this incident. Lt. John Welsh:

"We saw somebody in the water, and the Captain said, 'Go out in the whaleboat to pick them up. And I saw this Japanese, and like most other people, I thought they were pretty slick people; thinking they had knives up their sleeves, and so forth. I broke out my .45, and the poor guy was frightened as we approached. He put his head under the water, and you could see his bubbles."

Omer Emond, S1/c, realized that "he was trying to commit suicide by swimming into the ship's propellers."

John Welsh felt that "he thought better of it after awhile, and put his head up, and we got him in the boat. I was nervously holding a gun on him all the way back to the boat, but he was done in. We searched him, but they couldn't find any weapons or

---

[1] Action Report on Ryukyus Operation, 24 March; dated 4 May 1945
[2] Ibid

knives."

The Battle Report continues:

"All survivors were transferred to the ship by stretcher from the whaleboat after it had been hoisted to the rail. They were disrobed and treated for exposure in the wardroom. The two officers responded rapidly, and one was found to have a fracture of the left humerus, which was immobilized in a traction splint.

"The enlisted man responded more slowly and continued to exhale quantities of frothy water. He improved after 250cc plasma and, when fully conscious, was started on sulfadizine again for pneumonia. All the men spoke a few words of English, but the CincCPac booklet of terms to aid in treatment of Japanese patients was of value in establishing contact." [3]

Lt. John Welsh:

"All three were in the Japanese Naval Air Corps. Two of them were officers, one being a lieutenant, and I think there were two ensigns also. One of them I remember talking to very well. We put him up in Chief's quarters. A lot of people went up to talk to him. They talked him to death, almost."

Lt. Tom Parkerson:

"The one had been educated at the University of California in Berkeley. He spoke better English than any of us did, but he said that he had returned to Japan before the war broke out. He told us, 'I'll really never be able to return to Japan. I should not have let myself be taken alive.' That always impressed me, because he sounded like he really meant it. I don't remember what I said to him. I just didn't know what I could have said. The idea of this great humiliation of being taken alive was not really comprehensible to me. But, that was how he felt; and a fellow that had been educated over here, no less, that's the Bushido Code, that's what it sounded like to me."

Waino Johnson, GM1/c, had the dubious distinction of watching over the prisoners:

"Two of the Japanese were sent down to a pea–coat locker, because it had a heavy mesh screened–in door. I was given the job of guarding the two Jap pilots. They were both college graduates, and one had attended college in San Francisco. They spoke good English... and I had a good conversation with them while stand-

---
[3] Battle Report, Op. Cit

ing guard. They spoke mostly of their doings, and how they became aircraft crew. They had been sent out to gain information on our ships, but were shot down. They sat down in the locker room and seemed to be worn out tired. They didn't move, just talked, but seemed to be healthy. I wasn't nervous, but I had a pistol in my hand, outside the screened door, just in case..."

Lt. Art Repogle:

"We were amazed at their uniforms when they came aboard. They had silk scarves, and little zipper pockets all over their uniforms. They had unusual looking identification... and money-things that were very personal, such as which we were told not to carry with us if we were ever to be taken prisoner."

The third prisoner, who may have had a broken collarbone or something similar wrong with him, according to Orville Hiles, S1/c, ended up in Freeman Phillips' bunk. This didn't make Freeman too happy:

"I raised a stink like you wouldn't believe! I was mad when I found that guy in my bunk! That's when they put him in the locker. I had come down to my bunk, and here he is shackled to my bunk..."

LeGrand Van Uitert, CFC:

"He was in the bunk right above me, and I talked with him. He wanted to commit suicide. We told him to forget all this nonsense, and he would be all right when the war's over. 'You're out of the war now, you know,' I told him, but he was very much affected by his family honor. They (the crew) had spoken so much verbal anti–Japanese all the time, and here are the same ones spoon-feeding into his hands, treating him like a king."

Freeman Phillips believed that the man in his bunk had a broken arm because of trying to swim into the ship's screws while in the process of being captured. And although the men of the *Luce* apparently treated the prisoners very well, this wasn't the case when Marines came aboard to take the Jap aviators off the ship, according to Orville:

"When the Marines came, they had an entirely different experience than what we had (given them). I remember one of them had a broken collarbone or something wrong with his arms, and they just pushed him right down into this little boat that was alongside. It was about ten or fifteen feet down in there, and they weren't very gentle in getting them. That was quite a rude awakening for these California–educated pilots…"

When the prisoners came topside for the transfer, Bill Lietz TM2/c, noted "their amazement at all the ships around. There were hundreds as far as one could see."

The Battle Report concludes:

"The wounded officer was kept overnight in CPO quarters under guard. The other two slept on mattresses in the small storeroom just forward of the shipfitters' shop. All ate well, were docile in demeanor and eager to talk, and were in good condition when transferred to the USS *Baxter* the next day." [4]

That night, 2 April, after refueling at Kerema Retto, the *Luce* was assigned to screen Picket Station No. 4 with Task Force 54 to the northwest of Okinawa.[5] For the next few days, DD 522 routinely patrolled her section and served as well on picket stations 1, 9 and 10. Tom Parkerson (LTJG) remembers that there was plenty of sunshine to go around:

"Everybody got sunburn. If you wanted to watch the waves or whatever, no matter where your station was, if you were on the bridge, or the main deck, or engine room, or anywhere, you got sunburn!"

Bill Fotie, RM3/c, found time to continue teaching Art Powers, S1/c, how to copy code. Art was "striking" for radioman. Bill and Art had a good time at it and enjoyed "horsing around" a lot. "I also used to spar with Art a bit. We would go out on the little radio deck and try to get some exercise that way. We were all such 'cut–ups'."

Art's best friend, Stephen Pramick, RdM3/c, was a radarman, and in their talks together had encouraged him to try for radioman.

Freeman Phillips, S1/c, was also trying for rank, striking for torpedoman, third class. He passed his test, but as there were no openings, he did not obtain the rank. Studying, and whatever recreation they could set up helped pass away the hours when there was no action. But as they continued their radar picket duty, the action seemed to increase day by day. J.C. Phillips, SC1/c, recalls the set–up and purpose of picket duty and what the duty was like:

---

[4] Battle Report Op. Cit.
[5] Ibid

"There were at least 12 stations. They had them all the way around the island of Okinawa, every so many miles. Every thirty miles there was a destroyer, and they were using their radar to screen the skies and make sure the Japs didn't get any planes in there on our Marines, or our Army. As soon as we would get contact on the picket line, we would call the aircraft carrier that was nearest to us, and they would send up pilots and shoot them down. That was our job out there; and also to pick up any information, such as prisoners, to take them in for interrogation. We worked on almost every picket station. Some of those ships would come out today on the picket line, and tomorrow they were gone. They wouldn't survive twenty–four hours. We lost at least fifteen destroyers in Okinawa that were sunk. I believe eighty–something destroyers were damaged, I'm not sure, but in that neighborhood. Okinawa was the most expensive operation the Navy had in the Pacific. They lost more men there than anywhere else. The next most expensive one was Guadalcanal. They lost the same amount of destroyers down there, but they didn't get the damage to the ships that we got in Okinawa. All this time that we're going back and forth to these picket duty stations, and sometimes for two or three days we'd be down there shooting up all our ammunition. Then we would have to come back for more ammunition, load the ammunition, take on stores and get the mail, and go right back out there. And we'd stay out there. When you got on the picket line, sometimes you'd be at general quarters, for twenty–four hours... They'd secure us from the battle stations, and in five minutes you'd be back, because in would come another plane, and you'd have to go to G.Q. They also used this harbor of Kerema– Retto as a graveyard, or a staging area for all the ships that had been hit. Every time we would come in this harbor to get our supplies and everything, we'd have to pass right by all those ships that were all torn to pieces, all busted and killed and bombed. The crews would try to get things together and get organized and patch up the holes where they could move it and take it back to get it repaired. That gave you a sobering thought. I remember the last time that we went in for fuel and took on new ammunition I was standing outside the galley right by the winch, and somebody was standing by me. I believe it was 'Moose' (Marty Nyholt, FC2/c), but I'm not sure, and we went by the USS

Aaron Ward I believe, or one of those ships that had just had the life knocked out of it the day before, killing about half of the crew. And old Moose said, 'Them guys must not be able to shoot, the planes shot the stuff out of them.' I just sort of smiled and looked at old Moose. I had some sobering thoughts come to me as I turned around and went back to my duty station. I thought to myself, 'Well, it's just a matter of time. It's not if you're going to get it, it's when. We had been blessed so far. And I thought to myself, 'Well, 'It's just a matter of time, just a matter of time', and the very next trip out, we got it. I had made up my mind that they might get me, but I'm gonna take just as many of them as I can get with me. After so many days out there, and going to G.Q. day and night, and trying to eat, and trying to get a bath—just to take a bath was a daring act. I mean, you get in there and you get all soaked down, and here are these guys trying to kill you. We'd been up about three days there one time, and I hadn't had any sleep for that three days.

"There was one episode and I was so tired and so weary, I thought well, death would be a relief. It would actually be a relief. It would be over. I had the thoughts, 'Well, look man, just don't shoot at me no more, and you can have this whole thing.' You get that kind of feeling. Then you get the feeling that if you could just lay right down here, and take all of this out of your head, and just relax, and not have to worry about someone trying to kill you, or just kill me, it would be a relief. Those thoughts come often. Of course, they don't stay with you. The day we got sunk, I really expected it. But I was determined that I was going to do all I could to take as many of the enemies with me, so if he did get me, the guys behind me would have fewer to cope with."

During those days when everyone was on edge and knowing that devastation could come any time from the skies, the men grew short–tempered. Fights and arguments become more commonplace. Gnawing uncertainty and fear caused some to take special precautions, as did Freeman Phillips:

"I slept topside through the whole thing. I wouldn't go below decks. It was eerie going out to a picket station to take the place a destroyer that we knew had just been badly damaged or even sunk."

Sometimes a break in the routine would bring a bit of welcome relief from such disturbing thoughts. Such an event took place on 10 April and described by the Action Report:

"1200—sighted two horn type drifting mines. Commenced maneuvering to keep mine in sight and to sink mines by 40 mm and rifle fire. When visibility decreased in heavy rain to such an extent as to make further operations extremely dangerous, we dropped dye sea marker and directed supporting LCS's to search for and destroy mines. These operations continued until nightfall, but were unsuccessful because of increasing seas and decreasing visibility. At sunset we moved our patrol five miles west and our support ship resumed normal patrol." [6]

And while the weather on 11 and 12 April was poor enough to discourage most enemy activity, 13 April was clear enough for an enemy aircraft to close in on the *Luce*, as detailed in the Action Report:

"On R.P. #10. No CAP assigned. Just prior to sunset alert, enemy aircraft approached from southwest. We twice fired on aircraft which approached within gun range, and each time the attack was immediately broken off and plane withdrew. 1900—One Jill made torpedo run from about 10 degrees forward of our starboard beam. Fire was opened at about 8000 yards with 5" battery and about 3500 yards with 40 mm battery; plane was shot down at 1600 yards. During approach of the plane ship's speed was increased to 25 knots and at time plane was shot down, rudder was put hard right to present small target to possible torpedo. Some minutes later, a violent underwater explosion was felt, apparently caused by torpedo exploding at the end of its run." [7]

Freeman Phillips, S1/c, credits Captain Waterhouse for saving the ship from the torpedo:

"The word came down from the bridge that he (Captain Waterhouse) was the only one that saw the plane release the torpedo... I saw the torpedo when it left the plane from down where I was, and Waterhouse called a hard right rudder toward the torpedo and that torpedo passed just astern of us. I was on the fantail, and had it hit the fantail, it would have been good–bye. It was very, very scary, because it came so close."

---

6 Action report, Op. Cit.
7 Ibid.

Omer Emond, S1/c, thinks that a PBY aircraft kept the Jill from the *Luce* for a time:

"This PBY was pushing him out of the way, and as the PBY was keeping it away from us for quite a while, we were ready for it. Then when it finally got away from the PBY and came at us and dropped its torpedo, we were shooting like a son–of–a–gun at it. We weren't hitting it, but after it dropped its torpedo, it banked and that's when we got it. I recall that very vividly... I was stationed at 40 mm No. 5 then, and they had picked him up from the starboard side. (John Charles) Lake, S1/c, and Lionel Berthiaume, S1/c, were there with me shooting at the plane."

The Daily Deck Log also records that on 28 April a twin engine enemy plane approached the ship from the island of Kume Shima. Its course was steady and, as Tom Blanck, Y1/c, continues:

"It was a Betty, I think, and this bomber evidently thought he had us dead to rights... we picked him up on radar when he took off from the island... he was coming in right on our beams and of course, was up to no good. I'm sure he was going to drop a bomb down our smoke stacks if he had the chance. Anyway, they picked him up and followed him all the way in. All 5–inch 38 guns were trained directly on that poor guy, and they caught him, I would say, 500 yards from the ship, or so... all you could see were 5–inch 38 shells converging right on that dude's nose, and he went VOOM! Blew into pieces! He didn't even know what hit him!"

The new gunnery officer, Lt. Cliff Jones, who had the responsibility of giving the order to fire, could not get a good sighting on the aircraft:

"It was dark, no moon. I could not fire by the search radar. I could not depend upon the fire control radar because the plane was so low the 'sea return'—what the weather people today call the 'ground clutter'—of the radar made it impossible to sight through radar on that plane. I had to wait until it became visible. Pretty soon I caught a glimpse of the moon on its wing and I gave the command to open fire. After one round from the 5–inch guns—and the 40's were also firing—the plane burst into flames and fell astern of us in the water. It was a Jap Betty plane, a bomber, and I believe it dropped a torpedo at us, which missed. As we steamed away, that fire was visible for some time, until it finally disappeared over the horizon."

Jubilation was expressed on the bridge after the plane was downed:

"So perfect was the range that the Nip burst into flames suddenly, and plummeted to the water about 1,500 yards off the starboard beam. He burned in the water for about fifteen minutes, and was soon joined by a Jill and a Jap torpedo bomber. During that time, a war dance was going on aboard the *Luce*. The ship's gunnery officer, Lt. Cliff A. Jones, ordinarily a shy, quiet fellow, kept shouting with joy. On the bridge, Lt. Welsh, standing next to Commander Waterhouse, ran to the loudspeaker system.

'We got him!' He shouted. 'We got him!" [8]

The next few days saw little enemy air activity because of poor weather. Things perked up on 3 May, however, as the weather began to clear. The log notes that ships on the picket station No. 10 had undergone heavy attack. (The *Luce* was on picket station No. 12) All ships were ordered to move their radar picket stations closer to the beach area, and the *Luce* moved to within 30 miles, along with her supporting smaller craft. (Some of these smaller craft came to be known as "pall bearers" because of their rescue activities in picking up the dead and survivors of ships sunk by kamikazes.)

Another unforgettable incident involving kamikazes was impressed on the mind of Lt. Cliff Jones:

"Another time, the Korean pilot of a plane we probably shot down was rescued by us. We saw him swimming in the water, so we stopped the ship and threw a line to him. Some of the deck crew stood by with rifles trained on him as he climbed up. He was quite a muscular fellow, and had been a farmer a few weeks before when the Japs had picked him up and told him he was going to be a kamikaze pilot, whether he wanted to or not. His only chance, he told us later through an interpreter, was to follow their orders. They gave him flying lessons on how to fly the plane and guide it, but not on how to land. There was a bomb strapped to his plane that was sensitive, and would go off if he tried to land. Up in the air over him there were other planes ready to shoot down any kamikaze pilot who defected. So he felt his only chance was to do what they said, and go to the paradise they promised him (after he crashed). It was interesting how the doctor examined him. They

---

[8] Pinkowski, "The *Lady Luce*." Our Navy, Mid-December, 1946, 60-61.

were afraid that he might have concealed some sort of a small bomb in one of his body cavities. That poor fellow was searched from stem to stern!"

The ship's doctor, Lt. Shaffner, found something interesting to do while the destroyer warded off attacks:

"We spent a lot of time going to General Quarters and shooting at planes that came in over our radar picket station. We were very active in the CIC, and there was no question that that was a very busy and dangerous situation we were under. I, of course, didn't have much to do at those times, except to be in my battle station, which was the wardroom. I was given an 8mm movie camera to take pictures of the air attacks on us. This was from Naval Intelligence, therefore, I would go out on the main deck during these times and get pictures of planes coming toward us and our own tracer fire funneling down on them. It was really quite spectacular. I wondered many times, when I'd see movies later of some of these kamikaze attacks if any of those films were any that I took. All I did was send the undeveloped film in when I got back to a spot where I could."

A few years after the war, Bob Moyer, FC3/c, met a Marine friend who was an aide to the captain of one of the larger carriers stationed just off Okinawa at the same time the USS *Luce* was on patrol. The first time that they were placed on alert because of incoming kamikazes, Bob's friend noticed that his captain was standing there very calm and nonchalant, casually watching out to sea. The Marine was becoming a bit nervous about the situation, and said to his superior, "Captain, aren't you getting excited about this?" "No", the Captain replied. "You see those little boys out there on the horizon?" "You mean the destroyers?" asked the Marine. "Yes, the destroyers," the Captain returned. "Destroyers are the work force of the Navy. They get the tough details. Those planes have to get through those little boys out there first, then we get excited. But up to that point, don't worry."

Every day, the men of the *Luce* would hear horror stories of ships sunk, and of men being mauled and killed off the shores of Okinawa by kamikazes. The uncertainty of what the next day might bring, and the knowledge that they very well could be next, caused many to probe deeply within themselves. Some came forth with good answers to their own questions. The certainty that what they were doing was not only necessary, but just, gave them the stability and determination they needed in these uncertain days. One of the crew, William Burns, MoMM1/c, penned his thoughts in a poem he entitled "Prayer Before An Attack":

"It ain't as I 'opes 'ell keep me safe While the other blokes go down; It ain't as I wants to leave this world And wear a 'eros crown; It ain't for that as I says my prayers When I goes to the attack; But I pray that whatever comes my way I may never turn me back. I leave the matter O' life and death To the Father who knows what's best; And I prays that I still may play the man Whether I turns East or West. No sooner that it were east, ye know, To Blighty and my gal Sue; No sooner be there wi' the gold in 'er 'air And the skies behind all blue. But still I pray I may do my bit And then, if I must turn West; I'll be unashamed when my name is named And I'll find a sailor's rest."

And Walter Fischer, CTM, could have spoken for many of the crew in the closing paragraph of his last letter to his wife, which he dated "Sat. aft'n Apr. 21":

"The past several weeks have brought home to me, more forcibly than ever, just what it is that I'm fighting for. I hope I live thru it all to profit from its lessons."

Walter Fischer would not be able to realize his hope. In just a few days, he would give his life in an attempt to save some of the crew from going down with the ship.

About 1 May, Orville Hiles, S1/c, saw something which gave him—and possibly some others—the feeling that things just might turn out alright for their destroyer:

"One time we had the radar going around, and there was a dove sitting up on top of the antennae and we thought, Boy, that's our symbol of peace!"

Three days later, this "symbol of peace" was to be savagely shattered by the murderous all–out onslaught of determined enemy suiciders.

CHAPTER 11
4 MAY 1945—"BOGIES CIRCLING!"

The fourth of May dawned clear and bright. The *Luce* was patrolling on Radar Picket Station Twelve, sixty–one miles northwest of Point Bolo on Okinawa. The crew of DD 522 had been up much of the night, and they were dog–tired. One of them was Fire Controlman 2nd Class, Martin Nyholt, otherwise known as "Moose":

"On the night of May 3/May 4, 1945, I had the 1200 to 0400 watch and was relieved in the Main Battery at 0400 by Dick Flaum, FC2/c, as usual. We had been annoyed several times during my watch by bogies dropping foil (window) but nothing serious enough to go to G.Q. Shortly after I was relieved, the ship was called to G.Q. and we stayed on G.Q. until about 0700. I was pretty tired, so I decided to forgo breakfast and hit the sack fully clothed. My battle station was the operation of the main battery 5" guns Director Optical Range–finder. Its function was to send down to the computer in Fire Control Plot… (1) target angle, (2) elevations, (3) speed of the target; and to keep a steady input of these data, so that the computer could develop a Fire Control Solution, which aimed the guns with the correct time of flight of the projectile and lead–angle (as in leading–the–target). Once the ship commenced firing, I had the responsibility of spotting or correcting the bursts of the shells to bring them onto the target. My sights contained lighted reticules; the main one was a large diamond in the center, which I lined up over the target. There were smaller lighted vertical lines on each side of the large diamond, which I could use to suggest corrections in parallax or side correction. The essential purpose of a combat ship, in my opinion, is to bring its guns to bear on the enemy and to quickly, efficiently destroy that enemy.

The USS *Luce* fulfilled that description. She was an efficient combat ship with an excellent, highly-trained crew who loved her. She, on many occasions prior to May 4, 1945, quickly and efficiently destroyed every target that came under her guns."

Lt. Cliff Jones relates that he and other officers were enjoying "a good breakfast and were about halfway through when Lt. Hutchinson came and told the Captain, who was there, that they had sighted many bogies coming in some 50 or 60 miles away. Captain Waterhouse said, 'finish your breakfast, gentlemen, we have plenty of time.' Well, we gulped down the final bit and rushed to our battle stations. The whole ship went to General Quarters."

J.C. Phillips, SC1/c, was trying to get breakfast for the enlisted men:

"I was in the galley making buckwheat cakes for breakfast. Then the general alarm went off, so I took time to turn off my grill, instead of rushing down to G.Q. because I had had some bad experiences the day before. I had gone to G.Q. for about two hours, and when I came back, the pancakes were all charcoal on the top of my grill. It took me about 30 minutes to clean it up, so I could make some new ones. So, this morning I said the heck with it, I'll just turn off my grill."

Paul Wallace, F1/c, had just come off duty and was settling into his bunk:

"I no sooner got to my bunk when they rang General Quarters again. I jumped up, got some clothes on as quick as possible, and I ran down to my G.Q. battle station, which was in the after fireroom. I no sooner got down there, and I snapped my life jacket on, when the lights went out. My first thought was to get down in the bilges. Our chief water tender always told us that if we got in trouble down there, because of the steam's tendency to rise, the best place to get is in the bilges. That was my first thought. My second thought was, 'I better get off this thing, because something drastic was happening!'"

Up in the Director, Marty Nyholt, FC2/c, could sense what was coming:

"The people on the *Luce's* Bridge, Fire Control Plot and in CIC knew this beautiful May 4th morning was going to be a busy one. Ships were already under attack on several of the picket stations, and a lot of intense chatter was on the TBS and other radio lines, which could be clearly heard in the Main Battery Director. Down in my bunk in the forward port section of the ship, I had just slipped into a nice restful sleep when the G.Q. horn goes off with its ear–shattering 'Bong–Bong–Bong.' Here we go again! I race up the forward hatch (near the bow) back down the port side of the deck, up three ladders to the Flying Bridge, up one short ladder on the side of the MBD, down the overhead hatch in a drop… where I was then in my spot behind the optical range–finder. On with the sound–power phone and ready to go to work… all in less than 1 1/2 minutes. We had been to G.Q. (real or simulated) hundreds of times and at Okinawa, with ships getting hit every day, we didn't need additional motivation to 'get there quick and go to work.' Lt. (JG) Cliff Jones was the Gunnery Officer, Bob Moyer was the Trainer, Len Rhule was the Pointer, Dick Flaum was the Fire Control Radar Operator, and I was the Optical Range–finder operator and spotter. With the exception of the Gunnery Officer, the rest of us were all at these positions since the ship had been commissioned, and we worked very well together."

All over the ship weary men who had hoped to get some rest were rudely interrupted by the harsh sounds of GQ:

Tom Blanck, Yeoman First Class:

"We had been up all night at General Quarters. There were raids coming in from most directions the previous day, and I know that everybody was kind of punchy at the time, kind of dead on their feet. I went down as we secured from GQ to my bunk in the ship's office, and I no sooner got my head on the bunk when GQ rang again. I jumped up and went topside, and the first thing I heard was that there were 90 planes coming in. Our flight director crews had picked them up maybe 100 miles away. Our fighter planes were directed to them and followed them in all the way, picking them off. They were knocking the heck out of them all the way in, but it was such a huge raid that some broke through. They always did… "

Bill Lietz, TM (Torpedoman) Second Class:

"The night of May the third we had been at General Quarters mainly because of the intensive attacks on the previous night. I was on the fantail depth charge when word came over the phone system to set Condition One Easy—meaning half the crew would be able to get to chow. About fifteen minutes later, our radar picked up bogies at 95 miles. General Quarters."

Freeman Phillips, S1/c:

"I relieved 'Pappy' (John Joseph) Malone, TM2/c, from watch on the port side K–gun and he laid down right at my feet and he said, 'Freeman, if any bogies get within five miles of us, wake me up.' I was putting the phones on which he had just taken off, and he laid down on the deck with his life jacket under his head, and instantly he was out. We were all so tired. About ten minutes later, they started reporting bogies all over the place... and I said to myself, 'I'm not going to wake that man until just before they ring GQ! Then it rang!"

Down in the galley, J.C. Phillips rushed topside, placed his hand on top of the steel shield enclosure near Freeman Phillips, and vaulted over. As he did so, he called to Freeman, "Phil—buckwheat cakes in the galley when we secure!" Freeman recalls that "the crew that was down there just jumped up and left their breakfast on the table. They never got back to eat those pancakes. None of us did... "

As the sounds of GQ continued to reverberate throughout the ship, sailors and officers, like so many bugs scattering around, flew to their assigned battle stations.

Bill Lietz, TM2/c:

"I ran up the starboard side to the No. one torpedo tube along with Torpedoman First Class Jim McGuigan and Second Class Torpedoman Ken 'Whitey' Sturm. Torpedoes being useless in an air attack, I moved to the duo–40 mm anti aircraft gun amidships, starboard of the No. two stack. I could see planes everywhere—theirs and ours. We were Fighter–director for our Navy carrier-based planes. I still had the phones on for our JU circuit, which included both torpedo tubes, port and starboard depth charge K-guns, fantail depth charges, and smoke screen generator."

Joseph J. Billie, RT2/c:

"I reported to my GQ station outside the Combat Information Center (CIC). We did have Corsair fighter planes under our control. Japanese planes—bogies—were picked up on our radar screen approximately 50 miles northeast of the ship. Our Fighter Director Officer radioed and directed the planes under our control towards the bogies."

Freeman Phillips:

"I woke up 'Pappy' Malone just as the gong started to go off, and he ran up the ladder to where Jim McGuigan was. That was the last I saw of them."

Tom Matisak, Radarman Third Class, spotted a group of planes on his radar screen:

"We were just about on the end of our four to eight watch. I had been on the aircraft radar... and had detected, as imperfect as the radar was, what we thought was a large number of Jap planes coming down from the north. The alarm was given. As a fire-director ship, we had an Army officer on board, for what I think were P–47's circling above us. He was called in and he vectored the Army aircraft to the area where we thought were enemy planes. In the course of their getting there, and us keeping track of them, we had constantly flipped on our IFF's, which is called Identification Friend or Foe, to determine what these planes from the north were. The results were negative. Our suspicions were right. The planes we spotted did not prove to be ours."

As gunnery officer in the Director, Lt. Cliff Jones had a ringside seat to what was beginning to take place. He noticed other small ships around the *Luce* were getting into position:

"We had three small ships—we called them 'meatwagons'— and they were there to pick up any survivors in case a ship went down. (I learned later that during the Okinawa campaign we lost seventy or more destroyers either sunk or so badly damaged, that they were out for the rest of the war.) We could see these three little ships astern of us, widely separated. Radar kept tracking the planes and then my fire control radar picked them up; but they were still too far away to fire on. When our 5–inch guns were new their range was about 20,000 yards, or about ten sea miles. Now that they were quite well worn they were not as accurate at that range. We could see splashes at great distances as planes were shot down by our CAP (Cover Air Patrol) which consisted of about four or five aircraft at least. Finally they began coming into range."

Dozens of pairs of eyes on the *Luce* were glued to the scene, slowly but steadily approaching them. Men began to grow tense as they realized the inevitable. In just a few moments they too, would be drawn into the raging conflict. For a few moments all was very quiet on the ship. Then suddenly Tom Matisak heard the dreaded warning from Robert Abbruzzese, S1/c, on number two stack as he shouted into the phones, "Here they come!"

Joseph Huss Jr., QM3/c, who was on the bridge with Commander Waterhouse, noticed that the skies were suddenly full of aircraft. "It's only a matter of time," he thought, "until we're sunk." He watched fascinated as the kamikazes began attacking the other smaller ships in their area. Joseph Bille noted that two of the gunboats with them on patrol began firing back. Robert E. Stanley, S1/c, whose GQ station was no. two 40 mm on the starboard side just below the bridge, looked out over port side and saw some planes which seemed to be heading right towards them. Norman Foland, MoMM2/c, had, just before GQ sounded, left his station on the no. seven 20 mm between the aft depth charges. He wandered up through the port side of the ship and was standing in the hatchway that led down to the galley because breakfast had been called. "While I'm standing at the hatchway, I look out and see many, many aircraft flying around out there. Suddenly I realize that those planes are not on our side! So I run down the quarterdeck heading for my 20 mm, hollering 'Japs! Jap aircraft!' I was trying to set the alarm, as I had not heard nor was aware that the GQ went off. J.C Phillips, the cook, running out of the hatchway of the galley, looked at me like I was nuts. I reached my gun, threw the lanyard down, and cocked the 20 mm myself as the loader had not gotten there yet. I know that you can't do these things, but I did it that morning. It takes two men to cock a 20 mm, but when you're scared, you can, I found out, do it yourself!"

Lt. Cliff Jones saw "two planes peel off and come toward us. Then we opened fire. They kept coming closer." Both J.C. Phillips (who by now was at his station at no. five 20 mm) and Freeman Phillips heard through their earphones a hair–raising report: "Twenty–eight bogies circling! Twenty–eight bogies circling!"

"And," thought Freeman, "every last one of them bent on taking us down!"

PHOTOGRAPHS

⇐ *Bert Alton,*
Chief Radio Technician

⇑ *Ernest Carpenter, WT2/c*

⇑ *John Carpenter, WT2/c*

⇑ L to R: H.M. Demenchuck, F1/c; Burr McFarland, Wt1/c; J.M. Hill, MM1/c; P.B. Dodge, MM2/c; Marty Nyholt, FC2/c

⇑ Omer Emond, S1/c

⇑ Norman Foland, MoMM2/c

⇑ Leo Greco, SM1/c

PHOTOGRAPHS

James M. Gory, WT3/c ⇒

⇑ *Robert D. Harrison, RM2/c then and today* ⇒

Joseph Huss, Jr., QM3/c ⇒

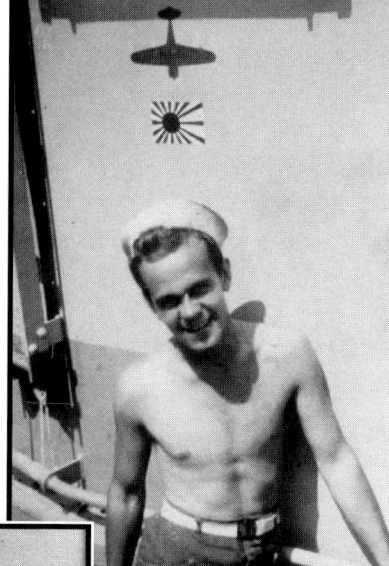

⇑ *Waino M. Johnson, GM1/c*

⇑ *William V. Lietz, TM2/c*

PHOTOGRAPHS

⇐ *Bill Lietz and buddies with Russell Miller in background*

⇑ *Russell Miller, TM2/c*

⇑ *Anthony Marchitelli, GM3/c*

DD 522: Diary Of A Destroyer

⇐ *Thomas Matisak, GM3/c then and today* ⇓

⇑ *Jack McCormick, S1/c*

PHOTOGRAPHS

⇧ *Burr McFarland, WT1/c*

⇧ *Burr (L) with John A. Carpenter, WT1/c*

⇧ *James McGuigan, TM1/c (MIA)*

⇧ *Joseph McGuigan, RM2/c (brother of James)*

⇐ *Freeman Phillips, S1/c then and today* ⇓

James (J.C.) Phillips, SC1/c (L) with John Borack, BKR3/c ⇑

PHOTOGRAPHS

⇧ L to R: Len Rule, (Pointer Main Battery Director;) Marty Nyholt, FC2/c; kneeling: Robert Moyer, FC2/c

⇧ Lt. Louis Shaffner, ship's medical doctor

⇧ Captain Hinton A. Owens, second skipper of USS Luce, with Lt. John R. Welsh

⇧ Robert E. Stanley, S1/c

L to R: Marty "Moose" Nyholt, FC2/c; Legrand Van Uitert, CFC ⇓

⇑ *Clarence Vanness, MM2/c*

⇑ *Back row, L to R: David L. Appleby, CMM (MIA); Norman Foland, MoMM3/c; Richard Schneider, MM1/c; Hershel Freeman, MM2/c; John M. Hill, MM1/c (MIA); Calhoun (?); John R. Wickens, MM1/c (MIA)*
Front row, L to R: Art Whitney, MM1/c; Clarence Vanness, MM2/c; Patterson (?); Don Stranger, MM2/c; Frank M. Maloney, F1/c

PHOTOGRAPHS
MISSING IN ACTION

⇑ *James P. Appicelli, CMM*

⇑ *Edwin Gould, MM3/c*

⇑ *L to R: George Graff, WT2/c with Edwin Gould*

⇧ *Arthur Powers. S1/c*

⇧ *Francis A. Malinowski, BM2/c*

⇧ *John Rechkemmer, F1/c*

PHOTOGRAPHS

⇑ *Lawrence L. Stowe, S1/c*

Paul J. Zwick, MM2/c, with friend ⇒

⇑ *Walter Fischer, CTM*

DD 522: DIARY OF A DESTROYER

REUNIONS

⇐ Bill Lietz with wife Rita at Norfolk reunion 6 May 1989

L to R: Gerald Perdue, Don Stranger, Clarence Vanness, Art Whitney - May 1988 on USS Kidd ⇒

⇑ John A. Carpenter (L) and Hershel R. Freeman at home

Burr McFarland (L) and Dick Burlingame at 1992 Philadelphia reunion⇑

⇑ L to R: Bob Moyer, Marty Nyholt, Dick Flaum, Art Replogle

⇑ L to R: Waino Johnson, Bill Lietz and Cliff Roberts at 1993 Baltimore reunion

⇑ L to R: Freeman Phillips and author Ron Surels at 1993 Baltimore reunion

⇐ *The five sisters of Art Powers - 1992 L to R: Joan Deflorio, Lorraine Gallipoli, Helen Brandt, Marilyn Delaney, Ethel Scanlon*

Marilyn Gallipoli Miceli, niece of Art Powers, S1/c, rings memorial bell at Mobile, Alabama reunion in 1990 ⇒

⇑ *USS Luce survivors at the 1990 Mobile reunion:*
Row 1, front, L to R: Paul Wallace, William Lietz, J.C. Phillips, Carl Fernandez, Dick Burlingame
Row 2, L to R: Roger F. Bernice, John A. Carpenter, Joe McGuigan, Arthur L. Whitney, Michael Heon, Robert E. Stanley, Bob Harrison, Tom Blanck, Burr McFarland, Orville L. Hiles
Row 3, L to R: James M. Gory, Gerald Perdue, William Fotie, Fred Matteson, Harry Snyder, Omer Emond, John Welsh, Kenneth Sturm, Arthur Doaust, Tony DeFrank
Row 4, L to R: Art Replogle, George V. Graul, Milton L. Cathey, L.G. Van Uitert, Leo Greco, Joe Bille, Tom Matisak, Louis Shaffner, Anthony Marchitelli

Chapter 12

KAMIKAZE ATTACK

<u>The First Plane</u>

The pace of events now became fast and furious on this 4 May for the crew of the *Luce*. (The next three chapters describe events which took place in just a matter of minutes.)

The group of kamikaze suicide planes circled about like a swarm of angry bees, searching out targets for their lethal sting. Suddenly two or three broke away to begin their suicidal run on the destroyer.

Marty ("Moose") Nyholt, FC2/c, quickly dropped down behind the range–finder in the forward section and began ranging as the director swung out to focus on an oncoming kamikaze:

"Instead of a smooth, quick ride it was jerky, almost a frantic movement around to port. No sooner did we get to target–point then Bob Moyer, FC3/c, begins to train the director rapidly to starboard. I had yet to see the target and quickly got the feeling that there was something radically wrong. I didn't know that a kamikaze was diving at the bridge and, while we were training to the starboard the Skipper put the ship into a radical starboard turn to throw off the pilot's aim and unmask our guns. This combination of actions forced both the gunnery officer and the trainer to use compensating actions which accounted for the frantic, jerky ride. It also put the planes coming in on the port side to now be coming in more towards the port quarter, or stern."

Captain Waterhouse appeared very much composed on the

bridge:

"He was calm as if he were waiting for the start of a horse race. There were several others with him. 'Two planes on the port beam, Sir!' The shout came from a seaman lookout on the port wing, and Waterhouse hastened to get in touch with the main battery officer. As the planes closed in on the *Luce*, they split. One veered off to the right, taking approximately the opposite course from the ship. The other plane changed course to the left, then turned and headed directly for the ship. The gun crews frantically tried to aim at the suicider, but Waterhouse noticed that the entire main battery could not be brought to bear. 'Hard right rudder!' he ordered, and the ship quickly turned to meet the oncoming plane.[1]

When the kamikazes had started to come in, Captain Waterhouse turned to his Executive Officer John R. Welsh and calmly said, "You handle the guns, I'll handle the ship." As Welsh relates:

"So I handled the guns. By handle, I mean get the word to the gunnery officer, Lt. Cliff Jones, who was up in the Director. There was a kamikaze on the port bow, and Jones was already on it. They were pointing in the right direction, and everything seemed to be progressing fairly well, even though things were beginning to happen fast and furious."

Tom Blanck, Y1/c, was a talker on the bridge, and as such he would give range readings and bearings:

"I remember a guy I knew that was the gunpointer on the port side of the bridge, Kenny Marks, and he was yelling, 'He's coming down! He's coming down!' He followed him all the way in."

Then the guns opened up. Derry Moll, Lt. JG, remembers "that day I was in the forward fireroom. I heard the 5–inch fire, followed by the 40 mm, then the hell of the 20 mm's opened up... the blast of the earth's end."

Robert E. Stanley, S1/c, was at his GQ station in number two 40 mm starboard side just below the bridge:

"Looking out over port side, I saw the planes were getting closer. Several guns immediately opened up. All the action was coming from port side."

Norman Foland, MoMM2/c, swung his 20 mm around and began shooting at the first approaching aircraft:

"It was a Betty bomber, approaching off our port bow very high

---
[1] Edward Pinkowski, "The *Lady Luce*. Our Navy, Mid-December, 1946, 60-61.

and in a steep dive. J.C. (Phillips) was pumping some bullets in him, but I couldn't reach him with my 20 mm because the stops prevented me from getting low enough to aim at him. The stops on any gun mount were to keep anyone from depressing low enough to shoot into the masts, or whatever."

No doubt intending to crash into the bridge, the suicide plane came so close that several men could see distinct details of the plane and its pilot.

Marty Nyholt:

"I began running the range down with my knob while the pointer was trying to locate the target. I knew it would be close and took this action in anticipation. Suddenly, the target was in my scope. I mean, covered my scope! It was so close I couldn't see anything but the underside of the forward fuselage and wings. All I could do is count the rivets because it was too close to get a range on."

Robert E. Stanley:

"All of a sudden I saw this Jap plane coming straight for the bridge. The plane was so close I could actually see the Jap pilot smiling as the plane missed the bridge."

Tony Marchitelli, GM3/c:

"I was able to actually see the pilot with a scarf tied around his neck... and then saw him coming right at us... I looked right into his eyes, and then I hit the deck."

Omer Emond, S1/c:

"I was stationed on the port side, on the number two 40 mm practically underneath the bridge. The Skipper... headed towards the plane to give it less of a target and it came so close that it seemed I could have reached out and touched it. It missed, but it hit some of the signal wires... "

Bill Lietz, TM2/c:

"I could see the shells from our guns hitting the plane. You could tell by the gray puffs of smoke. We drove him off in the water about fifty feet amidships starboard—close enough so I could see his smile and white handkerchief around his neck. I could see the bomb that he was carrying."

Meanwhile, the 40 mm guns were firing as fast as they could, while "the plane swerved as if to avoid the lightening–like streams of ack–ack. When it was almost ahead of the ship, it banked quickly toward the ship. It missed and crashed into the water less than a hundred feet off the starboard side.'[2]

Tom Blanck, Y1/c, following the plane's trajectory, "heard this big 'WHOOSH!' He almost hit our radar antenna, but he splashed off the starboard side." The kamikaze's bomb went off as it hit the water, causing the power on the *Luce* to be lost.

The plane crashed near enough to inflict casualties, as Tony Marchitelli relates:

"It seemed to me that the tail section of the plane had been badly damaged. When this plane blew up, I got splashed by water, and after speaking to members of gun crews number forty-one and forty three, I was led to believe that there were some shrapnel casualties to men of those gun crews.

Freeman Phillips, S1/c:

"This also hit men in the open on the port side. It killed the men on number two repair party, who were also on the open deck. And I believe it spattered shrapnel along that whole side of the ship. Any man that was on the top deck was probably hit and wounded, if not killed."

Leo Greco, SM1/c:

"I thought for sure we had had it, but he missed the bridge, and went over the starboard side. When I got up, I went over to that side. I had hit the deck, because they taught us to put our hands under our stomach and cover our faces, and that's where I was and what I did. When I looked down over the side, all I could see was blood…"

Robert E. Stanley:

"… It hit the water near midship's starboard side and exploded. The shrapnel hit my helmet, knocking me down to the deck. When I picked my helmet up, there was a big dent on its left side Boy! You can imagine how lucky I felt being only 5' 5" tall, for if I was any taller, I probably wouldn't be around."

The power failure was big trouble for the guns. Waino Johnson, GM1/c, who was manning the 40 mm on the starboard side opposite from Omer Emond, S1/c, noted that the ship "didn't run correctly. The guns were no longer on automatic."

John Welsh, Executive Officer:

"He crashed… so close, and he had such a big bomb, that we felt

---
[2] Edward Pinkowski, Op. Cit.

a tremendous blast—shock, like a depth charge—and I believe that kicked out the circuit breakers for the main battery computer."

Joe Bille RT2/c, concurs that this was the blast that "knocked out a good portion of our electrical system, and made it difficult to maneuver the ship."

And the crew in the forward boiler room was having its problems, as well. One of the men who had also tried to get some breakfast that morning but couldn't because of GQ being called, was John A. Carpenter, WT1/c. Reporting to his station in No. one boiler room, John had an eerie feeling that he had better put on his lifebelt—something he had not been in the habit of doing. "I reached back where I had the lifebelt snapped around a diesel oil line and snapped it around my waist. That happened to be the time I needed it. The first thing that happened we took a sudden jar, which put the fires in the boilers out—just like you would blow out a match. So we proceeded to light those boilers back on and we were very busy. None of us were scared that I know of, and I didn't know if we had been hit. My first thought was that somebody had dropped a bomb down by the side of us, that we had a near miss, and the sudden jar had put the fire out in the boiler room. We finally got it lit back on and didn't lose too much steam pressure; and we kept that pressure up."

Marty Nyholt:

"Frank Fratello (FC3/c), on my phones in Fire Control Plot, was yelling: 'Moose, you've run the darn thing into the stops!' I started to answer 'I know', when there was a big explosion which knocked out all our power.. While the trainer, Bob Moyer (FC3/c) was trying to train around on the second bogey coming in on our port quarter, I looked out and saw the wreckage of the plane about 50 yards off the starboard side of the ship about even with our No. two stack. Close by the wreckage, I saw what looked like the body of the pilot floating face-down."

Observers from other ships in the area also took note of the kamikaze attack on DD 522. James Ries was aboard USS LCS (L) (3) 118, which was accompanying the *Luce*. From about 2000 yards, Ries observed:

"The explosion when the plane hit the water disabled the destroyer so she was still in the water. This made it so she could neither move nor fire her guns." [3]

(It seems unlikely that the *Luce* was dead in the water until she started to sink. All other testimony from survivors and reports indicate that the ship was going full speed when the first plane splashed off the bow, then slowed somewhat, but was relatively still only when she actually sank.)

A log entry from this same LCS states that the destroyer "did get the bomber."[4] This agrees with several *Luce* crew members who remember either scoring hits or seeing shells hitting the plane. Several of the *Luce* crew were also convinced that the exploding bomb from the kamikaze did severe damage to the ship's side.

Bill Lietz, TM2/c:

"It exploded, killing most of the starboard mid–ship repair party. At first I thought he had hit us and the wing of his plane was sticking in our mid–ship at the waterline, but the explosion had ripped our starboard plates loose from amid–ship to aft."

Tom Blanck, Y1/c:

"I walked over to the starboard wing of the bridge, and looking backwards, there was a huge plate metal, screen of plate metal, right perpendicular to the ship, sticking out there, so the ship had to be taking water very quickly."

Robert Stanley, S1/c, also noted the "steel plate hanging out into the water." Waino Johnson, GM1/c, looked down where the side of the ship was blown out... "and from a distance, it looked like the side was bulging out."

Tony Marchitelli, GM3/c:

"I was standing mid–ship on the starboard side when the plane crashed... about 30 yards off starboard mid–ship. It was always my impression that the plane did some damage to opening us up. I personally thought that's what caused us to sink—that he opened our seams. But others I've talked to have different ideas."

Several felt that some of this damage could have resulted from another plane which hit seconds after, and that its exploding bomb ripped open the ship aft, but most also seem convinced that the exploding bomb in the water opened up the side of the ship at least somewhat, and caused the ship to scoop in seawater. Joseph

---

[3] Earl Blanton, "Boston To Jacksonville", p 88.
[4] Ibid.

McGuigan, RM3/c, believes that this eventually caused the sinking:

"The one that missed us, with the bomb, did the most damage to sink us....That really did us in... it opened the side like a sardine can."

The evidence seems conclusive that the starboard side was indeed ripped open by the exploding bomb of the first plane. The speed of the ship scooped in the sea, thereby at least beginning the sinking process, which was accelerated by other planes. Scant minutes, or even seconds later, the other suiciders bore in. And this time, they didn't miss.

<u>Planes Two, Three—and Four?</u>

The partner of the plane just splashed had swung back, and was now heading for the ship from the port quarter.[5] Other suiciders were also heading for DD 522. Omer Emond, S1/c, stationed next to the bridge on 40 mm No. two spotted one coming in near midships on the port side:

"It was on pontoons. I saw the pontoons; and it was so low it was skipping on the water... We were trying, with no power on, to crank the 40 mm... trying to get it, and my 40 mm would turn just so far... we couldn't shoot at it. It was heading right into the side of the ship."

Lt. John Welsh agrees with Emond and believes the aircraft was an old biplane that they had dug up from somewhere.

J.C. Phillips, SC1/c, on the fantail at gun number five 20 mm, saw the other suiciders:

"There were two coming down the port side of the ship where this other one had peeled off to come along the bow. They continued on around, and one of them turned to come in, and he came in from dead astern. The second one was in his flight path and continued on around and turned over on the starboard side to come toward the ship. I didn't concentrate on him because I knew the one on the fantails was coming on faster than he was, because he had to turn to make his run. Then I saw two more coming in on our port quarter."

Freeman Phillips, S1/c, was on the number seven 20 mm near J.C.'s position:

"The ship, by that time, was in such a tight circle that even

---

[5] Edward Pinkowski, Op. Cit.

though the planes had been coming in more on the port side, the turn of the ship put the planes coming in dead astern, as mentioned earlier. I was on the fantail with Richard LeBrun (SM3/c), John Tremback (S1/c), Urstle Keck (S1/c) who was my closest friend, Cyril T. Olsen (F2/c) and others. LeBrun and myself both saw two planes come in on the port quarter low in the water and straight in. We both know that one at least, hit at about number four 5–inch gun. One plane, I don't know where it ended up, was coming in straight at us. Dick Flaum (FC2/c) thought that it had turned and headed for the focsle, but we don't know for sure."

Meanwhile, as previously mentioned, knowing that torpedoes were useless in an air attack, Bill Lietz, TM2/c, left his torpedo tubes and moved just a few feet over to the dual 40 mm guns midship starboard of number two stack to see if he could assist the gun crew position the gun on the incoming kamikazes:

"As we swung the gun aft, I saw two planes—the first one coming in low from the stern with the second plane right behind. One—or both—hit on the aft 5–inch guns. I saw the two planes at the same elevation coming right in to get us, right from the stern, and I even told that when there was a Lt. Commander and a Commander who asked me about it in the hospital in Honolulu. They said that they had a couple of other reports that there were two planes. I replied that I didn't know whether the second plane, that was coming in at the same elevation as the first, hit or went off the side, or what, but I saw two planes coming in there."

Freeman Phillips picked up a full canister of ammo and started to load his 20 mm and then just froze. "Those two planes were so close that I just knew they were gonna hit me. I just froze, with the canister in my hands, watching those two planes—one slightly behind and alongside the other—coming in low right at me." Transfixed, unable to move, he watched as the kamikazes bore in on their target. There was nothing he could do except wait out the few scant seconds before the fatal impact occurred.

From the Director, Lt. Cliff Jones "tried to slew the guns around to the two planes coming in on our port side. The 40 mm were already firing on it, and it looked like they were very accurate. My slew sight could not work—no electricity. The 40's could work without electricity, and so could the 5–inch, but I couldn't slew them around. I gave the command to the trainer to train port. I watched those gun barrels slowly moving to where those planes were coming in, but I could see that they weren't going to get there in time to open fire on them. With my head out of the Director, I had to watch that plane boring in on us with the 40's and now the 20's sending up a hail of these smaller shells, riddling that plane, but it kept coming. We might have knocked the wings off it, but it wouldn't have made any difference—it was hurtling towards us. There was nothing we could do."

Meanwhile another observer on LCS 118, which was now less than 2,000 yards from the *Luce*, trained his gun on the planes bearing down on the destroyer. He had some frightening moments as he noticed where his shots were going:

"We could see hits (on the kamikaze) and knew we had him... We never stopped firing until he (hit) and our last shots, maybe four or six (40 mm fire rate is approximately five or six per second), hit the sea between us and the *Luce* and I watched in horror as the rounds ricocheted off the water and the tracers floated toward the *Luce* passing just over her deck and between the stacks as the huge fireball (from the crashing kamikaze) erupted. Later, survivors that had been on deck confirmed that we did not hit her, thank God for that, but I guess I will always ponder over this."[6]

Leo Greco, SM1/c, remembers that the ship was still making its sharp turn, and when he stood up after being knocked down from his position on the bridge by the starboard near–miss, he saw "the planes coming in as I went over to the starboard side. Actually, I saw three, but the other one was further away. I don't know whatever happened to the third plane, but two hit. The third... might have come in from the stern."

Tony Marchitelli, GM3/c, in talking later with the survivors who were aft, came to the conclusion "that everyone that was on the fantail, anyone that was on that port side, saw those two planes come in. There was no way that second plane didn't hit us. Yet there was just one big explosion, so they must have hit close together. Paul Wallace (F1/c) stated to me that he definitely saw two planes: the one that came in over the fantail and clipped its wing on mount five, cartwheeled onto mount four, and blew up the whole magazine section of 40 mm number five, the super-

---

[6] Statement in a letter to the author by Earl Blanton, gun captain on LCS 118.

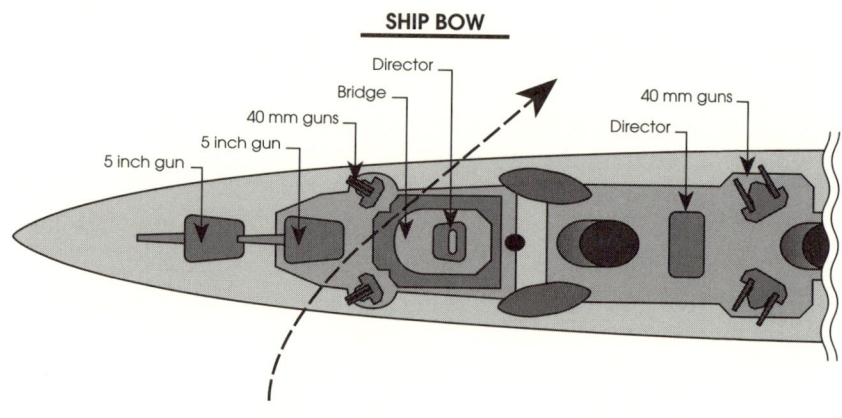

First Kamikaze

(ship turning to starboard)

structure, and possibly did damage to mount three. I think that those planes hit so close together that they produced one big explosion. And there seems to be a consensus that one of the planes had a five hundred pound bomb on it. That bomb most probably went down into the magazine and blew it..."

Just before the planes hit, J.C. Phillips had earnestly concentrated on the kamikaze closest to him off the stern:

"The planes were making a circle around us, and they were just a few yards behind one another. They would go round and round as they had a command plane up there, and he would order them in from different angles... I saw this one coming in astern of us, sneaking around, and it looked like he was going to be successful—and he was. But when I thought he was in range, I received no orders to fire. Nobody said anything. When I thought he was where I could get him, I fired. He was low off the water, almost making a wave. When I fired the first burst, a little smoke came out from around the cowling. I think it was a Zeke, as there were Zekes and Vals. When I saw the smoke I thought, 'Well, I've hit the dude.' So I hesitated before I fired the next burst. He lowered his nose just a bit, so I must have hit him. It was still smoking, but also still coming. So I gave him another burst, and I got more smoke.

CHAPTER 12: KAMIKAZE ATTACK

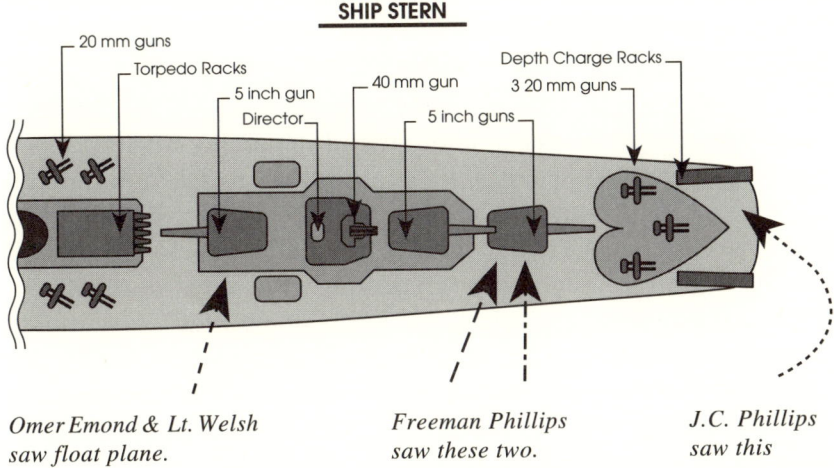

Omer Emond & Lt. Welsh saw float plane.

Freeman Phillips saw these two.

J.C. Phillips saw this

He raised his nose up a bit more. I just emptied the gun on him. But even though I kept hitting him I couldn't stop him. If you kill the pilot and he turns the controls loose normally the plane would come on in on a glide pattern to hit the ship. You had to get the wings or the engine. I saw he was sure to hit us, but everything was coming so fast there was nothing anyone could do."

Norman Foland, MoMM2/c, was also concentrating on the same plane as he saw it "coming in from the port quarter and it looked like a Zeke 51 or a Zero. I thought I saw a 500 pound bomb on his belly but it might have been a gas tank. My loader threw in another magazine of 20 mm, and I started shooting and so did J.C. He kept coming and we couldn't stop him. I knew our rounds were hitting him but he just kept coming in."

Meanwhile, Freeman Phillips and Richard LeBrun, SM3/c, were firing to the right of J.C. at the two planes coming in on the port quarter.

It was during this time that the planes were bearing down on the ship that Vernon C. Downs, S2/c, had a rather unusual experience with one of them, as recalled by his wife, Betty:

"My husband was a gunner on port side. He could see that the kamikaze, if he kept coming in the path he was on, would hit directly where he was at. He raised his hands up in a pushing upward motion and shouted, 'Get up! ' And he did. The plane angled up, and therefore hit the top of the ship instead of right in."

After J.C. Phillips fired his whole magazine into the oncoming kamikaze, his gun malfunctioned. While his loader, Virgil W. Degner, BKR2/c, tried to overcome the trouble and reload, Norman Foland managed to pump another full magazine into the ever-nearing aircraft. As J.C. recalls, "Foland was firing at him right up until he hit us. I know we had him punched full of holes, but he just kept coming. We didn't hit him in a vital spot where we could kill the engine or knock out his hydraulics. We did all we could do. That plane came in at around 300 knots. He pulled up, just high enough to clear the fantail, then the starboard wing on the aircraft just shaved the top of mount five, about where the cannon came out of the wing of the plane. It hit right underneath mount four. The plane cartwheeled."

Lt. Cliff Jones, who had stuck his head out of the Director to watch to see where the planes were headed, ducked back just in time:

"Just before they hit, I pulled my head back into the Director, which was fortunate. Lt. Ken Heuck, the torpedo officer, was up there by the Director, and he had two fingers sticking out as he held on. There was a tremendous explosion, and looking up, I could see a sheet of fire go right over my head through the open port in the Director where I had my head a second before. Ken's two exposed fingers were burned some.

"We lost all aft guns. I continued firing with the forward guns. I nearly hit an American plane, but stopped in time when told by one of the spotters. I tried to get contact with the after guns, but there was silence. Gun one and two responded, but three, four and five did not. The talker with the 40's reported that the forward 40's and some of the 20's were functioning."

Just before the crash, Norman Foland ran out of ammunition, and "turned my back because I had run out of the 20's. Right then a kamikaze hit number four mount up on the torpedo deck. Something exploded, and the ship raised up in the air as I hit the deck, and then came back down again. His bomb I believe, went right down into the magazine room. There was this terrific explosion, and the fantail was forced right under the water. It devastated mounts three, four and five and the 40 mm. It killed all hands there. On the fantail there were ten of us, but only two or three of us remained."

Foland stood up and noticed that "there was no one moving except myself and J.C. Phillips. There was a lot of blood and such around the gun mounts." For years afterward Freeman Phillips, S1/c, thought that only himself and Richard LeBrun, SM3/c, had remained alive. Then at a reunion years later he spotted J.C. Phillips, and in the course of their conversation they learned that there were five men that survived and five that were killed. The five survivors were both Phillips, Foland, LeBrun, and Cyril T. Olsen.

A bit further forward Bill Lietz, TM2/c, with the crew of 40 mm number three, was "knocked down by the explosion and rolled up the torpedo deck to the number one stack. I still had my head phones on, but the cord had broken and severely damaged my mouth, with the loss of five teeth and the two front teeth broken."

Art Whitney, MM1/c, who was in the forward repair party, noticed that "the shrapnel came sweeping up the deck from a hit on the aft section. We were fortunate in that we hit the deck just before this, when we heard the explosion. But there were several people killed in our party. Paul Zwick, MM2/c, was laying there on the deck. It looked like he was badly hurt. I picked him up and set him against the bulkhead, but I could see he was already gone. Then I saw another man, a friend of mine, and I laid him against the bulkhead as well; but he was also dead. I looked around and saw several other men lying around. Some might have been from the midship repair party."

Marty Nyholt, a bit forward in the director, also received some injury from the explosion, but was horrified at the scene in back of him:

"Bob Moyer was training manually to port, so I looked around aft and saw the plane just before it hit and knew we were not going to get the gun around in time. I ducked down into the director just as the plane hit—probably at the waterline between mounts three and four. There was a tremendous explosion and I ended up with large bumps on my forehead and knees. I jumped back up and peered aft out of the overhead hatch. The after–part of the ship from stack number two all the way back to the depth charge racks on the fantail was total shambles. The decks were ruptured; the 51 director and part of the deck and railing were gone. The torpedo tubes were pointing skyward, and it looked like 5–inch mounts three and four were gone, as well as 40 mm mounts forty–three, forty–four, forty–five; and at least seventy–five feet of the side hull plating was sticking out into the sea at a 60 degree angle. There was fire everywhere. I was in shock—I just couldn't believe it."

Everyone on the ship felt the crash. Lt. Arthur S. Replogle and everyone in the director felt the hit. There was much concern on the bridge:

"Waterhouse was thrown back against a steel bulwark. He was down for no more than a minute. When he got up, his first thoughts were for the men in the aft sections. He found the telephone disrupted at the aft repair station. He rang the forward repair party and said to the officer in charge: 'Go aft and see what you can do.' 'There's not much chance', the officer replied. 'Our men can't get through on account of the debris and the ruptured decks. They're already up to their waists in water The ship's leaking like a sieve.'

"Various reports reached the bridge. 'The port engine is okay', someone cut in. 'Another plane is closing in on the port beam, Sir!'"[7]

Some of the planes circling were friendly, trying to shoot down the kamikazes.

"In spite of the damage, the guns opened fire on the closing planes. Waterhouse recognized the other planes following... and almost immediately ordered the guns to cease firing. For long, awful moments there was a dogfight on the *Luce's* port bow, and it wasn't until minutes later that the last Japs were driven away."[8]

The enemy aircraft may have been driven away, but seconds later they came back to plague the men of DD 522 who were struggling to put up a fight. It had been only a very few minutes since the first suicider had crashed off the starboard bow, followed seconds later by the hits astern. Marty Nyholt was relieved when "power was restored and we still had 5–inch mounts one and two forward, so we picked up a couple of bogies and com-

---

[7] Edward Pinkowski, Op. Cit.
[8] Ibid

menced fire. The firing was slow and erratic and generated a lot of smoke, making it difficult to see the bursts, so as to spot our fire. Suddenly, a Navy Corsair flew right through our flack and onto the tails of two bogies, so we ceased fire. By this time, however the *Luce* was dead in the water and listing about 15 degrees to 20 degrees starboard. We commenced fire on still another bogey, but the MBD (Main Battery Director) and both forward guns ran into their elevation stops (couldn't depress any further) and we stopped firing."

In less than a minute after the first plane splashed off the starboard bow, at least two other planes had simultaneously hit the aft section, and possibly a third crashed close to midships on the port side. From Freeman Phillips we get the picture of two planes coming in at port quarter aft, crashing at about number four 5–inch mount; from Tom Blanck that a hit was scored on both number four and five mounts, and that yet another plane as testified to by others, hit somewhere at about the number five 5–inch gun near the top. Several men saw two planes coming in very close to each other, and most feel certain that two planes hit together, both blowing up in a corporate explosion. The possible third plane, which could have been a companion of the two deemed to have hit together, may have been the float plane seen by S1/c Omer Emond and Lt. John Welsh. It could have hit on the port quarter close to mid–ship or just skimmed the ship. Counting these three and adding as number four the first plane which splashed off the starboard side, it could be concluded that possibly as many as four kamikazes did damage to the ship. One of the planes that hit, in all probability, carried a bomb which blew up in the aft magazine, the combined explosion of the ammunition and the bomb blowing out a section of the bottom of the ship, thereby giving it the coup de grace, as the ship had probably already started to sink because of the damage caused by the first plane which splashed close to the ship and exploded.

Bob Moyer up in the director with Marty Nyholt remembered that the crew had called their ship "The *Lucky Luce*" because of their fine shooting record and action in the Philippines and off Okinawa, and "because we always seemed to come by with the skin of our teeth." But when the planes hit, he thought to himself, "Well, the luck just ran out."

As Lt. John Welsh gazed back from the bridge to see just what had happened, he couldn't see the stern of the ship. It was debris and smoke and obscured. All over the ship stunned survivors did what they could for each other and the ship, which wasn't much. Things were just too messed up and changed. In several areas—especially the stern section— the destroyer was not recognizable. And neither were some of the crew. Carnage and chaos were everywhere.

For a few seconds, there was some confusion in the director and the bridge as to just how serious the damage was. Men from below decks inquired about the situation, as Lt. Cliff Jones relates:

"One of the lower handling rooms called up to ask if we should abandon ship—were we sinking? I relayed this to the Captain immediately, and asked if the men should leave their stations and come up on deck. He called back, 'Stand fast! Stand fast!' He had not yet received the damage control report, and couldn't determine from the bridge the extent of the damage. I could see more than he could, and it was a shambles. I passed the word to stand fast. Those poor souls in those lowest rooms never had a chance to get out. We sank within three or so minutes of the hit. In less than a minute, the Captain did give the word to abandon ship, and I saw that a few did make it from the handling rooms below, but most just drowned. I do not hold the Captain responsible, because he needed to know just what the situation was from the damage report before he could do anything."

Robert Blondin, GM3/c from Vermont, was stationed on the Mark 51 Director close to the bridge. With the power gone and harnessed to his gun controls, he felt very helpless as the kamikazes swirled around the ship. He had watched fascinated as the first kamikaze near-missed and crashed off the starboard bow. He then turned to see another plane hit the aft section. At almost the same time he noticed a third kamikaze hit near amidships. Then the corner of his eye shifted his attention to a fourth plane coming in low off the water-- and suddenly realized that it seemed to be headed straight at him! His brain became numbed as he pictured the scene which must take place in the next two or three seconds. He felt trapped--this was it, he thought. Breathing a prayer, he grabbed the wooden cross around his neck which his mother had given him. "Wear this and you will come back to us", his mother had said. Then--blackness! That was all he remembered.

And when the smoke began to clear a bit, Vernon Downs, S2/c, at his station on the 20 mm port side, was horrified as he looked around and realized that he was the only one standing there.

CHAPTER 13

THE CARNAGE

During the attack one of the "pallbearer" ships with the *Luce*, LCS 118, as mentioned earlier, had also opened fire on one of the planes bearing in on DD 522. One of the crewmen[1] aboard this amphibious gunboat describes the scene around him:

"We opened up on him and fired all the way down. We hit him, and he was on fire, but he just kept coming. (Later the fellows we picked up said we knocked off his wing.) He hit the *Luce* just behind the second stack. There was a hell of an explosion and a big balloon of orange flame shot up at least two hundred feet, and a huge cloud of black smoke rolled up to at least five hundred feet. You could only see her bow out of the smoke, and she was cutting in a tight circle, burning like everything.

"The planes kept coming and in spite of four fighters and ack–ack, the same thing happened to the LSM(R). I saw two planes hit her and at least four miss her and crash into the water or they were

---

[1] Note: The observer aboard the LCS was Earl Blanton, gunnery captain on the 40 mm in director control. In a letter to the author he gives some details he received from the LCS association's historian Ray Baumler concerning the valuable service these small craft provided: "One hundred thirty were built in nine months, between June 1944 and March 1945. Most were immediately deployed to the Pacific. Between February 1, and June 30, 1945, six were sunk and twenty–two suffered battle damage. The twenty–three year old Captain of the No. 122 (Richard McCool) was awarded the Medal of Honor and lives in Seattle today. LCS's were credited with the downing of one hundred three Jap planes, fourteen probables, and ninety assists. Also forty–one suicide boats destroyed, 1,990 survivors rescued, forty–one prisoners captured, eighteen salvage operations and eight amphibious landings made. In addition individual ships were awarded Presidential Unit Citations (three) and Navy Unit Commendations (eight). Personal awards are unknown by number, but were in the dozens; at least six on my ship alone."

shot down. The "M" was burning and smoking bad. The planes were all around us but we couldn't shoot for fear of hitting our own planes."[2]

The suicide hits came as Virgil Degner, BKR2/c, and J.C. Phillips, SC1/c, were frantically attempting to fix their malfunctioning 20 mm and reload. As previously mentioned by Norman Foland, MoMM2/c, many of the men around them were instantly killed and Degner, who was shouting something to Phillips, never got to finish what he was trying to say. J.C. would never forget what happened next:

"He was trying to tell me something. His lips were moving—I had the earphones on—and I didn't know what he was trying to say. For some reason he wasn't able to load the gun—probably because of the malfunction. Then the explosion came... a piece of metal flew by and decapitated him. Just like that, his head fell off at my feet. I looked down, and to this day, I believe his mouth was still trying to tell me something. His body was still up, holding onto that magazine for what seemed like thirty minutes, but I know it was just a few moments. Then the body began to shake, and it just fell over. Soon it just floated away as the water came up."

Ken "Whitey" Sturm, TM2/c, and James McGuigan, TM1/c, were with Bill Lietz, TM2/c, next to the No. one torpedo tube on the starboard side. Ken remembers the tremendous feeling of hopelessness that came over him when he viewed the chaos about him caused by the explosion. He felt that "all the training and drills that we went through just went completely out the window. We always had drills of what to do in an emergency, over and over and over again. Everything happened so fast, and all this training and drill was just completely surpassed and forgotten, mainly because of the sights of mangled flesh... Bill was hit with shrapnel. I was standing six feet away from him and didn't get anything. I knew that he was hurt, and he didn't have his life jacket on. He had a phobia against life jackets, I understand, but I got one around him and we were both capable of going down one of the ladders to the main deck. Doing this, we executed some of that so–called training..."

Bill Lietz had just been blown off the gun mount by the explosion, as mentioned earlier, with some damage to his teeth. After

---
[2] Earl Blanton, "Boston To Jacksonville", 88.

picking himself up, and just before Ken Sturm helped him, Bill noticed James McGuigan "hanging on the torpedo tube rail. He was badly injured. He asked me what happened, and then just died in my arms. I laid him on the deck. I then noticed my right shoe, sock, and pants leg was missing. I could see the blood running from my right leg. Ken Sturm put a life jacket on me, and we went over the side."

Leo Greco, SM1/c, on the bridge as a signal man, looked back and saw "all this money around… somebody said it was payday that day. There was money all over the guys and the blood. One guy stood up, and half of his face was gone… Guys were laying all over the starboard side. Then the Captain said something to somebody…it was to abandon ship because we were starting to list."

Michael Heon, MoMM3/c, a talker on the phones with the forward repair party, had trouble making himself talk because he was scared. Just plain scared. "I actually felt the hair on my head go up and down. My voice didn't sound the same. They were hollering for power over the phones. They couldn't shoot their guns." Then Mike saw a sight that horrified him. He looked over to a gun mount near him and saw no one except a guy on the gun with no body—just shoulders—no head, no nothing. Nobody was moving."

Grisly scenes like this were repeated all over the ship. In later years, PhM3/c Charles Roger Bouley would tell Freeman Phillips, S1/c, and Richard LeBrun, SM3/c, that a man with his face half blown off had clutched him in a death grip, and then died in his arms.

Bob Harrison, RM2/c, jumped out of his seat in the radio room when "we got hit the first time… we got hit with three kamikazes, I think. I knew we had taken hits, but I didn't think our ship was going down, so I was planning to stay at my station. I went back and sat down. I was the only one in there, everybody had gone. The big transmitter had fallen over onto my chair. I had my I.D. card and my wallet wrapped up in a waterproof thing in preparation for this, and had it in a drawer—but I forgot about that. Here I am, this ship is going down, and I'm still at my battle station not knowing it. All of a sudden, Joe McGuigan, James' brother, who was a radarman, comes running back in and says, 'Let's go, Harry!'

(They called me 'Harry' for Harrison). I realized then that this was it, that I had better get going. Besides, the ship was listing badly to starboard. McGuigan's warning probably saved my life. I ran out of the radio room to the starboard side… and I saw guys lying all over the place. There was money floating on the main deck… I observed a sailor wounded with a hole almost through him. He was Glen Foulks, MM3/c. He didn't make it. He took about three steps and collapsed. He went down with the ship."

Gerald Perdue, MoMM1/c, began leaving the forward engine room with some other crew members when he remembered that he had on a brand new pair of shoes. He turned to Clarence Vanness, MM2/c, who was beside him, and said, "I hate to leave these!" But if they were going to end up in the water, and it had sure begun to look that way, shoes would be a problem, so off they went. And as he went up past the laundry room and into the long galleyway, he noticed that it was full of money, near where the paymaster's safe was. Burr McFarland, WT1/c, remembers someone telling him that "when that plane hit, the explosion blew the door of the safe off…and it went right through our phone talker of the damage control party… and blew that money all over the place!'

Bill Fotie, RM3/c, who was also on his station in the radio shack, was guarding the 500 KC's—the emergency circuit:

"Nothing was coming over so I stood up and leaned against a bulkhead. Suddenly, there was an explosion, and the rivets behind the seat of the radio set popped out, and I really believe that had I been sitting down, they would have killed me. With my set destroyed, I told Chief Page I was going to peek out and see what was going on. When I stepped on deck, nothing was alive except me—there were a number of sailors laying dead on deck, and I thought the galley had broken open and chunks of beef were laying on the deck… they weren't beef. I felt panic starting, and a hand was on my shoulder. It was an old chief, and I can't remember his name, but he said, 'Keep your head, and you'll be okay.' From that minute on, I kept my head."

Burr McFarland, whose GQ station was on the starboard side in the midship damage control party, "was blown out from under the starboard 40 mm guns by No. two stack where we had taken cover as ordered by the bridge. I was blown out and landed up on the main deck under the whaleboat and knocked unconscious. I was the last one to go in under and take shelter, and I was the first one blown out. I came to, and I was laying on the deck under the whaleboat. I looked down, and my leg was bleeding. It was twisted to the side, broken, and the first person I saw when I turned over was Chief (Walter) Fischer. I don't know where he came from. He had a line in one hand and a knife in the other. He put his knife down. I don't know where he got the line. I have no idea, to this day, I have been trying to rack my brain as to where there was some line hanging or laying around that he could cut a piece off from, and he put it around my leg, tied a knot on the inside where it should be to make a tourniquet to keep me from bleeding to death, gave me a shot of morphine, called for a stretcher, and made sure the stretcher bearers headed for the wardroom with me. Chief Fischer saved my life then, with the tourniquet and the morphine, and made sure I got some help. Then Bill Fotie made sure I got off the ship. But Chief Fischer, in my estimation, saved many lives, and sacrificed his own, with no thought of his own safety, whatsoever. He knew he was gonna go down with her, and I think there was only one medal given for heroism from our ship. Lt. Derry Moll got it—a silver star, deservedly so. I think Chief Fischer also deserves a minimum of a bronze star."

Orville Hiles, S1/c, was in his place as assistant to the gun captain on No. five 40 mm and, therefore, was very close to mount No. four where the kamikazes exploded:

"Next thing I knew, I was standing on my head in the corner of the turret, in the safety net, and my clothes were all burned off. I only had about a six inch strip around my belt with my keys, and the rest, I think, was basically nude, with the exception of my life jacket, which was burning. I threw that right off. Suffering from burns, I wandered towards the wardroom to get some medical attention."

Back on the fantail, James C. Phillips, SC1/c, was still trying to clear his head from the shock of the explosion and seeing his friend, Virgil Degner, decapitated before his eyes:

"That concussion addles ya. It blows your thoughts right out of your head. When I came to my senses, I was still strapped in fine 20 millimeter. I unhooked the strap and noticed the shield was cut off. Degner's head was on my right foot, his body had fallen over. S1/c D. McKay's body was over against the splinter shield. His head was also off. I looked around and I thought, well, maybe I'm dead. You really don't know for just a second. Then I heard somebody calling. I looked to the right, and mount five was on fire. The water was beginning to come up on deck. I thought the ship was still turning. I didn't know it was sinking. Malinowski (Francis A., SM2/c), the gun captain on five-inch No. five had fallen out of that little hatch on his belly, where you get into the mount. His legs were the last to come out of the mount, and they flipped up and were on his back. So I knew he was broke up. He got himself up on his elbows, and he was looking at me, and he was burned. You wouldn't believe it. I can still see his face. There were big huge burns on his face, both his hands were burned off or cut off. They looked like burned limbs. He was pulling himself up on the deck. And he looked up at me, and he said, 'J.C., can you help me over the side?' Well, in the meantime, LeBrun was asking for help and I had his leg in my hand. The water was coming up on the deck, and it began to get deeper. I finished the tourniquet quickly on LeBrun's leg. I looked back, and Malinowski said 'J.C., can you just help me?' I started over but then the water caught him, and washed him up underneath the depth charge rack on the port side. He was still calling and he was drowning, with the water going into his lungs. So that really has haunted me all my life. I never can get that voice away from my mind. In the meantime, I put the tourniquet on LeBrun; and I held him in my arms. I was burned by all that gasoline that rained down on us like fire. It burned all my hair off and burned my shoulders."

Norman Foland, MoMM2/c, had noticed that J.C. went to help Richard LeBrun, SM3/c, who was badly hurt:

"I heard some of the men screaming in No. five mount. About that time, a shipfitter came up out of the after hatch and asked me what he could do, and I said, 'Anything at all.' Phillips called me and said, 'Give me a hand with LeBrun.' He was a gunner on No. six 20 mm on the starboard side. His leg was just about gone—what a mess. I looked around. Besides LeBrun breathing, there was just myself and J.C. Phillips. J.C. put a tourniquet on his leg and I gave him a shot of morphine out of the syringe we carry. Then I noticed my loader, the Swede (Cyril T. Olsen, F2/c)—we called him 'the kid', as he was only 16 years old—was in bad shape. I thought he might be dead, but I gave him a shot of morphine anyway, just in case he did make it. About that time, I heard J.C. call, 'Look out!', and here comes a wall of water down the starboard side. Apparently what happened was that we got steam up to the forward engine room and the starboard screw, and they got underway again. Most of the men in the after engine rooms and after guns died. I could see the carnage—it sure looked bad. This wall of water came down and I reached around to pull the chain loose from the stantion so we could jump off. There wasn't any jumping off to it. We just got hit by this wall of water."

Ernest Carpenter, WT2/c, was down in the fire room, and was knocked out by the jolt of the first plane that crashed in the water and exploded. He woke up just before the second plane hit on mount No. four and made it to the wardroom, but not without some difficulty:

"I went to go up the starboard side, but I couldn't get up the ladder, because it was crushed in. So I went back down and went over to the port side. As I went to go up, one fellow was there, and he froze to the ladder. I think his name was Manning. So I hollered, 'Come on, Manning, let's go!' We were the only ones left and it was all dark in there. He said, 'I can't move!' So, I pushed him in the back, and then he ran up the ladder. I went up behind to first level, where the fellow tending water, O'Neill (William, WT3/c) was stationed, and I'm hollering for him, running across the catwalk, and he wasn't there. I went on up to the top, and I don't know who had opened up the hatchway to let us out, but it was already open. When I got up top, the air hit me and knocked me down. Some kind of pressure, I guess. I fell flat on a burning deck. It was red hot, and burned my knee. I was burned all over, and I was taken to the wardroom where the wounded were. I was laid down. It was filled up in there. They were all laying on the deck, and what they were doing was opening their legs up, putting your head between your legs, to make room. Hill (John M., MM1/c) was there, Machinist, and he had a big hole in his shoulder. I found out later that he died. The guys were all hollering and everything, they couldn't move. So, then all the sudden, it sounded like another plane hit. Whether it did or not, I don't know. That's what it sounded like."

All of the wounded that could make it continued to head toward the wardroom, where the ship's doctor, Lt. Louis Shaffner, did what he could for the injured. After he had heard and felt the explosion of the suicides' hit, he opened the door—"the only one that opened onto the starboard main deck. Almost immediately injured crew began to come in. One fellow particularly, who had a large hole in his upper chest and having difficulty in breathing, collapsed and died right in front of me before I could do anything. Another man was brought in on a stretcher who probably had a broken leg. There were others who came in and sat on the couch. I saw that they were burned and gave morphine to one or two of them. About that time, the ship began to list to starboard and didn't roll back again."

In a later report, Dr. Shaffner identified some of the men he had treated:

"Two casualties from forward repair had already run into the wardroom through the passageway, one (Hill, J.M., MM1/c) complained of chest injury and appeared very pale, but no external wounds were seen on rapid examination. The other (Mason, Richard, EM3/c) was found in extremis with a perforating sucking wound of the chest above the clavicle and massive hemorrhage, probably from the aorta. An effort to close the hole by hand was of no avail and he died within thirty seconds of his injury. Hill was given morphine, and by that time, two ambulatory patients (Hubbard, M.E., TM1/c and Wallace, Paul L., F1/c) and one stretcher case (Gareffa, Bruno, MM3/c) with fracture of both legs and burns had come in. Hubbard had a fragment wound of left arm, on which a tourniquet had been placed. A battle dressing and morphine were given. Wallace had severe burns of face and arms having come from the after fireroom. He was given morphine also. Up until this time, the medical officer was assisted by Schneider, R., MM1/c, a member of forward repair party. The Pharmacist Mate had not returned, but it was learned later that he was administering first aid on deck.[2] Trying to find his way out of the fireroom after trapping himself there, Paul Wallace, F1/c, was injured by steam and fought his way to the wardroom:

"I looked up to see whether the hatch was open, from where I came down into the fireroom, and I was the last one down there, so I remember shutting the hatch. I knew it was shut, and I said, 'Well. I can't get out there.' So, I walked across the fireroom to the starboard side, and looked up. All I could see was just a little light

---
[2] Special Action Report On 4 May •945, Lt. Shaffner.

in there. I said to myself, 'Well, I can't get out there either.' I could hear the steam escaping all the time. So, I had to walk back across to the port side of the ship, and try to get out that hatch over yonder. I did, and I was walking across where the boilers were, I could feel the steam hit me, and my skin would just crawl on my face and my hands, I got to the end of the port side of the ship, and looked up, and lucky enough, that hatch was open. I went up to top side. I remember being told if we got hurt, we were to go to the wardroom, and that's where I headed. Just as I got to the wardroom, I noticed a guy standing there with a big hole in the side of his groin. Two or three guys were trying to put tourniquets on him. I went into the wardroom and the doctor gave me a shot of morphine (for my burns) and told me to lay down, but I didn't for some reason. Then the ship began to go over..."

The sailor with the hole in his groin was Tony Marchitelli, GM3/c, who had arrived at the wardroom just after Wallace. Two or three minutes before, Tony had been with the repair party amidships under the bridge when the first suicide plane splashed off the starboard side:

"When the plane hit the water and blew up, I got showered with water from the burst, but that was all—I wasn't hurt. Walter Fischer, CTM, was standing just outside the hatch going into where the pay officer was and our sick bay. I turned to him and said, 'Chief, the guns have stopped firing. I'm going to go forward and see what happened.' (Fischer would be one of the many listed as MIA). As I started to take the few steps forward, I happened to see Malone (John J., TM2/c), a torpedoman, running along the torpedo deck, running forward, and glancing over his left shoulder as if watching a plane coming in.[3] Just then, there was this terrific explosion. I was still on my feet. All I felt was this hot blast hit me—the whole back side of me—and picking me off the deck. I actually was picked up in the air and thrown down, or blown down the deck, and landed on my feet in front of the bulkhead leading to the focsle. The one person whose name I can remember was Chief Boatswain's mate, Armond Beausoliel. I said to him, 'There's something hot and sticky on my neck.' And with that, I put my hand up and felt blood. He said, 'You're bleeding.' I opened my life jacket and took it off and sure enough, blood was

---

[3] John J. "Pappy" Malone was not seen again and was listed as missing in action.

spurting out my neck in several different directions. Chief grabbed the pressure points and was holding me there. While standing there, I looked down to see that I was standing in a puddle of blood. My pants leg and shoe was covered with blood. I dropped my trousers to see what the problem was, and there was a hole in the side of my groin about two inches by four inches, and blood was running out of me with every heartbeat. This meant that an artery was severed. There was another person with the Chief and I directed him to go and get a bandage from one of the first aid ready boxes... He went over to get it. Just about this time, Bruno Gareffa, MM3/c, came staggering down the starboard side dragging a couple of fire hoses. 'Somebody give me a hand, somebody give me a hand,' he was saying. I made a move to go over to help him, but Chief Beausoliel told me to stand still until he got the bleeding stopped on my neck. At the same time, my leg was still bleeding, and by the time the man came with the bandage, we managed to get it in a tourniquet. I started up, crossing over to port side to give Bruno a hand. Chief grabbed me and pushed me into the passageway and told me to get into the wardroom where the Doc was set up. As I walked into the wardroom I noticed that the fantail was slanted slightly but I figured that the compartments were watertight back there, and even though the fantail had sunk a bit, I thought that the ship would not sink. While in the wardroom, one of the men on the table had just died, and I recognized him as one of our electricians. He had multiple chest wounds. Doc told me to lie down somewhere, and there was blood all over the deck, so I sat in one of the armchairs which belonged to one of the officers—leather covered and all. While I was sitting there, Bruno was brought in by two other men. His legs were shattered. The Doc went over to him, gave him a shot of morphine, and laid him down... The ship seemed to still be settling astern. I was a bit dazed at the time."

The *Luce* had been zigzagging at 25 knots when the attack began. The near–miss had jammed the rudder so that the ship began to circle starboard. The hits of the other kamikazes accelerated the intake of water and the settling of the stern. The ship had also began to roll to starboard. Throughout the destroyer, men began to sense what was happening. A simultaneous thought swept through many minds: If they didn't leave the ship now, they wouldn't make it.

Chapter 14

"Abandon Ship!"

The USS *Luce*, a once proud fighting ship, had become within seconds a floundering mass of steel and human wreckage. Executive Officer John A. Welsh, with Captain Waterhouse on the bridge, looked towards the stern of the ship. He remembers that "all was smoke after the second plane hit. For a few seconds I couldn't see a thing." Suddenly the smoke blew away and Welsh was surprised to see that the stern was beginning to sink. Then both men began to feel the destroyer starting to list down and over to the starboard (right) side. Seeing that the 376 foot destroyer was helpless and that the stern was fast going under, Waterhouse turned to Welsh and said "You'd better abandon ship." "Abandon ship, Captain?" asked a stunned Welsh. "Yes," Waterhouse calmly replied, "Abandon ship!" Welsh went into the pilot house, flicked on the loudspeaker and shouted. "Abandon ship! All hands abandon ship!" Welsh doubted the word got out. By that time the ship had listed enough and rolled so that he couldn't walk on the deck. He had to pull himself hand over hand to get up to the high side of the bridge. "I proceeded to get over what would have been the railing and walked down the side of the ship. Suddenly I heard someone hollering from down into the passageway from the focsle to amidships. I helped him up out of the passageway, and noticed that something was wrong with his leg. Suddenly he began cussing at me and I didn't understand why until I realized his leg was broken and in helping him my foot kicked his leg. He was an engineer, but I didn't know who he was. Everything happened so fast. We went off the ship together."

The ship continued to list heavily to starboard and seawater was backing down the hatch to the forward engine room. The crew began to get off the ship as best they could. In some parts of the steam room several men lay on the floor to escape being burned by escaping steam from fractured pipes. The men below decks reacted in various ways. Some waded around in the water until it was too late, trying to do something to hopefully save the ship. Still others were doing what they could to help those who were injured or trapped by debris. And although most of the crew did not hear the order to abandon ship because of the communications failure, it was obvious that this was the only thing left to do with the ship listing badly and the stern rapidly sinking. It became, as Lt. Art Replogle in the Director realized, "every man for himself." Some of the survivors, like S1/c Freeman Phillips, were blown off into the sea. Still others had to struggle to leave the *Luce*. Such was the situation with Thomas Blanck, Y1/c:

"The order to abandon ship was given. From the bridge, I yelled into my phones to the IC room and whoever else was on that circuit. The ship was listing to starboard so hard that I had to pull myself up onto the bridge hatch on port side and on the side of the 5-inch 38 director. I went right into the water. She was going down quickly and I think I was one of the last ones off. I remember looking back, and the bow was beginning to go straight up."

The listing motion of the ship signaled to the men in number one boiler room that the ship was sinking, although some of the men were so intent in keeping the boilers lit that the danger didn't register with them at first. Hershel R. Freeman, MM2/c, ran up to his friend, John Carpenter, WT1/c, and said, "Hey, Carpenter! Get out of here! This thing is a–sinking!" John noticed that the gauges on the panel board were swinging:

"They went wild. The hands on each one of them were playing back and forth. When they finally settled down, one of them was reading flank speed and the other was reading flank astern, which was the fastest speed we could travel, and that would turn you in the water at a very sharp turn. This would make the ship list to one side. I thought that this was what was taking place—that the ship was listing only because of this speed and turn. So it didn't alarm me. I was in charge of the boiler room and wore the headset phones all the time, so I could get the messages straight. Our messages came from the bridge to the forward engine room and from there to the boiler room. As the ship kept listing over, I still thought that we were making a sharp turn—nobody had said otherwise over the phones—until someone hollered at me."

Carpenter always felt after this that Hershel Freeman had saved him from a watery grave by his shouted warning.

Carpenter then shouted to the men to hit the ladder and helped some of them out.

While the men were clearing out from the boiler room, Carpenter began securing the boiler. George V. Graul, WT2/c, was helping him. Then finally, over the telephone, they heard the order to abandon ship. George went behind some other men towards the starboard hatch. They were surprised to find it under water already, and the sea rapidly coming in. They turned and began pulling each other over and through a grate. George frantically kicked his feet to get his shoes off, and finally succeeded. (For years afterwards he would always fix his shoelaces so he could easily kick off his shoes.) Then it was up the side of the ship to get out. Graul thought he was going to be trapped, as it was with some difficulty that had made his way towards the outside:

"I was, along with others, trying to keep ahead of the rising water. There was a man ahead of me blocking my way. I pushed against him with all my strength, finally pushing him outside. I followed him and then ran with him down the side of the ship. I noticed that the sound gear, which would normally be about ten feet under water on the bottom of the ship, was clear up out of the water. I said to the man in front of me, 'C'mon, let's get going!' and off into the water we went."

Meanwhile John Carpenter was having his troubles in attempting to abandon ship. By this time the ladder to the hatch and freedom was on the ceiling, or upside down. Only he and one other—an officer—were left in the fireroom:

"We had a ninety-day wonder down there, and I always felt that in a situation like this he would be the first man out. He was a fellow by the name of Moll (Derry O., LTJG). Well, he fooled me. He stayed. He was standing on that ladder reaching down with his hand to help me. I climbed up to where I could reach him—and slipped."

Moll grabbed his hair as Carpenter slipped, but lost his grip and Carpenter went down. As Moll relates:

"Twice more I grabbed onto his hair, and finally on the third try succeeded in getting him onto the ladder. I don't think he knew I did that. He looked at me and said, 'Go ahead—get out.' I replied, 'No, no—you go!'"

Carpenter didn't stay to argue. He shed his shoes, climbed out and Moll came after him.

Marty Nyholt, FC2/c, was having his troubles in the Director:

"After we ceased fire, we were all wondering what to do next when the Gunnery Officer announced: 'Looks like everyone else is gone, so I guess we better abandon ship.' Everyone else was reaching for their life jackets, but, like a total idiot, I unjacked my phones and began to coil the lead and hang them up... just like we do when we come into port. Dick Flaum (FC2/c) said: 'Forget them, Moose, let's get out of here.' Dick kept his life jacket (the rubber type that goes around your waist and which you blow up by pressing a gas cylinder) in the canvas weather bag around the starboard arm of the Optical Range Finder where it exits the Director. When he pulled his life jacket out, we noticed that the bag and his life jacket were full of shrapnel holes. Dick said: 'Now what do I do, I can't swim!' I suggested that he take mine...which he did, and we both left through the bottom hatch of the MBD (Main Battery Director). The ship was listing so bad that we didn't use the ladder. I simply dropped down and landed in a heap. Then I scrambled forward to the bridge. By this time, the ship's stern was going lower in the water and the bow started to rise. I could see the water start coming in the starboard hatch of the bridge. The rising motion of the bow gave me some traction on the after bulkhead of the bridge, and I used the phone jacks to pull myself up to the port hatch and climb up on the outer bulkhead where I stood up and tried to grab the splinter shield around the deck of the bridge. It was a foot or two beyond my reach, and I kept jumping up until I finally got a hand–hold. Pulling myself up onto the splinter shield required a tremendous effort, as I recall, because it seemed that I was being pulled downward by some kind of gravitational pull. I stood up on the splinter shield and looked out into the water where I saw a number of people swimming frantically to get away from the ship. I could also see the red–lead bottom of the ship. I had a problem: I was standing on the splinter shield surrounding the deck of the bridge, and I had to jump and clear the sixteen or so feet between there and the hull of the ship. Fortunately the bow had risen high enough so that I got a running start. A few steps and I did a belly–flop right onto the red–lead bottom, which knocked the wind out of me and scraped my belly. I slid into the water in a heap and out of breath… sucking in mouthfuls of seawater and fuel oil. When I came to the surface, the ship's bow was almost straight up and sliding over on top of me… I rolled over on my back, put my feet on the ship, and kept pushing myself away from her in a kind of running motion. I also learned that Dick Flaum, instead of going out the top hatch as I suggested, had followed me down the lower hatch of the director, climbed up the aft bulkhead of the bridge, but could not reach the splinter shield of the bridge. Instead, he climbed back up to the top of the main director, got ahold of the fire control radar 'basket', climbed in and went down with the ship until the director hit the water. He let go when it went under, but the vacuum created as the ship went down pulled him under about fifty feet below the surface. Then he was released and popped to the surface half drowned. So much for my good advice. Dick eventually married my sister, Maryann, had a long productive life with a flock of great kids."

Clarence J. Vanness, MM2/c, was manning the throttle in the forward engine room. "We were known as the 'Black Gang', a name from years ago in Navy circles. All of a sudden the ship was tilting more than normal and water started rushing in from a hatch that had been left open. One of the men was sent up to see what was going on. He yelled back that everyone was abandoning ship. We had not heard the order to abandon, as all communications were out. So I automatically secured the throttle—just basic instinct from good training—before I left my post. By that time, I was the second last man to go up the ladder out of the engine room. The rest did not make it. After I climbed up through the hatch and reached topside, the ship listed at such an angle that I slid down the side of the ship into the oily water. I tried to swim away from the ship as quickly as possible, but got sucked under. Somehow I did manage to escape, and when I reached the surface, my life belt did not inflate. A man nearby—Lt. Emerson P.

Hempstead—told me to hang onto him until I could get my life belt inflated."

Burr McFarland, WT1/c, being carried to the wardroom, was unceremoniously dropped by his stretcher bearers when they got word to abandon ship. He managed "to get myself turned over and out of the basket and crawl over to the port side and tried to climb over the life line. That's where I got all tangled up."

On his way out of the radio room, Bill Fotie, RM3/c, noticed that McFarland, with his broken leg, was struggling to get free of the life line ropes that had trapped him. Going down to him, Bill began to cut the ropes, but it seemed to be a fruitless task:

"I cut and cut and he still seemed trapped. That's when he turned around to me and said, 'Look—there was somebody else here, and I don't know who, but he took off.' I stayed with him and kept cutting. Finally he said, 'Look, we're going under. There is no use you being here. Both of us can't go, so you go and get off.' Well I did and years later when I saw Burr, he told me that I had indeed cut him free, and when the ship sank, he got off. Meanwhile, I went down and off the side of the ship." It was at the 1987 reunion in San Diego that Bill saw Burr, went over to him and said, "McFarland, I'm sure glad to see you—that you made it. The last time I saw you, you were all tangled up in the life line, and I was trying to untangle your legs so you could get over the side. I've wondered for forty–two years whether you made it or not." To which Burr replied, "and I wondered all these years who it was that untangled me." That's when McFarland told Fotie that his efforts were indeed successful. Just before he went off into the water, McFarland observed the actions of Walter C. Fischer, CTM, who, as previously noted, had a few days before written his wife that he knew what he was fighting for and hoped that he would live through the war to be able to profit from his experiences. Fischer, McFarland noted, "was still there, working to drag other guys out of CIC and that area and tossing them overboard. The last I, or anyone, saw of him, he was still throwing guys over the side. He saved several lives. In doing so, he could not get free of the ship, himself, in time, and went down with it." Lt. Louis Shaffner, the ship's doctor, noted in his Special Action Report of this day that "first aid by non medical personnel was invaluable. The Chief Torpedoman's Mate (Fischer. W.C.) was seen calmly administering first aid after the initial blast."

Leo Greco, SM1/c, from the same state—Iowa—as McFarland, ended up hanging on the same life line with him. McFarland had been able to flip himself over the side of the ship into the water. Greco helped him over to the floating raft and helped him shed his shoes. By this time McFarland's leg wounds were causing him considerable pain. Shrapnel had badly torn up his leg.

Several men were caught in the suction of the ship as she sank. Freeman Phillips, blown overboard, found himself in the water being pulled down with the ship. He felt no panic, "just peace. It was a sensation of wonderful, perfect calmness and peace. Then suddenly, I shot up to the surface, and when I broke out into the air, I grabbed three empty ammo cans floating nearby and put one under each arm and straddled the other one."

John Carpenter, WT1/c, who was already in the water, suddenly found himself in a very serious predicament: He was pulled back into the ship, and then realized that the ship was plunging to the ocean bottom—with him in it:

"The aft of the ship went under and the bow went straight up. It started coming down, and the bulkhead that went across the spud locker came down on top of me. It dragged me down and back in the ship. We had a hatch that went out on the deck and beside it was a hatch where you went down into the mess hall. That hatch had a little hallway in back of it, about ten or twelve feet long, where you raise the hatch up. I thought, 'If I swim around and get in back in that hallway, I'll never get out of here.' I couldn't see where I was. I said to myself, 'I can't see where I am. I got to get out of here!' So, I scrambled around, and shortly I got loose somehow, and rose to the top. By that time, I had swallowed a lot of water and came up coughing and a–snortin' because I had run out of air. I had to keep swimming to stay up until I could get my breath so I could blow up my preserver. I then took the little hose out of my life belt and blew it up. When I got that done, I was alright."

Orville Hiles, S1/c, jumping off the port side amidships, feet first, felt himself "going down and down, and I was waving my arms up and down trying to change the direction in which I was going. I was being sucked under, and I thought that I wasn't ever coming to the surface, but I finally did."

Mike Heon, MoMM3/c, had heard the order to abandon ship, and as he was getting ready to walk off into the water that was coming up to meet him, he was horrified to see "Manning (Manuel Medeiros, F1/c) come out of the forward fireroom, and I looked at him, and he didn't have a piece of skin left on him. It just all peeled off. You couldn't touch him. Then he went off into the water." Then Mike jumped into the water with a group of people that included Roger F. Bernier, F1/c.

The Captain's command to abandon ship was heard over the gun crew's phone in No. two 40 mm starboard by S1/c Robert E. Stanley. Looking over the starboard side and back to where he saw a steel plate hanging out into the water, Stanley crossed over "to port side focsle and jumped into the water. I didn't want to get caught by the steel plate and be taken under."

Two of the men in Combat Information Center, Lt. John Hutchinson and RdM3/c Tom Matisak, were looking for directions to come over the voice tube from the bridge. Inquiry had been made through this device because all other communication systems were not functioning. Hutchinson kept looking at the voice tube, waiting for a response. Matisak, noticing that the ship's list was becoming more pronounced by the second, kept hoping that Hutchinson or someone would order the men to leave. He thought to himself, "Well, this is getting a little scary. The minute an officer leaves this CIC room to go outside, I will be right on his tail—the first enlisted man out of here." Then suddenly Matisak noticed that Lt. Hutchinson was moving toward the hatch to the outside, and, true to the promise to himself, Matisak was on his tail. On his way out, Matisak noticed LTJG Thomas Hopley struggling to free himself from a phone line wrapped around his kapok preserver. Coming behind Matisak was RdM3/c John F. Murzycki, who, as he came up to Hopley, noticed that the lieutenant was apparently free and beginning to exit with the rest of the men. But he was later reported as Missing in Action, and apparently went down with the ship.

Tom Matisak was still following Lt. Hutchinson through the passageway:

"We were between the CIC and the outside hatch, midships, which is probably 25 feet or so. I know, because I had to wire brush it every morning, you know, keep it shiny all the time. On my way out toward the area where he was going, right near the hatch is the hatch leading down to Fire Control. He came to the hatch opening, which is about a foot off the main deck. You have to step up to get out. You can't slide your feet out. He had spread his arms across the hatchway. Now, I'm looking outside, and I can see over his shoulder that this water is getting precariously near the top of the deck near the life raft on the starboard side. I said, 'Mr. Hutchinson, Let's go! This thing is sinking!' I got no response. Well, it wasn't two seconds afterwards, I repeated myself. 'Mr. Hutchinson Let's go! The ship is going down!' Again, no response, so you know, I'm not gonna sit there and go down with the ship. I'm looking for my own skin. I crawled between his legs. Now, it was a very small space between his crotch and the top of that opening, between the deck and the opening of the hatch, but I got out. I immediately started up the port side. They always told us to get off the opposite side of that which is sinking. I glanced to the left, and the waters were awash of the life raft. I made one attempt to go up, and slid down. I had leather shoes on, which was a big mistake. Made another attempt, slid down again. I came down to the point where I had previously exited, near the spot where it goes up to the radio shack area, to the second deck. I don't recall how, but I got up on the second deck, not knowing how I got up that ladder. When I got up there, I'm walking along the four torpedo tubes. By that time, that's where the water had risen. So I squeezed my little CO^2 tube life preserver, found out that only one had exploded, so I was operating on that little air supply. I walked into the water, didn't dive, just walked in, and got out of the area as fast as I could."

(Lt. Cliff Jones remembers one of the men telling him that Hutchinson finally did go over the side.)

Joseph Bille, RT2/c, also in the CIC area, looked into the wardroom and saw the water was almost at the level of the deck. The wounded sailors from the wardroom, who were able to walk and myself abandoned ship from the hatch of the wardroom."

Lt. Jones, in abandoning the Director, "looked longingly at the binoculars I had hung up. I sure wanted to take them with me, but I thought the strap might get me tangled up in something, so I left them. The water came up and just floated me off. I started swimming the breaststroke, carefully avoiding the halyards."

Ensign Frank Scudder, who was near the wardroom and noticing that the water was engulfing the ship, turned around and said "Doc, you gotta get off—we're going down!" It was becoming difficult for the ship's doctor, Louis Shaffner, to continue to treat the wounded in the wardroom. He remembers:

"As the ship rolled, it listed more and more to starboard, and it was impossible to stand on the deck. Those of us who were able were forced to leave on the down side of the ship, with the water lapping on a deck normally fifteen feet above the normal waterline. I dove overboard fully clothed and swimming vigorously straight out, for fear the superstructure would roll down and trap me. Fortunately for me, the ship still had enough headway to pass me by, and I found myself treading in a mixture of warm seawater and fuel oil and watching the ship complete its roll, up–end its bow, and sink, stern first, as other survivors slid off the hull or jumped off the vertical decks."

One of the wounded who had still been patiently waiting for help, and a little dazed and sitting in that nice leather chair, was Tony Marchitelli, GM3/c. As the ship rolled over on its starboard side, he heard the Doc shouting, "We're going over, get out!' He and Wallace (Paul L., F1/c) "headed for the hatch on the starboard side. I was there for about ten seconds before realizing that I'd better get off, too. I thought about Bruno (Gareffa, MM3/c), but couldn't see anyone on the table. I went to the hatch. In talking to Doc and Paul Wallace, they both said they went out the hatch. I would say that the ship was at about a forty–five degree angle when I went out. I came out and was about ten feet above the fast approaching waterline. I tried to release the life raft, but could only reach one of the handles because of the steep angle of the ship. I told myself, 'Tony, you'd better get off—she's going down.' So I worked my way up along the cable lines, that we have along the side of the ship to keep people from falling overboard. Just opposite mount number one, I dove into the water with my life jacket in my hand and started swimming away. I looked up and saw the radar screen coming down on me. I let go of my life jacket and swam and I could feel the splash of the mast hitting the water. After I was picked up, I talked with another torpedoman (Melvin E. Hubbard, TM1/c), and he said he dove right behind me and got caught in the radar screen. Then when the ship righted itself somewhat, he was pulled from the water and got off the ship for the second time. He told this to me aboard the rescue craft."

In the rush from the wardroom to the outside, Paul Wallace, F1/c, didn't have to jump off the ship—"I was thrown from the wardroom into the water!" And by the time another injured man, Ernie Carpenter, WT2/c, went out of the wardroom, the water was already up to his hips and "then I just started swimming with the whole group of us. We tried to swim real fast to get away from the ship."

When Lt. Arthur Replogle left the Director through the sonar room and out into the bridge area, he discovered that "the deck was now a bulkhead, and I had to scramble to reach the flying bridge. The water was already up to my feet as I eased over the side without a life jacket. My CO^2 belt came off as I hit the water (you were not supposed to inflate it until after you got into the water) so I swam around, grabbing onto whatever flotsam was handy."

Several of the men had problems with the CO^2 cartridges. They would either just not respond or blow the life belt apart because, as one of the men stated, "the rubber was old."

Some of the crew, probably most of those who couldn't swim or were afraid of the water, climbed ahead of the rising water further up on the bow section as it lifted out of the sea. A few finally jumped or slipped off the ship. Others, like RT1/c Max W. Wannowsky, a violin player,[1] simply froze where they were. Bob Harrison, RM2/c, ran to the "port side on the boat deck and there is Wannowsky on the rail. I said, 'Come on, let's go!' I didn't realize for a minute that he was frozen at the rail. I jumped on the rail with my feet. I stomped on his knuckles. I grabbed him by the hair, pulled him, and got a clump of hair in my hand. He just wouldn't let go. So, I finally took off.'"

Others, who were stricken immobile with fear, were being helped off the sinking vessel. QM3/c Joseph Huss, Jr., was in a small group with Captain Waterhouse which "literally pulled crew members loose from the rail as they held on and threw them in the ocean." The skipper turned to Joe, ordering him to jump overboard so he would have time to safely swim away. Then Lt. Tom Parkerson and the Captain stepped on the port running light and slid down the ship into the water.

---

[1] Max had been a musician in the famous Xavier Cugart's band.

Lt. Harry Snyder, communication officer, looked back while treading water and noted that "quite a few men were caught in the superstructure, but some wriggled loose. A few guys froze to the spot, clinging to whatever was near when they knew the ship was going down. Other men would shout to them, 'Come on, get off!' You'd think they were following, then you'd get in the water and they weren't there. I suppose after a ship had been a man's home for a year and a half, there's something in it he doesn't want to leave."

Snyder knew that there were many men below decks who were not able to get out:

"No one got out of the engine room. Some steam lines broke, and live steam sprayed over everything in nothing flat. Nobody got out of the plotting room, either."

GM3/c Robert Blondin regained consciousness and found himself in the water, his damaged life jacket just barely keeping him afloat. The last thing he remembered was being harnessed to his gun control station on the Mark 51 Director trying to fire back at the kamikaze bearing down on him. Now here he was in the water--and all alone. No one else seemed to be around. He noticed that the wooden cross around his neck had been damaged--a piece of wood was missing. (He was not yet aware that his body was peppered with bits of shrapnel.) Blondin alternately passed out and revived again. He was aware of intense activity around him. Jap planes were strafing but were also being shot down by Navy Corsairs. He noticed the sinking Luce not too far away and he saw several men clinging to the bow. Once he came to and was horrified to see and feel sharks 'bumping' him. After what seemed like hours he was finally rescued. He wondered if his best friend, Jim Appicelli, who was stationed below decks, made it out. Later he discovered that his friend went down with the ship. Blondin's horrific ordeal was shared by many of his shipmates.

Well over one hundred crew members of the USS *Luce* went down with the ship; either killed by kamikazes or trapped in the destroyer. Typical of these was WT1/c Burr McFarland's acquaintance, F1/c John ("Jack") Rechkemmer, who was down in one of the magazines servicing the 5–inch guns. He was not able to get out. He was the one who had joined the Navy from Oelwein, Iowa, to stay free of trouble.

CHAPTER 15

IN THE WATER

As the survivors struggled in the oily East China Sea to get as far away from the sinking destroyer as possible, the accompanying "pallbearer" ships, LCS's and an LSM, started immediately towards them. These ships were LSM 190, LCS (L) (3)'s 81, 84, 118. The kamikazes had been bothering them as well, and shortly after the *Luce* went down, the LSM was sunk by three near misses. It slipped beneath the waves at 0905. Now, in addition to the *Luce*, other "pallbearers" had to contend with the rescue of survivors of the LSM. Tony Marchitelli, GM3/c, found himself with these men "whom I didn't recognize and, came to find out that they belonged to another ship—LSM 190—which had also been sunk. I clung to these fellows until I got my wind back and then went out on my own. Strangely enough, I never kicked my shoes off, figuring I would swim to a beach and need the shoes for walking. I was confident that if I had to swim it, I could. I floated around a bit and finally picked up a cushion from a whaleboat. I believe that I was in the water for about two hours before being picked up, probably one of the last ones."

Tony would have had quite a swim, as the *Luce* was sinking several miles from the small island of Aguni Shima and some sixty miles northwest of Point Bolo on Okinawa. It was certainly not the best of situations to be so far from land without a life preserver, yet several of the men were not wearing one when they hit the water. Some had had them blown off and others were still having trouble making them function. Orville Hiles, S1/c, swam for some time without a preserver and then met up with "a fellow from aboard our ship by the name of Lawton (Wayne J., RT1/c.) We said the Lord's prayer together, and that was a kind of help for me. I finally got over to one of those little donut life rafts that had the webbed bottom and got aboard that. The men in it tried to get me to stand up, and I said, 'Arrrgh! That burns!' I didn't know why then, but soon found out that I was severely burned on about 70 percent of my body from being too close to the kamikaze explosion."

Bill Fotie, RM3/c, believes he was in the water for quite some time and "kept looking for help and there was absolutely nothing on the horizon that I could see except Jap–held islands. That worried me that I might be taken prisoner. Later I was picked up by an LCVP, along with Chris Stanley, RM3/c, who died, and Lewis E. Hall, S1/c, who was wounded (with burns)."

Lt. John Welsh had talked the captain into letting him wear a CO^2 jacket preserver instead of a kapok because "I have to run through the bridge and all around to make sure I'm on the proper side wherever the action is coming in. It was a very bad mistake. I had run around the bridge so that I had worn that jacket just about off. When I got in the water and squeezed the CO^2 it inflated and then went flat—just no good. But I had a buddy next to me who had on a kapok, and I 'hitch hiked' with him."

Omer Emond, S1/c, noticed that Russell P. Coleman, S2/c, also had "one of those rubber things that wasn't working properly. He was wounded (serious burns). I had him hang onto me and my kapok." And Marty Nyholt, FC2/c, also without a preserver, would be forever grateful to Bob Moyer, FC3/c, who said it would be okay if he held onto him. "We saw some people climbing into a small life net (none of the rafts got off the ship that I know about and both gigs were blown into splinters), so we swam over to them. We were swimming and floating around the life net, but it was overcrowded and many of the people clinging to it were seriously wounded, so we let them have it. When I got tired, I merely took a light hold on Moyer, who had on a kapok, and rested."

The men were trying to help each other as best they could. Typical was Alexander Interlande, S1/c, who, while treading water, heard his name called. Swimming over in the direction of the voice, he spotted a wounded shipmate. Although wounded in the leg himself, Alexander applied a tourniquet to his friend's arm to stop it from bleeding. There were others in the area who were wounded or otherwise struggling. Interlande did his best to help them all.

Joe Bille, RT2/c, had a rather gruesome experience while swimming around: "I was looking for a kapok or buoyant material that would hold me up. I am an accomplished swimmer and had no problem swimming. I swam to a loose kapok, and when I turned it to put it on, there was a portion of a man's chest inside. I quickly let it go. Then I saw a shipmate swim towards the same kapok. I was about to yell over to him, but then thought he may think I wanted it for myself. When he saw what was in it, he swam away also. After about ten minutes in the water, I found another usable kapok. Along with other survivors, I began swimming towards a lifeboat (pallbearer ship)."

One who did have a good life jacket on as he slid off the bottom of the fast sinking destroyer was Leo Greco, SM1/c. He and Lt. Harry Snyder were among the last to leave the bridge. By this time, the ship's stern was deep underwater, and the bow was rising almost straight up. To their horror, both men noticed that as the bow rose up and began to slide under, it seemed to be coming straight over on them. Leo had never felt so helpless as "that bow came at me. I didn't realize it at the time, but it was pushing us away—until the bow slid under. Then there was this huge suction. It pulled me down, down, down. I felt things hitting me—probably the debris. Everything was going down with the ship. Blackness, confusion, no air... then suddenly, it just let go, and voom! I shot up to the top. My life jacket sure helped! When I came to the surface, I didn't have a scratch on me! And there was Burr McFarland (WT1/c) about five feet from me! He called to me and I answered, 'Mac, is that you?' He said, 'Yeah!' We went over to where there was a raft, and two or three guys on it helped lift Mac onto it. After about two or two and one-half hours we were picked up. We helped Mac up the ladder of the rescue ship, because one leg was just hanging there almost cut off."

J.C. Phillips, SC1/c, didn't have a life jacket, but was next to Richard LeBrun, SM3/c, who had a good full life jacket. "I was trying to hold on to two empty aluminum powder cases to keep myself up. LeBrun kept saying, 'Now, Phillips, don't let me drown if I faint. I think I'm gonna faint. Don't let me drown, now!' I said okay. His head fell over in the oil in the water, and I turned loose my powder cases and went over and pulled his head up. I stayed there and treaded water until he came to. The oil was getting into my eyes, and I couldn't see where my powder cases were. After the second time, I told him, 'Don't faint again.' He" said 'I think I'm gonna faint, J.C., don't let me drown.' I said, 'Go ahead. I ain't got no life jacket. I want your life jacket. As soon as you drown, I'm gonna take your blasted life jacket!' He didn't faint no more!"

Then Norman Foland, MoMM2/c, broke the surface next to the two men:

"I came up gasping for air and close to J.C. Phillips. He had LeBrun in a life jacket and mine was gone. It had blown off of me in tatters. I hung onto a 5–inch shell casing that floated by, but it started sinking and I started swimming over to LeBrun and J.C. Don't know how long we were in the water. The ship was about 500 feet away from us and sinking by the stern. It was down to the number one stack by the time I came out to the surface of the water. I could see men strung out from our position to where the ship was. I was told later that some of the men just stepped off into the water."

LTJG Derry Moll swam a few strokes and then felt something surround his chest which began pulling him down. He attempted to roll over to free himself, but whatever it was that trapped him held fast and pulled him deeper after the ship. Thinking he was doomed, he thought to himself, "Adieu world!" Then suddenly, when it seemed he could not hold out any longer and he would have to open his mouth and take in seawater—snap! He suddenly felt free and shot up to the surface. "That sounds like a light bulb exploding", he thought. He broke through the surface, took a deep breath of beautiful fresh air for his tortured lungs, and then looked back just in time to see the bow of the *Luce* go under. For over forty years Derry would wonder just what it was that ensnared him and dragged him down:

"At a reunion when we visited a Fletcher class destroyer I went up on the bridge to the part of the ship that was closest to me in the water as it went down. I spread out my arms. My hand hit a cable and then I knew It was the mainmast cable that had wound around me. But I still don't know what made it snap. The good Lord was looking out for me."

As Lt. John Welsh was swimming away from the ship with the man he had helped, he inadvertently would kick the man's injured leg, who would then curse. Fifteen minutes later they were picked up, which greatly relieved the situation.

Several other men swimming away from the ship turned to watch as the bow pointed straight up in the air. Just before the ship disappeared they were horrified to see that there were still men on it, climbing up the bow trying to escape the swirling waters. Someone yelled, "Jump off! Jump off!" But no one did. The *Luce's* doctor, Lt. Louis Shaffner, noticed that "as the stern sank and the bow went up into the air, holding the forward gun out of the water as well, I saw one sailor hanging onto the hatch on the bow, apparently afraid to let go because he was some twenty or so feet up above number one gun. If he had let go, he would have fallen right on that gun. But before the bow went under, a great blast of water came out of the hatch, hit him square in the face, and he disappeared. I never knew who he was or what happened to him, but obviously some waterproof door below had given away and this blast of air and water came out and knocked him off the hatch."

Swimming with Doc Shaffner was Ensign Frank Scudder who had just "flipped over on my back, because you're safer on your back rather than your stomach in the water and I saw the bow come up and go straight down. Two guys were hanging on, and one was a black man, one of the stewards. I heard later that they couldn't swim. They froze and went down with the *Luce*. They were hanging on the life line." Tony Marchitelli, GM3/c, heard one of the men identify the black man as one "Jives", who "just kept going up the life line. The water kept coming up to him, and he ran until he ran up the jack–staff. There was nothing left for him to go to, and that's how he went down, wrapped around that jack–staff for dear life." (This could very well have been SM2/c Willie Brown Jr., whom the casualty list reports as being seen on the focsle and refusing to abandon the ship.) Freeman Phillips, S1/c, and Robert Stanley, S1/c, also saw men hanging onto the bow. So did Tom Matisak, RM3/c, who "could see the ship, probably seventy or seventy-five feet of the bow, in typical Hollywood movie script fashion, sinking down, down, with this one guy on the top forward hatch, hanging on for dear life." Lt. Art Replogle thought the bow slipped under "just like a pencil. The ship went starboard, then stern, followed by the bow. I can still see that '522' as the last thing to go under."

Bob Harrison, RM2/c, had looked back from the water to see if RT1/c Max Wannowsky, the violin player, had unfrozen himself from the rail. He was saddened to see his friend still there, holding tight until the waves engulfed him. He then turned his attention to the bow and noticed the guns were still active:

"Number one and number two 5-inch guns were still blazing. Some of the crew of those two mounts were also the stewards (serving in the magazine), and they stuck to their guns and fired until either the ammo went out or the angle of the bow prevented them. They all perished, and there were at least two colored boys. Their living compartment was forward and that is why they were crew members of those guns. During General Quarters they could get to their battle stations the quickest." (One of these men could have been StM2/c Bob Jones, whose GQ station was number one magazine.)

Because so many men watched the bow slip under, Freeman Phillips believes it quite possible that "the bow was sticking out of the water for some time, but how long, nobody knows."

As the bow of DD 522 sank out of sight, the struggling men heard someone shout a warning: "On your backs!" Ken Sturm, TM2/c, didn't know who it was, but would be "forever grateful to him." Ernie Carpenter, WT2/c, heard Richard Schneider, MM1/c, exclaim "Get your head and your privates out of the water!" Most of the men who heard obeyed and rolled on their backs. No sooner had the warning been given when there was a tremendous explosion. The ship's doctor, Lt. Louis Shaffner, had been busy squeezing his life belt cartridges and was beginning to feel "somewhat relieved; although there was a lot of oil in the water; when all of a sudden there was a severe underwater explosion. It was quite frightening and shocking. I thought at first that we were being bombed or shot at by the Japanese planes above, since there were dogfights going on above us. But I subsequently realized that it was probably depth-charges—our own depth-charges—going off as our ship went down."

Ernie Carpenter was blown out of the water about six feet and received a concussion. Freeman Phillips, who was floating with a powder case under each arm and straddling another between his legs, had quite a scare because he "thought that the powder case between my legs had blown up! If it had, there wouldn't have been a piece of me left as big as a dime." And Joe McGuigan, RM3/c, felt sure the explosion tore his legs off "and the only thing I could think of was, 'I'm short enough without losing my legs!'" Joe would be one of the few to come out of his experience unscathed.

Lt. Tom Parkerson remembered his training "and one of the things that we had been taught was that when you are getting away from a sinking ship, you put one hand over your anus to prevent any explosion from getting in you. But the water was very oily, and to avoid that oily enema I swam away." Parkerson was with Tony DeFrank, Jr., WT3/c, and had just helped him inflate his life jacket when the explosion occurred. Parkerson was not hurt, but DeFrank had been seriously burned and was in shock. The explosion only added to his problems.

Apparently at least one of the stewards survived. Lt. Art Replogle was swimming next to him; and he "was very excited and frightened. I tried to calm him down. I grabbed a float nearby, and we clung to that and repeated the 23rd Psalm. I don't remember his name, but he survived." This could have been Ernest Mims, STM1/c, who was seen alive in the water.

Lt. Cliff Jones, Jr., witnessed the scene and noted that "the man had gone out of his life jacket somehow and was threshing about in the oil pockets, screaming hysterically. Replogle, who was keeping himself afloat with a life ring, persuaded him to take hold of the ring, talked to him quietly and calmed him down until both were picked up." Jones believes that Replogle's actions saved the man's life.

As the ship slipped under the waves, two of RdM3/c Tom Matisak's friends who had bunked next to him went down with it:

"Steve Premick, RdM3/c, was one of my friends, and was a laid-back sort of a person. He was in turn best friend to Arthur Powers, S1/c, who also bunked near me. I remember Art as being a real likable kid. Steve went down with the ship in the CIC room, and Art went down fighting, manning his 40 mm number 5 gun on the port side."

Some forty–six men from the *Luce* were listed as suffering injuries from the underwater explosion; and some of these were also badly burned from the explosion on board the ship. Others in the water also sustained burns, broken bones, and internal injuries.[1] Typical of the struggles the men faced was that of Joe Bille, RT2/c, who received a severe stomach concussion due to the underwater explosion. Although in severe pain, he did manage to swim to a rescue craft; just about making it. Some of the crew speculated that the explosion was caused by the boilers because, it was thought, they were not secured. John Carpenter, WT2/c, however, did secure the boiler in number one boiler room before he left. Others believed that it was the ship's depth–charges that blew up. Lt. Cliff Jones, who had received reliable training and information on the subject, is probably the best source among the crew as to just what caused the explosion:

"I remembered in school they had taught that you must not be upright in the water when a ship goes down, especially a destroyer with depth–charges. Those depth–charges will explode at 600 feet even though they are set on safety. The pressure of the water depth will detonate them. I watched the ship sink—one of the saddest sights I had ever seen...the black mess steward... clinging to the jack–staff. The depth–charges exploded...I was not injured. Then I saw one of these little ships coming to a standstill and waiting for us."

Ernest Carpenter, WT2/c, believes the explosion came from the boilers in the after engine room, as they were, in all probability, not secured because of the suddenness of the sinking and the men's thoughts of escape. George V. Graul, WT2/c, agrees with Carpenter that a boiler or boilers caused the explosion because if it were the depth charges there would have been a series of explosions. Also, according to Graul, boilers would still explode even if secured, when water and pressure hit them. What ever the cause, the explosion was of such magnitude that it greatly added to the distress of the survivors. But even now, after all this, they were not yet safe. Two other incidents arose to harry the flounder-

---

[1] Casualty list of USS *Luce* DD 522. This figure was gained simply by adding up the number of men so afflicted.

ing seamen.

The first came from enemy planes still overhead. Although Navy Corsairs were shooting them down left and right a few of the Jap planes with the ability to strafe did so. Tony Marchitelli, GM3/c, "witnessed planes swooping down to the water and I am almost certain that they were strafing, with the Corsairs coming in and firing at them." When the strafing began, Omer Emond, S1/c, with Russell P. Coleman, S2/c, hanging onto him, was struggling to reach a large life raft filled with sailors. Glancing at the sky above, Emond saw "a dog fight going on, and it looked like the (Jap) planes were coming to strafe, so me and Coleman swam away from the raft. Then they started strafing towards the life raft."

Bob Harrison, RM2/c, was with Joe Topor, RM2/c, and they both decided, as Bob relates, "to get away from, at least for a while, large groups of men to avoid the strafing. As we heard planes come down, we would duck under the water. We were both good swimmers."

Tom Blanck, Y1/c, also tried to stay away from "large groups of men because I figured they would be the targets for anyone strafing. We were very vulnerable at that point." Lt. Art Replogle was in the water less than thirty minutes and was among the first to be rescued. He scrambled aboard the small rescue boat and "then, as we took off, planes came in and strafed us... and the men in the water." Ensign Frank Scudder took evasive action because "the word was that we were being sprayed by another kamikaze. So I dove under the water for a few minutes. I knew the water could deflect the bullets." Freeman Phillips thought that "there were two Corsairs above us shooting down the Japs." And he also counted "three strafing runs within five minutes." Tom Matisak didn't hear any aircraft in the area, but suddenly here are these little spurts of water in front of us, going 'bom, bom, bom.' It was a Japanese plane strafing the guys in the water. He didn't last very long, however, because right on his tail was a Marine plane which fired two bursts and boom! down he went." Marty Nyholt noticed "occasional Jap planes coming in on strafing runs on groups of people and then a Corsair fighter firing at the Japs. This Corsair flew in circles over the survivors and there were no more Jap strafing runs."

Although a few of the water–bound sailors were hit, several of the men felt the same as Joe McGuigan in that "if it wasn't for the Marine Corsairs there would be a lot more of us dead. The Marine Air Corps—they were something else. They were good. Knocked those remaining Japs right out of the sky." The danger of strafing was now past. But there remained one more problem for the survivors. Tom Matisak spotted shark fins in the area, and "immediately cringed at the thought. I had kicked my shoes off, but my white socks were still on. Those two little white things kicking around in the water could flag the sharks toward me."

All the blood and action in the water had apparently attracted these fearsome creatures of the deep. Lt. Art Replogle had seen the sharks coming around just as he was rescued. Hershel R. Freeman, MM2/c, saw the sharks attack some of the men who were bleeding. For years afterward this would give him terrible nightmares. Tom Matisak, RM3/c, got aboard a small rescue craft before the sharks could grab onto his little white feet, but they continued to circle the ship. "I never saw such huge sharks in my life. They would come to a dead body and just give it a nudge, so apparently they were not that hungry… "

The call went out to get into the oil, and Freeman Phillips did just that. The sharks appeared to him to be very hungry:

"The smell of the oil would keep them off of us, so we were told. There were the sharks circling all around us. They were hitting men left and right, just tearing them up. They were hitting men that were still alive, taking their arms and legs off—really just slashing into us. I felt that in a matter of minutes I was going to get it; so I got into this very thick oil. I made sure that I was plastered with the stuff. I feel that there were quite a few men who would have made it if it had not been for the sharks. Then I floated quite a ways from the other men. As the day wore on, I became very scared. I kept trying to stay in that oil. It seemed that I was in the water for hours, and I thought it was getting dark. It probably was because there was oil in my eyes."

Lt. Cliff Jones witnessed a very gruesome shark attack: "As I was helping a man get aboard one of the little ships, two long grey shapes quickly went under me through the water, about ten or twelve feet down. They were sharks, going for our barber—I can't recall his name—and while he had his life jacket on, he was bleeding. He was swimming toward the ship when those two sharks got him. It was an awful, bloody mess as they chopped him and pulled him under. He disappeared. I never wanted to go into the ocean again. The fear of sharks was imbedded in me."

The men were scattered over quite a large area, struggling to keep afloat by whatever means possible; and keeping an eye out for strafing planes and sharks. There was at least one large life raft with several wounded men on it who were being helped by Lt. JG Derry Moll. A few months later Moll would be awarded a medal, not only for remaining at his station in the fireroom and assisting men to abandon ship, but for his assistance to men in the water. As the citation reads, Moll "proceeded to rescue and to administer first aid to the wounded; saving at least two lives by his timely application of tourniquets.'" On the raft Moll had on only a white jumpsuit, as he called it:

"I used my jumpsuit to make tourniquets, and when was picked up I had nothing on except my watch and class ring, which I wear to this day."

Just a few miles away, another destroyer, the USS *Morrison*, was also hit by kamikazes, and sunk within two hours of the *Luce*. As the news went out concerning the sinkings, it was heard by a former crewman of the *Luce*, Seaman John McCormick:

"I was aboard the *Luce* during the Aleutian campaign, then transferred to the USS *Erbin* (DD 631). We were operating about twelve miles off Okinawa when I heard over the TBS radio (Talk Between Ships) that the *Luce* had been sunk. It was a rather shocking thing for me to hear and I was very much concerned for my former shipmates. I was sure glad to meet some of them at future reunions. I later met a friend of mine who survived the sinking, Art Doaust (SM2/c), and he told me that Captain Waterhouse and he walked down the side of the ship together and into the water."

The pallbearer ships had reacted quickly to the sinking and were the first on the scene to begin picking up several of the more than one hundred and fifty survivors. It was just in time for some. The rescue was in full swing.

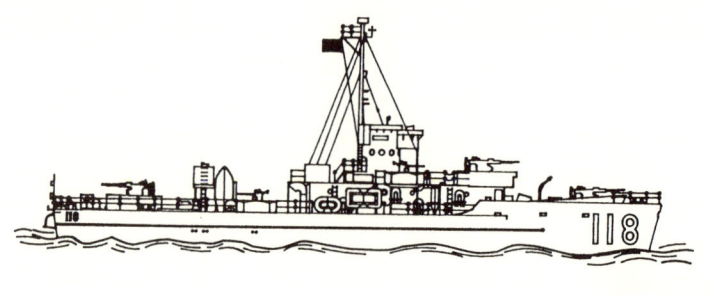

CHAPTER 16

THE RESCUE—AND HOME

There were several men in the water with J.C. Phillips, SC1/c, and one or two thought that they were not going to be rescued. They couldn't see any ships. J.C. encouraged them, saying it was only a matter of time before they would be out of the water. Richard LeBrun, SM3/c, was having a problem trying to keep from passing out because of his fractured leg, but J.C. kept on helping him. Then J.C. and the men with him "saw the most beautiful thing I ever saw in my lifetime. I believe it was the USS *Wiley* coming towards us. There was no earthly thing more pleasing to me than the sight of that ship coming for us—beautiful, beautiful sight!"

To many men it was a beautiful sight indeed, to see a ship coming to the rescue. Omer Emond, S1/c, who was helping badly burned Russell Coleman, S2/c, to stay afloat, was relieved when "a small ship came alongside and threw me a rope. I tied it around Coleman, and they pulled him aboard. Then they came back around and hauled me aboard." A few minutes later the ship came alongside Manuel Medeiros, F1/c, who had been seriously burned on his head and arms. Omer remembers that "Medeiros, the poor guy, was hollering, 'Help! Help! I can't swim!' He was struggling to hang onto something that was helping him to keep afloat, and when the ship came close to him, he let go of that, and began swimming towards the ship. Maybe he thought he couldn't swim, but he swam to the ship and was picked up."

Alexander Interlande, S1/c, found a destroyer heading his way. When it came alongside, he was very much surprised to find that the man leaning down over the side to pluck him out of the water was a very close friend from his home town.

One of the earliest men picked up was Lt. John Welsh, who believes he was in the water for less than a half hour: "I was in the water with a wounded man, an engineer, I think, and I was accidentally kicking his broken leg. As if that wasn't bad enough, when we were picked up, to my dishonor, I got aboard before him! And then they grabbed the guy with the broken leg and pulled him up as well. Doc Shaffner had people laid out on the deck and was tending them... l went to the focsle, sat down, and noticed that the *Luce* was still afloat. Must have been air in the bow holding her up. But soon after I noticed the bow sticking out, she slid right under."

Several of the wounded, especially those badly burned, were experiencing difficulty being rescued. Tom Matisak, RdM3/c, was trying to assist Paul Wallace, F1/c, aboard a rescue craft. Tom took Wallace under tow and "I would surround him and try to comfort the guy, he was so badly burned. Shortly, one of those small ships appeared; and we had a very difficult time getting him on board because he didn't want to be touched. He was so sensitive to pain. So finally one of the guys from the ship grabbed him by the hair; and that way we got him aboard." Having similar difficulties was Bob Harrison, RM2/c, who had just been rescued, and being unhurt himself, turned around to help others aboard LCS 84. One of these was Christian E. Stanley, RM3/c, also seriously burned. Bob reached over and grabbed ahold of his arm at the elbow. "It just pulled the skin right off, he had been burned so bad. I had a handful of his skin. I got him aboard. The wounded were lying in a row, the dead in another row. I laid him down."

Bill Fotie, RM3/c, aboard the same ship, heard that Chris Stanley, his friend, was dying. "I held Chris's hand until he died, then stayed with Hall (Lewis B., S1/c), who had flash burns on his face until we returned to Okinawa. Chris, Hall and myself had made liberties together... Sometime later Hall called me one day and said, 'Do you remember that you went back and forth between Chris Stanley and myself?' I didn't remember that. He said finally I came over and told him that Chris was dead; and that I stayed with him. He had called to thank me for that." Fotie himself was "bleeding fairly profusely from my rear." This was, no doubt, from the explosion of the ship in the water, which seemed to Bill like "a huge board hitting me across the back. I drifted in and out of consciousness... but was awake when rescued."

Orville Hiles S1/c, climbed aboard a rescue ship with "my skin dripping off my arm. I wandered down below deck and laid down. Some corpsmen came over and asked what my problem was. I told them I thought it was my back and they turned me over on my side and gave me about three or four pints of plasma." Ernie Carpenter, WT2/c, also found himself a bit handicapped in climbing aboard a rescue ship because "the skin on my hands was hanging off." They had been burned by escaping steam in his fireroom.

Freeman Phillips, S1/c, thought that he might have been one of the last of the men to be rescued because he felt that it was getting dark. It could have seemed that way to him because of the oil in his eyes; plus the fact that in such a situation, all comprehension of time is easily lost. Whatever, Freeman finally did see a ship coming his way. The craft came close and he started swimming.

"I was splashing around the water, and so on, and they saw me. Of course, they were looking for survivors anyway, and when they spotted me, they slowed down. They never stopped, but they slowed down. All the time these fellows had to worry about subs torpedoing them, and also, they needed to be moving in case another kamikaze came at them.

"I was off to the side of the ship and I thought it was gonna get by me and not stop. I think because of the oil in the water and the oil on me, so much black oil, that they didn't see me, and I thought it wasn't coming toward me. I remember thinking, 'Now, if I dropped these canisters and swim, I probably can't get back to the canisters. So my only hope is to get to the ship.' At that point I almost had to pry my arms off of those canisters. I had been holding on to those canisters so hard, that I barely could get away from them; and at first, I couldn't even kick my feet. But once I got going, I swam like I never swam in my life. I had super human strength. I had so much strength that when I got to the side of the ship, I was able to help them get me out."

There were still one or two enemy planes around to strafe or crash the ships while the rescue was going on. Lt. Tom Parkerson, on a crowded rescue ship, suddenly spotted one coming in:

"Here we are, crammed on board, and here comes another kamikaze low on the water, right for us, and I thought good-bye. But out of nowhere came a Marine Corsair plane and shot that kamikaze down; and I remember thinking to myself then, 'Boy, anything after this is just gravy!' I saw no way out of it, nothing to do, but here comes the Marines! So no matter what they say about the Marines, I love them!"

Martin (Marty) J. Nyholt, FC2/c, whose feelings after being rescued were probably typical of many, found himself going back in the water again:

"After some time in the water, we were picked up by a Marine transport, a converted WWI four-stack Destroyer. I remember climbing a rope-net to get aboard.. I helped some others to climb aboard but was asked to find a seat somewhere because the ship's crew didn't need the help. I remember sitting on hatch, feeling lousy... full of fuel oil... no shirt or shoes and with everything hurting... especially my stomach and rear. They were pulling the bodies of some of the fellows that had died in the water and laying them side-by-side on the deck. Must have been between ten and fifteen bodies. Looking at them... it suddenly hit me that those Japs had sunk my ship and killed most of my shipmates. I could only see twenty-five to thirty survivors. I can remember feeling guilty that I survived and so many didn't. Later on, of course, I found out that other survivors were picked up by other ships. However, for the next forty years I believed that there were only fifty or sixty survivors. I learned at our first reunion that over one hundred and eighty men survived.

"I do remember a sad incident when we were aboard that Marine transport that picked us up. There were still Jap planes in the area and the ship was at G.Q. while performing the rescue. Her skipper started to steam away toward Karama-Retto when we saw an obviously badly wounded man in the water. Our people were pointing him out to the ship's crew and yelling for the ship to go back. For some reason the Skipper didn't want to turn around so myself and another survivor (I don't know his name) dove off the moving ship and swam back to the man. I recognized him as a fireman from one of the engine rooms. The top of his head had been blown off and he was badly burned, with the skin on his face, arms and chest hanging down in strips. As I approached, I could hear his steady, rhythmic moaning, and I swam up to him with the intention of rolling him over on and his back and 'towing' him in that position back to the ship. I started to roll him when he reached out and got me around the head in a bear–hug, and both of us started to go under. He was covered by oil, blood and mucus and, because of this, I was able to slip free and get him on his back. The other rescuer arrived and joined in the effort. I remember him saying, "Moose... I was yelling at you to take him from behind...you're lucky he didn't take you down with him.' In the meantime, the four–piper's Skipper had come back to get us. He stopped alongside us and, with the help of several guys aboard, we tried to lift the dying man to the rope–net. But, as soon as we were holding on to the rope–net... with most of our bodies still in the water and our trying to lift the dying man high enough for those on board to grab him and pull him up, the ship got underway. We were not only struggling with the dead weight and slippery body of this man, but the force of the wake of the moving ship threatened to pull all three of us back into the water and maybe into the screws of the moving ship. Finally, the men aboard said that they had him and my exhausted friend and I let go in order to climb aboard. As soon as we released him, he slipped out of their grasp and fell back into the water and was quickly astern... lost in the wake of the ship. My friend and I climbed aboard expecting the Skipper to turn back and get him. One of their officers shouted something to the effect that they were under attack and couldn't risk the ship for a dead man. I admit that I didn't know all the facts regarding enemy planes or perhaps a sub... but I've never forgotten the incident and never forgiven that Navy skipper. I sure wish I knew the name of my *Luce* shipmate who tried so hard to help in saving that unfortunate man."

The crews on the rescue ships were shocked at the condition of the survivors. This quickly turned into compassion as they tenderly assisted them on board, as reported by one of the crew on USS LCS (L) (3) 118:

"We were picking up the men from the Can (*Luce*). There was a lot of heavy black oil around and they were covered with it. The water was dotted with their heads. Some were waving their arms, but none were crying out. Everyone but just enough men to man the guns were helping to get them aboard. There were a lot of wounded around. One fellow's whole face was gone and he was swelled up from broken bones and burns and was floating among the survivors. Another man had his arm gone but was still conscious. They were cut and torn and burned and broken and they were naked or their clothes hung on them in rags, and they were all covered with black heavy oil except where the blood was running from their cuts and wounds. The ones who were not wounded helped their shipmates aboard. Most of them just sat down shaking like a leaf. They would look at you and their eyes seemed to say 'Thanks, Buddy.'

"Everything was quiet—as quiet as it was noisy before—and before everything was just one big volume of sound and noise. The wounded didn't even cry out. They were in sort of a daze, it seemed like. One fellow climbed aboard, and his whole body was cut up. He looked like he had been hit with a hundred pieces of something, and he was bleeding from each cut. He just sat down and waited. He seemed to know he would be taken care of as soon as possible.

"Doc had his hands full and when two more pharmacists mates were pulled aboard, they helped out too. We thought we had them all aboard and as we pulled away, we saw two more. One had a jacket and was holding on to a wounded buddy. I saw him die later. As they pulled the wounded fellow aboard, the line slipped and he fell back. He was burned so bad, he left chunks of skin hanging on the line. Two fellows went over after him and got him aboard and laid him back by my gun tub. He was bleeding from the nose and mouth. His right leg was torn all to pieces. Every inch or so a piece of the bone stuck out. His foot was just hanging on by some battered meat. When he did get first aid, the pharmacists mate finished cutting his foot off. He was unconscious though, and kept gasping like a fish out of water, then he just stopped. The sun dried the blood on his face, and his eyes came open.

"By this time, ships from the next patrol had arrived; and then some more planes came, but were shot down before they got in range of us. One plane just kept coming in on a destroyer no matter how much ack–ack was going up. It seemed impossible for a plane to fly through such a barrage, but he did and when they finally got him, the splash from him hid the can from us. Then we pulled up to another can and passed all the wounded over to them where they had doctors and more room. We had one hundred and fourteen men aboard, and forty-some of them were wounded. One of the other LCS's got there in time to pick up around forty-five. That means at least one hundred and fifty men from the *Luce* were lost. I don't know how many were picked up from the LSM(R), but only a few, I heard."[1]

Wounded men were in the rescue ships' bunks and scattered on the decks. Tony Marchitelli, GM3/c, settled himself in enough to give attention to his wound by "opening up my tourniquet, and saw that I had stopped bleeding. They gave me a shot of morphine, and put me on one of the bunks. Later I was transferred to the hospital ship, USS *Mercy*. Aboard the *Mercy* my clothes were stripped off, and I was cleaned up. Then I was put in one of their bunks, near to Ballantine (Peter D., S2/c) and Burlingame (Richard A., WT1/c). Both were wrapped head to toe in bandages. They had been burned by steam. Then I was taken to Guam."

Most of the men were quickly transferred to the other larger ships which had proper facilities to treat their wounds and burns. After being transferred to the hospital ship USS *Mercy*, Freeman Phillips had a visitor:

"I was put on the hospital ship *Mercy* and I was in a little two bed room. There were just two beds in it. Richard LeBrun, SM3/c, was in the bottom one, and I was in the top one. Then this guy comes in, and he was wrapped in gauze from one end to the other. There was just a little slit for his nose and eyes. He looked like a mummy; and he came walking in there all wrapped in bandages. He had gotten burned real bad. And he said, 'Hi, Phil.' And I looked at him and I said, 'Who are you?' He said, 'you know me, Jew Boy (Alexander Jacobs, S1/c)!' Well, there was no more way you could tell who he was than nothing in the world. You couldn't even hardly see his eyes. The guys always called him Jew Boy; and it really ate him up. He didn't like it a bit. If you were his friend and you called him Jew Boy, fine. But if you were saying it as a slur to him, he did not like it. Now this fellow was a pretty big guy. He was stronger than us. But he was quiet; and always reading. One

---

[1] Earl Blanton, "Boston To Jacksonville", pg. 88–99.

time while in the Aleutians, we got leave in Dutch Harbor and we went in the bar. You had to sit down with your drink, and Jew Boy got up and went over to talk to somebody. The shore patrolmen told him to sit down, so he did. In a few minutes, he got up again. He was drinking, and he didn't realize what he was doing, and he just kept getting up to go talk with someone, and the point was that when he was aboard ship he wouldn't say nothing, I mean, he wasn't a talkative person at all, but he had a few drinks that evening, so he started talking. About the fifth time he got up, the shore patrolmen grabbed him, and set him down hard, one man on each side of him. He got up and cleaned house! He took the clubs away from them, and he was beating them over the head, and so forth! And after seeing him all bandaged up on the hospital ship, I never saw him again."

Burr McFarland, WT1/c, on the USS *Mercy* headed for Guam also saw a shipmate whom he didn't recognize because of his bandages from head to toe. He was, to all indications, dying. The medical people left the room, and a priest came in and gave this person the last rites of the Catholic church. Then he left and the medical personnel came back in with slabs of ice and placed them over the bandaged man's body. The ice apparently did the trick, for the man did not die after all. But Burr "had no idea who this was, only that he was a shipmate. For years afterwards I would wonder who he was." It would be over forty years before McFarland would discover the man's identity.

Freeman himself wasn't feeling too well because of all the oil he had swallowed keeping away from the sharks:

"They had Dick LeBrun in the bottom bunk, and they were paying all their attention to him, which was rightfully so, because he was much more bad off than I was. Both of us were plugged with oil. Our eyes were plugged with oil, we had oil inside of us, we'd almost choked to death on oil, and I was laying with my back to the wall. This was just a little small room; maybe six feet wide. It was just the two of us in that room, only two bunks in that room, and as I said, I had my back to the wall. In comes a nurse, a female nurse, she had a lot of perfume on. She never should of had that perfume on to begin with! But she did. She leaned over me and put her face right down in my face, and she said something to me, I don't know what. When I smelled the perfume, the blast of that perfume, it went both ways. The oil went out of my rectum and plastered that white hospital wall black, and at the same time I vomited it up. All in one motion, and I recall she ran out of the room hollering 'Corpsman! Corpsman!' She didn't want to clean it up, or even hang around there! So she's calling the corpsman to come in and clean up the mess and take care of us. And when I vomited, it went all over everything. There was saltwater with the oil, and it was a terrible mess! I was so shy that I was blaming myself. I was saying to myself, 'What have I done? I got this wall all covered with oil!' That was the stupidest thing, but never–the–less, that's what came to me. It was really very funny, but at the time it was anything but that. Dick LeBrun down in the bunk underneath was getting it on him, too, and I felt bad about that."

The survivors were transferred to ships such as the USS *Mercy*, the USS *Lauderdale*, the USS *Karnes* and others, for treatment and transportation to Okinawa and Guam; and eventually to the United States. Some of these ships also carried wounded soldiers and Marines from various other battle areas. Orville Hiles, S1/c, a burn patient like many others, went first to a fleet hospital in Guam and then "they took us out of there on stretchers and flew us to Honolulu. After two weeks they then flew us to Oakland Hospital in California, where I stayed to recover from my burns. I had several surgeries for skin grafts. My lower right side of my back was burned almost through to the kidney. They tried regular skin grafts, but that didn't take, so they went to 'pinch grafts'— large pieces of skin—and that worked... I looked like a Ubangi, with my lips swollen way out. I still have several pieces of metal in my body, in my legs, arm and back. They did well with me in that hospital."

Art Whitney, MM1/c, after being picked up by one of the pallbearers, was transferred aboard the transport USS *Karnes*:

"They were to take us back to the rear area, and far as that skipper was concerned the rear area was San Francisco, so he kept right on going without stopping." Ensign Frank Scudder remembers that he had more wrong with him than what was recorded:

"I was taken aboard the hospital ship for observation and internal bleeding—not for just pain as stated."

On the hospital ship USS *Mercy*, Joe Bille, RT2/c, was bunked next to Allen C. McEachern, SoM1/c. McEachern not only had a serious stomach concussion, but had swallowed a large amount of oil while in the water. His body could not survive these two problems; and Bille observed that "he died a few days later."

Lt. Cliff Jones was appreciative of the treatment from the time he was "picked up from the water. We were a sorry lot when we were hauled aboard the LCI. Our clothes were smeared with grease, our hair was matted and even our ears were full of oil. They treated us swell on that rescue craft. Blankets, towels, raincoats, every kind of covering was given to us to replace our clothing."

Robert E. Stanley, S1/c, was transferred "to the USS *Karnes* where most of us, covered with oil, had a shower. Some of us went to sick bay with pains in our stomachs. In the course of the day we experienced bleeding from our rectums—the result from the water explosion."

In the harbor at Okinawa, Bill Fotie, RM3/c, and his group tried to find transportation from the battle area:

"The harbor was under attack at the time, so ships passing couldn't stop to help; but they would offer. We would ask where they were bound. One offered to take the wounded to the hospital ship, but the rest of us refused. One ship was going to Manus, one to Pearl, and finally, the USS *Karnes* came by and offered to help. We asked them where they were headed and they said Frisco. 'SAVE US!' So they threw down cargo nets and we (with concussions) climbed up and headed for home."

When Dr. Louis Shaffner had climbed aboard one of the small rescue crafts, he was surprised to find "other survivors that had been picked up, including some that I had left in the wardroom, I thought. I asked them, 'I left you over in the wardroom. How did you get here?' They said, 'Doc, we left before you did!' So, I think it was a reflex when none of us could stand up, when the ship was rolling over—and we just left. Later, there had been an order to abandon ship, but we left before that order went out; or at least it never got to us. I do have regrets of those who were in the wardroom who never did get out, and this has worried me and haunted me many times since. In all honesty, in retrospect, I don't know what I could have done to save them. We were eventually all put on a four-stack destroyer that had been out there mine sweeping. It took us back to base. I and the doctor aboard that destroyer ran a morphine plasma clinic during our three hour run back to base. He took care of those below deck and I took care of those on deck. When we got back to base, we transferred the injured to a hospital ship, and we were transferred to a receiving ship. All the survivors were mustered on deck to see who was there. We were a bedraggled-looking bunch of people. All of us were dirty with fuel oil, not having had a shave... hungry... we were a sad-looking crew. I remember standing by one officer and he made the comment to me, 'I wonder why the Lord wants to take the good ones and leave the bad ones.' He had looked around and had seen who was missing and who was surviving. I had felt the same way about it, but I commented to him that he and I were among those saved and we weren't in any condition, or position, to complain about the Lord's decision in the matter."

Like all the other survivors, the *Luce's* doctor was grateful it was all over, but the experience still haunted him:

"We were given fresh clothes and a little kit from the Red Cross that had a toothbrush and so forth in it. Somewhere along the line, we ended up on a ship going back to the States. I remember the first night after being all cleaned up and everything and beginning to relax and feeling grateful that we were survivors, we all went to bed. But I couldn't sleep. Every time I closed my eyes I could see that ship going down and see that poor fellow being blown out by the hatch from the water. So I got up and went back up over the wardroom and everybody else was already out there. They were all having the same experience that I was.

"In order to keep busy on the way back... we tried to reconstruct the roster of the crew—what battle stations we last saw them at, alive or dead, and so forth. I lost two of my hospital corpsmen. One of them was in the area of the original plane crash, and I am sure that he was killed instantly. Another one was seen dead aboard the ship; and the young fellow that was with me in the wardroom survived, but suffered... injuries. Some of the survivors on the receiving ship, on the way back... required surgically drained abscesses and the like.

"I went straight to San Francisco where I got back pay, a new uniform and a suitcase... All the paper work I did got lost... Everybody was mad at me for not having done it, and I know that I had done it. Nobody knows what happened to it, but that's the way things happen in the Navy sometimes. I really never saw any survivors of the ship after that. I did run across a doctor in Philadelphia who had his orders to replace me aboard the ship and was about to leave to come to relieve me when he got word the ship had been sunk. I told him that he was welcome to it; and he would find the sick bay a little messed up and about six hundred fathoms down in the East China Sea, and that the inventory was not in very good shape at the time.

"I did write to the parents of the two hospital corpsmen that we lost and got nice letters in reply from each. I had occasion to visit the mother of one of them later in California. She made the comment to me that she had sent a boy to the Navy, but that I had written to her about a man that I had known."

Except for some of the more seriously wounded, the ordeal of the USS *Luce* survivors was over. DD 522 was gone, fighting to the last for a cause that those who served aboard her believed in with all their hearts—and lives. As she settled to the deep bottom of the South China Sea with almost half of the crew still with her, the memory of those lost shipmates began to settle in the hearts of the survivors. The day after he was rescued, Bob Harrison, RM2/c, on board the USS Ft. *Lauderdale,* searched around to see if some of his closest buddies had made it. He didn't have much luck. Tears welled up in his eyes "as I realized that all this had really happened." And like so many others, Robert Stanley, S1/c, was happy to be safe again, patched up "and knowing we were headed back to the good old U.S.A. and home alive in 1945—but wishing all our shipmates who were still at their battle stations were here with us… " On their way back to the States the survivors had several days in which to rest, recuperate, and reflect… Bill Fotie, RM3/c, and several *Luce* shipmates eagerly strained their eyes from the deck of the USS *Karnes* for the first glimpse of their home land. They were only too glad to see the shores of California come into view and, as Bill relates, "most of us just cried when we saw the Golden Gate."

Ensign Frank Scudder believes that the USS *Luce* was the fifty-fourth of all ships sunk in the Okinawa campaign. At a terrible cost in lives and ships that went on for many weeks, the men of the USS *Luce* exemplified the courage and spirit of the crews of all ships in the Pacific sea battles. Norman Foland, MoMM2/c, perhaps says it for his shipmates on the *Luce* and all World War II Navy personnel:

"Somebody said one time that being in the Navy at sea was like being in jail with a chance of drowning. A lot of times it may be that way, but we had a lot of good times, too, even though we didn't make it back (with the ship). We would have liked to have brought the old ship back—we sort of had a fondness for her. You get acclimated to your home; and you don't want to change. We lost a lot of good men in Okinawa, but we got the job done, and that's what counted."

And Walter Fischer, CTM, as one of those who gave his life for "getting the job done", knew why he had to be there. Recalling again his last correspondence to his wife:

"The past several weeks have brought home to me, more forcibly than ever, just what it is that I'm fighting for. I hope I live through it all, to profit by its lessons."

Many of the survivors who did live through the sinking which took the lives of Fischer and scores of others have profited by its lessons, but feel that these lessons are being lost today. As one stated, "It's a different world, a different country today. The values of our day, when we as a nation were fighting for our very existence, have seemed to have just disappeared. And that's too bad, its just too bad. I don't know if we can survive this time..."

Epilogue

The News Comes Home

Three days after the *Luce* sank Germany surrendered to the Allies. With the battle of Okinawa ending on 21 June and the Philippines being declared secured by General Douglas McArthur on 4 July, the Japanese began to increase their home land defenses to thwart invasion. But the atom bombs dropped on Japan on 6 and 9 August convinced the Japanese leadership of the futility of continuing the war, and on 14 August Japan surrendered. The surrender canceled the necessity of invasion and several hundred thousand lives on both sides were saved. But for relatives of those who died fighting the sorrow would last long after hostilities had ceased.

Just a few short months before the war ended, telegrams were sent out in May to about one hundred and fifty homes all over the country, bearing the tragic news of sons and husbands lost at sea or missing in action from the sinking of the USS *Luce*, DD 522. Typical of those families being so notified was that of Arthur Powers, S1/c. Powers had received the brunt of the kamikaze's hit on the 40 mm number five gun. Helen Brandt, one of Arthur's six sisters (he also had five brothers), was with her father in front of their home "when Western Union arrived with the telegram. As soon as we saw him, we knew it was bad news. During the war if you had someone in active duty it was a fear you lived with. It was a terrible shock to all of us, but I think it broke our father's heart. I can still see him crying as he read the telegram. Years later I had a son and we named him Arthur after my brother." Another sister, Lorraine, was not home when the telegram arrived, "but when I came home I noticed that the street we lived on was very quiet. I knew something was wrong. My uncle broke the news to me. My feelings were at first that of anger, especially after just losing our mother. In my letters I used to tell Arthur we were going to have the biggest party when he got home..."

Joseph, one of Arthur's brothers, was also not at home when the news came. When he did arrive shortly afterwards, "there were neighbors standing in the street. My best friend tearfully broke the news to me. I have some wonderful memories of Arthur, as he was very special. I enlisted into the Army shortly after this." Another brother, Harold, had just turned fifteen on the very day the *Luce* was sunk. The birthday would always be a sad reminder for the family. Harold also joined the Navy in later years.

Similar scenes occurred in other *Luce* families throughout the nation during those months of May and June, 1945. As soon as the survivors could, they contacted their homes to let their loved ones know that they were safe. In some cases, men would contact their kin before any news reached them. This happened to the family of Joseph Huss, Jr, QM3/c. On a Sunday night after the sinking, Joe called home and said, "I don't know what you may have heard, but I'm all right." That was when his family first learned that his ship had been sunk.

Officers and shipmates contacted families of those who did not survive the sinking to try and offer some consolation. Lt. Emerson Hempstead, for example, wrote to the father of Allen H. Bixler, MM2/c, recalling that Allen "always kept the boys in good spirits and on their toes" and that he had "never seen a fellow like him before—always on the sunny-side of everything. He had made chief machinist on the *Luce* and always worked hard." As time went on a few families of those not yet accounted for still held out hope that somehow their loved ones might have survived, as many had received notices only that their men were "missing in action." In a letter dated 2 July 1945 Margaret Appicelli, wife of James Appicelli, CMM, wrote to Romaine Burns (whose husband William Burns, MoMM1/c, had spent a night on the deck of the *Luce* during an Aleutian storm and then had been transferred from the *Luce* on 25 November 1944 and up until then had been close friends with James) that she still had hope "that my husband might have been picked up and not reported yet... I have a daughter nineteen months old and she has never seen her father, so I hope and pray he will return soon to see her." But as the weeks passed and it became obvious that James had not survived, Mrs. Appicelli also received a letter written by Lt. Hempstead. Dated 8 August 1945, the officer stated that her husband James had worked with him in the "E" division on the *Luce*... "I had the highest personal regard and liking for him and thought him one of the swellest fellows on the ship. He and I used to talk about New England at length, as my home used to be in Providence."

After reaching the United States from the Pacific area the survivors had gone their separate ways. With the war's end most were discharged after any medical treatment needed was completed. They found jobs, married and/or settled down and raised children and became successful citizens. But deep down in their innermost beings the memories persisted. Several carried shrapnel in their bodies which served as a physical reminder of the ordeal they had suffered. They thought often of their shipmates who had not survived. Sometimes their memories became flooded with vivid details of the hell they had witnessed and lived through. They became involved in the details of building their lives and made the necessary adjustments to normalcy. And so the years passed on. But it took the reunions to finalize for many their emotional turmoil over the events of the sinking of the USS *Luce*.

Reunion

Twenty-five years later at least one survivor was trying to find some shipmates from the USS *Luce* and somehow get together with them. James C. Phillips, SC1/c, had tried for several years without success to find a shipmate. Then one evening he and his wife Christine attended a party in their home town of Ocala, Florida. He was introduced to the host whose name was Foland:

"I said that I knew a man named Foland—Norman Foland—from the Navy. The host stated that that was his brother. I got Norman's address and phone number. He lived about sixty miles south of me. I couldn't enjoy the party after that and we excused ourselves and left as early as possible. We went home and I called Norman. We talked until the early morning hours. That was the first contact that I had with any crew members that survived the sinking of the *Luce* in all these years."

The two men set out to find other survivors. They began to advertise and soon others were contacted. A reunion was scheduled for 1985 in Jacksonville, Florida. One man who saw an ad for the reunion was Francis A. Malinowski, Jr., whose father had served aboard the *Luce*. Francis was only two and one–half years old when his father went down with the destroyer. Hoping to meet with men who knew his father he called to inquire and was invited to attend the reunion. From various parts of the country survivors and family members began making plans to attend the first meeting of USS *Luce* crewmen since the sinking in May of

1945. Flying in from the West with his wife Fern, Bill Fotie, RM3/c, had a surprising coincidence take place:

"We took our assigned seats and while we were waiting to take off, the two passengers to the left of Fern were talking. She heard one say that he was going to a Naval reunion. Fern leaned over and asked him what ship. He said the USS *Luce*! When I heard him, I also leaned over and asked, 'Who are you?' He answered, 'Tom Parkerson.' Can you believe—my communications officer aboard the *Luce*! What were the chances of booking the same time, same plane, the same row of seats and even sitting next to each other!"

For many survivors, as they began their traveling to the reunion, feelings of apprehension were high, of which Fotie's were typical:

"I was very uncertain about meeting with everyone. Forty years had passed. Would the meetings be stilted? How should I act? Well, I didn't have anything to worry about. I saw Tony Martin (RM2/c) about a quarter of a block away and in a minute we were hugging each other. Same with Bob Harrison and Chief Page. I have to say, it was one of the big moments in my life. And you think of shipmates as they were, not as they are. Some changed little, others lots."

It was a release of deeply buried emotions for the men. Half–buried, and half–forgotten, memories came flooding to the top. Comrades in life and tragedy, they could now pour out their souls with others who had shared the same experiences. Immediately, there began to develop a unique closeness among the men and their families. For several like Bob Harrison, RM2/c, it was the beginning of a healing process:

"The memories of our demise bothered me quite a bit for several years. But I handled it, and survived. After this first reunion, however, which was very emotional, I was able to handle it much better. That was a breakthrough for a lot of guys. Some of us began to talk about meeting every year."

The USS *Luce* Association was formed and annual reunions were planned. These reunions also helped the men to obtain a clearer picture of events around the sinking, as they compared their experiences. The 1987 San Diego reunion was especially helpful, and by then, several more persons had been contacted and the *Luce* association membership grew. It was at this San

Diego reunion that Burr McFarland, WT1/c, learned it was Bill Fotie who had helped him to get untangled from the life lines that held him fast on the sinking ship. And Burr also learned, after wondering for forty-two years, just who it was that was all bandaged up and given last rites on the rescue ship, USS *Mercy*, as they sailed from Okinawa:

"We were in San Diego in 1987 sitting down with J.C. Phillips and Orville Hiles and our wives. J.C. said, 'Mac, how did you come back from the Pacific and all?' So I started telling him about the events, and told him the story about the bandaged man who had received last rites, only to survive, and that I wish I knew who that was. Orville broke in and said, 'Why, that was me!' And Orville went on to say, 'I'm glad to hear you tell that story because almost no one would ever believe me, although my folks were mad at the Navy for giving me the last rites, because we weren't Catholics! I thought it was communion, but my Dad knew better and asked me why I let them do it, to which I replied that it seemed like a good idea at the time.'"

Orville's wife Norma was glad to hear her husband's story vindicated. She could now back up her husband's testimony because she had heard it for herself from a surviving crew member who was there.

<u>The Breakfast That Never Was</u>

Just before the alarm had sounded on that fateful May morning in 1945, James C. Phillips (J.C.), SC1/c, was busy preparing a hearty breakfast for the crew of the ship. At the sightings of the kamikazes the men jumped to their battle stations and never had a chance to eat their breakfast. In just a few minutes they found themselves in the water with their ship sinking under them. Forty-three years later at their fourth reunion in Baton Rouge, J.C. prepared and served that breakfast which the men had missed. It took place on the USS *Kidd*, a destroyer on display which was the same exact type as was the USS *Luce*. Joining the forty-plus *Luce* survivors at the meal were over forty crew members of the USS *Morrison* which was also sunk that same day and in the same area. J.C. was only too happy to cook again for the crew:

"Paul Wallace, F1/c, and Cy Olsen F2/c, assisted me in cooking 'The Breakfast That Never Was.' We had pancakes, sausage and coffee—the same menu we had on the morning we were sunk. I had only served about a dozen people on that morning before we were called to GQ."

After the breakfast, the men toured the *Kidd*, reminiscing where they were just before the *Luce* sank. Bill Fotie was amazed at how small the destroyer seemed. When he asked Joseph McGuigan, also a radioman, how they could ever fit in the closet–like space of the radio room, McGuigan reminded Fotie that they were much slimmer back then and could squeeze by anyone.

Orville Hiles probably summed up for all the men as they wandered through the ship, remembering:

"When we all stood around on that ship, we thought, 'Well, this is where I was when that thing happened.' It was a good experience, the reunion, and when people ask, 'Why do you go every year?' I really don't know the answer, except that I have to."

The Five Sisters

Arthur Powers' (S1/c) brothers, James and Joseph, spotted one of the ads in a paper, concerning a *Luce* reunion in 1987. Ethel Scanlon and Lorraine Gallipoli, two of Arthur's five remaining sisters, planned to attend the meeting. It took some hasty planning, as their brothers told them about it only two weeks prior to the event. The two sisters flew to the reunion with much anxiety, hoping to find someone who had known their brother on board ship. The sisters knew that the *Luce* crew were the only persons who had been with their brother during the last two years of his life.

At first their inquiries produced disappointing results. No one seemed to know their brother, no one knew them and they, of course, knew no one. They were showing around a picture of their brother, taken with a shipmate. They showed it to Tom Matisak, RdM3/c. He studied it for a moment, then recognized the man with their brother as Stephen Pramick, RM3/c, who had also gone down with the ship and was Arthur's best friend. Matisak studied the picture a few moments longer and then his eyes lit up as he said, "Yes, I remember, I knew your brother."

As they sat down together, Tom "looked at each one of those girls, and they suddenly broke down, completely broke down, and I broke down, too. But they were so relieved to find someone that knew about their brother!"

Soon other crew members who had known of their brother

came to the sisters with bits and pieces of information on his life aboard ship. In talking with Tom Matisak, and meeting others, Lorraine and Ethel felt that "it kind of finalized things for us about our brother, 'Artie'. We were now more at peace about what had happened to him." Two years later the other sisters—Helen Brandt, Marilyn Delaney, and Joan DeFlorio, along with Lorraine's daughter Marilyn—joined Ethel and Lorraine in attending the 1989 reunion in Norfolk. At this reunion they met up with Bob Stanley, S1/c. Lorraine recalls that "he came over and asked our brother's name. We told him and he seemed to be a little startled. He said, 'Yes, I knew him.' His eyes filled up and he walked away. Later we had some good talks with him." The experience of the reunions caused the sisters to feel that they "had finally laid 'Artie' to rest. And even after all these years," related one, "Artie has brought us into this beautiful relationship with these people, his shipmates." Other survivors and their families have also found the reunions to be a similar experience of love and sharing, a healing process which provides a common bond of "family."

At the 1990 reunion, on board the USS *Alabama* in Mobile, J.C. Phillips, S1/c, announced that "Marilyn Gallipoli will now ring the bell for her uncle, Arthur Powers, S1/c, and all other men who are still at 'General Quarters' in the USS *Luce*." The shipmates and families have indeed "finalized things" and have helped each other come to terms—and peace— with the tragedy of the sinking of the USS *Luce*, DD 522.

And for the survivors, the reunions continue to be the highlight of the year for them because, as J.C. Phillips explains, "Men in combat develop a special bond—like brothers. Its a very unique alumni. Its almost sacred to me."

A Final Overview

In reflecting on their role in World War Two for themselves, along with other US Navy crewmen and the hardships and sacrifices made, perhaps Norman Foland, MoMM2/c, summarizes it for all:

"The US Navy has a lot of technicians and if you look past all the emotional sides of these things like a fighting, dying, and the guns and so forth, you realize our ship was essentially fighting machine. This ship was built for one purpose and one purpose only—and that was to carry out the policies of the U.S. and do away with the enemy as much as possible. Most of the men aboard these destroyers were highly-rated technicians. They not only were sailors but 'techs' and ran machinery and radar and so forth. They were radiomen, gunners and shipfitters. We had a lot of smart people on these cans. And that goes for most of the other ships. You can't run a can or battleship or anything without having a little common sense and a little 'smarts'. Most of us were proud of being sailors, but we were also those technicians... These things I remember and carry with me.

"None of us were indispensable, but we were typical of all the cans and DE's and men in the fleet. Destroyers were used as errand boys for everything, and if we, by sacrificing tin cans, saved a lot of carriers and their people (and they got it pretty rough, too) then I think it was worth it. A tin can is a lot cheaper than a flat top and a lot less vulnerable in many ways. Besides, those carriers furnished those air planes, God bless 'em, which wiped the noses off them Japs for us. They threw so many suicides at us that a few were bound to get through. But if we didn't have the Navy air arm we couldn't have stayed in Okinawa. God bless them all, as far as I am concerned.

"The old saying goes, 'As for man, his days are as grass, as a flower of the field, so he flourishes. For the winds pass over it, and it is gone, and the place thereof shall know it no more' (Psalms 103:15–16). I suppose if we went 60 miles due west of Point Bolo, where our ship went down, there would just be a peaceful ocean, no signs of the terror and the hell that reigned there at one time..."

AFTERMATH

Lt. Donald B. Allen, who helped put the USS *Luce* into commission in 1943; and was married that same year, was transferred from the *Luce* just one week before the sinking. The father of two boys, Lt. Allen became an attorney and settled down in Long Island, retiring in 1990.

Bert D. Alton, Jr., Chief Radio Technician, left the *Luce* in 1944 for the USS *Mindanao*, a repair ship then anchored in Seeadler Bay, Manus Island, in the Admiralties. He narrowly escaped death when the USS *Mt. Hood*, an ammunition ship anchored adjacent to the *Mindanao*, exploded on 10 November, 1944, killing scores of Navy personnel. Bert married in 1949 and had three children. Widowed in 1983, he remarried in 1984. Working as an electronic engineer for Raytheon Co., he retired in 1990 and lives in Ventura, California.

Joseph J. Bille, RT2/c, married in 1950, and became the proud father of four boys and one girl. Working for the New England Telephone Co. as an Engineering Manager, he retired in February 1987 and lives in Lexington, Mass.

Thomas G. Blanck, Y1/c, married in 1948 and had three children. He worked as an industrial cost accountant, retiring in September 1984. He now lives in Scotch Plains, New Jersey.

Earl H. Blanton, Jr., GM3/c, the observer aboard the USS LCS 118, which was one of the pallbearer ships with the *Luce*, continued working with ships. He became a draftsman and supervisor in the shipbuilding trade in Newport News, Virginia. Married on 20 July 1946, Earl raised three daughters. He retired at age fifty–nine on 1 April 1985, to Seaford, Virginia. In 1991 he published his account of life aboard the LCS entitled "Boston To Jacksonville: 41,000 Miles By Sea."

Donald Brockhoff, TM3/c, transferred from the *Luce* in February 1945. He married in October 1946 and had two children—a boy and a girl. He worked in computers and then for an insurance company as a claims adjuster. Don retired in 1982 to Cold Spring, Minnesota.

William A. Burns, MoMM1/c, survived the sinking and returned to his wife Romaine whom he had married in 1929. Their marriage brought three children into the world. Burns stayed in the Navy until 1963, returning to Sudbury, Massachusetts; and farming until his death in 1985.

Richard A. Burlingame, WT1/c, was one of the few married men serving on the *Luce*, having been married on January 17, 1942. He and his wife Marian have two sons and four grandsons. Working thirty years for Loblaw Inc. as a meat cutter first class, Richard retired in December 1976 and lives in Russell, PA.

Ernest Carpenter, WT2/c, was also married in 1942 on 17 August. He had four children—two boys and two girls—and boasts of six grandchildren and three great-grandchildren. Working as a foreman in a power plant for Bethlehem Steel, Ernest was forced into early retirement in August 1976 because of a stroke, He lives in Abingdon, Maryland.

John A. Carpenter, WT1/c, married on 15 March 1947, was a farmer from 1945 to 1954, and then worked as a boiler room fireman from 1954 to retirement in 1987. John lives in the town in which he was born—Rutherfordton, North Carolina.

Milton L. Cathey, BM2/c, married in January, 1942, and had three boys and one girl. He stayed in the Navy until December of 1959. Upon discharge, he worked as a letter carrier for the U.S. Post Office until retirement in April of 1972. Milton resides in Six Mile, SC.

Anthony DeFrank, Jr., WT3/c, married in December of 1949. He had one son and worked as a bank safe service man until January, 1985. Although he enlisted in Philadelphia, Tony lives in West Deptford, NJ.

Vernon C. Downs, S1/c, married the day after Christmas, 1951. He had four boys and worked as a heavy equipment operator, welder, and mechanic. He passed away in Rapid City, SD, on 3 March 1992 from cancer.

Omer Emond, S1/c, married in June 1948 and fathered a boy and a girl. He retired in June of 1989 from a foundry and lives in Nashua, N.H.

Richard F. Flaum, FC3/c, married the sister of his shipmate, Marty Nyholt, FC2/c, on 25 June 1947. He had five children and worked in the Test Bureau of the New York Telephone Co. until retirement in June 1980. He was born, raised, and then settled in Brooklyn, NY.

Norman Foland, MoMM2/c, settled down with a wife in December of 1945 and raised three children. He was a police officer in Ohio before he retired to Ocala Florida in May 1972.

William R. Fotie, RM3/c, married in 1945. After losing children in eight pregnancies, he and his wife were finally blessed with a girl. Bill owned his own print shop until retirement in 1988. He alternates his residence between California and Colorado.

Hershel R. Freeman, MM2/c, married in June 1945 and had three children. He worked in construction and the textile business until retirement in 1986. Living in Hildebran, NC, Hershel died on 4 April 1987.

James M. Gory, WT3/c, produced a boy and two girls from his marriage which began on 1 June 1948. Intensely interested in music, he was a band director as well as an insurance agent. Still operating his partnership insurance agency, Jim says he can't afford to retire but loves to enjoy the bayou and Cajun country around where he lives in Thibodaux,

Louisiana.

Leo Greco, SM1/c, married on 5 August 1945. The father of five children, he was also a band leader for twenty-two years before going into radio as an account executive. Retiring on the last day of December 1988, Leo settled down in Cedar Rapids, Iowa.

Robert D. Harrison, RM2/c, married in 1947 and then again in 1987. He is the proud father of seven children which have in turn given him seven grandchildren and two great-grandchildren. Bob didn't leave the Navy until 1962. He then went into the communications field with the Navy and the FAA until 1972, after which he developed his own furniture upholstery business. Still unretired, Bob lives in Palo Alto, California.

Michael Heon, MoMM3/c, tied the knot on 18 August 1947 and their family included two boys. Working as a foreman in a meter manufacturing company, Mike retired October 1984 in Somersworth, New Hampshire.

Orville L. Hiles, S1/c, married in 1948 and became the father of two girls and two boys. He was plant manager for Swift & Co. and then was director of the Student Union at Graceland College. Retiring in May 1990, Orville resides in the town of which he is mayor— Lamoni, Iowa.

Waino M. Johnson, GM1/c, said the vows on 26 April 1947. Father of two sons and one daughter, he was a firefighter for twenty-eight years in Fitchburg, MA before working for Digital for five years. Waino retired in 1984 to Tilton, New Hampshire.

Lt. Cliff A. Jones married Patricia in September 1947. Three children were born to them and they in turn have given him seven grandchildren. Cliff was chairman and president of the R.B. Jones Corp, the seventh largest insurance brokerage firm in the U.S. He is also chairman of Jones & Babson, Inc. and retired in September 1994. He has always lived in the Kansas City, Kansas area.

William V. Lietz, TM2/c, married his wife Rita on 19 August 1948. They had three children and Bill worked as bricklayer for forty-one years. He has also been a politician in his town of Wapakoneta, Ohio. Bill retired in July 1989.

Lt. Thomas G. Lynch was transferred before the sinking and served aboard the USS Remey (DD 588). He retired from the Navy as Lt. Commander. Married in 1949 (no children), Lt. Lynch also served as a sales and marketing official for railroads. He retired in 1983 and lives in Charlotte, North Carolina.

Burr K. McFarland's, WT1/c, wedding day to his sweetheart occurred while he was still a patient due to his leg injuries at a Navy hospital in Norman, Oklahoma. He was married by a Navy chaplain in a private home on 25 August 1945. He had three boys and one girl, and they in turn gave him nine grandchildren. Working for the Iowa Department of Transportation for nine years in highway design and then twenty-six years in data processing, Burr retired on 17 May 1984 and lives in Ames, Iowa. His leg, almost blown off during the *Luce* sinking, still gives him trouble and he remains under medical treatment for his injuries.

Joseph P. McGuigan, RM3/c, took a wife in February 1949 and became the proud father of seven children. Working for the U.S. government as a printer, Joe retired in February 1987 to Marlton, New Jersey.

Anthony (Tony) Marchitelli, GM3/c, married in 1949 and had five children. Working as a carpenter and in construction, he retired in 1986 and resides in Lakehurst, New Jersey.

Anthony F. Martin, RM3/c, married shortly after arriving home in 1945 and had five children—three boys and two girls. He worked as a dental technician until his retirement in 1983. Anthony makes his home in Boring, Oregon, which is near Portland.

Thomas Matisak, RdM3/c, took a wife on 30 November 1946 and raised three boys and a girl. A public school teacher most of his life, Tom retired in April 1986 and lives in Freeland, Pennsylvania.

Manuel Medeiros, F1/c, raised one child through a marriage which began in 1947. Working in a rubber factory, he retired in 1983 and lives in South Dartmouth Massachusetts.

Lt. Derry O. Moll remained in the Navy for several years, rising to the rank of Lt. Commander. In 1952 his service records and awards were re-examined. On 3 November 1952 a communique was sent to him stating that he was to return the Navy and Marine Corps medal awarded for his aid to the wounded on a raft during the *Luce* sinking. The award was to be upgraded to a Bronze Star. It was delivered to him on 17 November 1952 at the Brooklyn (N.Y.) Navy Shipyard. Derry married in 1947 and had three daughters with the beautiful names of Sari, Derry, and Spring. He was Chief Engineer and Senior Watch Officer aboard two other destroyers. After leaving the Navy he worked for a time as a construction engineer, retiring in 1986. Derry lived in Stony Brook, New York, but then settled in Burlington Junction, Missouri, where he lives today.

Robert F. Moyer, FC3/c, married on 5 June 1948 and raised two children. He worked in sales for Bethlehem Steel Corporation and retired in May 1982. He makes his home in Buffalo, New York.

Martin ("Moose") Nyholt, FC2/c, became husband to his wife Dorothy on 12 June 1948. They became the proud parents of six children. Marty was Regional Marketing Manager for Blue Cross–Blue Shield of Illinois before retiring on 1 April 1981. Having lived in Springfield and Palatine, Illinois, he and his wife now reside in Sun City Center, Florida.

Commander Hinton Allen Owens was awarded the Bronze Star and Gold Star in lieu of a second Bronze Star while he was still in command of the *Luce*. In February 1945 he assisted in the fitting out of the USS Columbus, and served as gunnery officer and later as Executive Officer of that ship. After serving as commander of a ship which participated in the Bikini atomic test of July 1946, he enrolled in the Naval War College in Newport Rhode Island for the senior course in Strategy and Tactics. He was assigned to the Naval Administrative Command, Central Intelligence Agency in May 1948. From December 1949 to January he was Commanding Officer of COMDESDIV (Commander Destroyer Division) 142; served in the Navy Department, Washington, D.C. from January 1952 to July 1954, and became the Senior U.S. Naval Advisor to the Argentine Naval War College in Buenos Aires, Argentina, in September 1955. Married with three children, Owens received his permanent rank of Captain on 1 July 1951. He retired to his home town of Augusta, Georgia.[1]

LTJG Thomas B. Parkerson, Jr., married on 4 June 1945 (one month to the day after the sinking) took family life seriously. He and his wife Jane successfully raised nine children. Working as a mechanical engineer, Tom retired in 1985 to McKinleyville, California.

Gerald Perdue, MoMM1/c, tied the knot on 11 June 1945, and the marriage produced one son and three daughters. Gerald was a truck driver, covering forty-eight states from Buffalo, New York. He retired to Edgewater, Florida in 1987.

Freeman Phillips, S1/c, became a married man on 23 September 1946 and had three children—two boys and a girl. Working in dry cleaning, then trucking and construction for over thirty years, Freeman retired on 3 March 1986. He lives in Wentworth, New Hampshire.

James C. Phillips, SC1/c, raised two daughters from a marriage begun in December 1946. Becoming a rancher and then working in the retail business, J.C. retired in 1973 and lives in Ocala, Florida.

LTJG Arthur S. Replogle married on 7 September 1946 and had two sons and one daughter. He became an executive with Replogle Globes, Inc., the world's largest manufacturer of geographical globes. In 1974 he became president of Oak Park (Illinois) Development Corporation where he still carries on. Arthur lives in Oak Park, Illinois.

Clifford A. Roberts, CFC, exchanged the vows on 22 October 1942 and raised two daughters who gave him four grandchildren and two great-grandsons. From 1949 to 1958 he was in the U.S. Army and retired from that service as Chief Warrant Officer. Cliff then went into civil service and worked at the Pentagon for sixteen years and with NASA for seven years. He retired in 1982 with twenty years in military service and

---

[1] Bureau of Naval Personnel, Naval Historical Center, Washington, D.C.

twenty-three years in civil service. He now resides in Mechanicsville, Maryland.

LTJG Frank E. Scudder was married in January 1944 and raised one boy and three girls. He was in management with the Hilton Hotel Corporation, then was an instructor in Hotel Executive Management. Retiring in 1992, Frank lives in Washington, D.C.

Lt. Louis Shaffner, the *Luce's* doctor, married on 27 September 1945, raised five children. He was a surgeon and Professor Emeritus of Surgery at Bowman Gray School of Medicine at Wake Forest University, North Carolina. Retiring in the last day of December 1985, the "Doc" now lives in Winston–Salem, North Carolina.

LTJG Harry E. Snyder lost his single status in 1947. His marriage produced four daughters. He was a career Naval officer and served on the USS *Badger*. Harry later commanded the USS Hazelwood. Both ships were the same class destroyers as the USS *Luce*. Retiring in 1969, Harry lives in Norfolk, Virginia.

Robert E. Stanley, S1/c, went to the alter on 15 September 1950. They had no children. Working as the chief import–export clerk for Union Pacific Railroad, Robert retired to New Orleans on 3 June 1983.

Kenneth Sturm, TM2/c, had two children from his marriage begun on 5 June 1945. He was a supervisor for the U.S. Post Office until his retirement in June 1973. Ken lives in Kirkwood, Missouri, in the good weather and in Oak Springs, Florida in winter.

H. Donald Sweeten, SoM2/c, who was transferred in the Philippines from the *Luce*, married in June 1945 and raised two sons. After the war he worked as an accountant controller and semi–retired into a two–day work week. Don now lives in Baltimore, Maryland.

Clarence J. Vanness, MM2/c, took a wife on 20 August 1945 and raised two girls and a boy. He worked as a tool and die maker first class until retirement in 1984. Clarence now lives in Oak Creek, a suburb of Milwaukee Wisconsin.

LeGrand G. Van Uitert, CPO, married on 8 June 1945 and raised two sons and a daughter. All three children became medical doctors. From 1946 to 1952 LeGrand attended college, earning a PhD in chemistry. He was employed by the Bell Telephone Laboratories in New Jersey as a specialist in Solid State Science and won a number of awards in the fields of lasers and optics and in other related areas. Listed in Who's Who, LeGrand retired in 1989 and lives in Morristown, New Jersey.

Captain Donald C. Varian was assigned to various other destroyers and ships after leaving the *Luce* on 22 November 1943. By 1953 he had risen to the rank of Rear Admiral. Varian continued his distinguished career when he became a staff officer to the Secretary of Defense from

1956 to 1961. In this position he directed personnel policy. Retiring in 1961 he became founder and president of Varian International Corporation. Making his home in Coronado, California, he died there in September 1969.

Paul L. Wallace, F1/c, had been married on 18 August 1944. He raised two sons and was a mid–west former for a time and also did cobbler work. Paul also found time to teach others in his fields as he spent some time as an instructor. Retiring from Indiana in 1980 he and his wife Darlene settled in Davenport, Florida. Paul passed away in February, 1992.

Lt. John R. Welsh began his married life on 25 July 1945 and raised six children. Remaining in the Navy until December 1967, he retired as a Captain. John then spent sixteen years as an engineer on the senior staff at Johns Hopkins University and worked in the Applied Physics Laboratory. Retiring on 31 March 1982, he now resides in McLean, Virginia.

Art Whitney, MM1/c, worked in Naval Ordinance in the DC area for about a year before returning to Detroit where he worked for the Michigan Consolidated Gas Company. He then moved to Clearwater, Florida, and worked for the city for thirty years. Art's first wife Lucille died from cancer and he later remarried to his present wife Bernice. He had two children, one from each wife. Art retired in 1975 and lives Clearwater.

Commander Jacob Wilson Waterhouse married Lucy Ann Hicks of Vulcan, Michigan. Obtaining the rank of Captain on 30 March 1945 while in command of the USS *Luce*, he was awarded the Silver Star Medal, as the citation reads, "for conspicuous gallantry and intrepidity as Commanding Officer of the USS *Luce*, assigned to Radar Picket duty, in action against enemy Japanese forces... With his ship a frequent target for many extraordinarily heavy hostile raids... (he) performed the vital functions of providing early air warning and fighter direction which, together with his ship's gunfire, accounted for large numbers of enemy planes and prevented air attacks in strength on the Naval forces off the beachhead. When his ship was severely damaged during a savage hostile suicide attack, he inspired his men to remain at their stations and carry on the fight until the order was given to abandon ship..."

Captain Waterhouse returned to the United States where he was assigned to Tangku, China for fifteen months. He then performed a three year tour of duty in the Training Division of the Bureau of Naval Personnel after which he served ten months, beginning in May 1950, as Commander Destroyer Division 202 (later changed to 22). He finished out his career by returning in 1951 to the Naval Officer Personnel Division, and retired to his home in Arlington, Virginia.[2]

---

[2] Biographics Section, Op–293C, Bureau of Naval Personnel, Navy Department, Washington, D.C.

Glossary

Enlisted Ranks

BKR1/c	Baker First Class
BKR2/c	Baker Second Class
BKR3/c	Baker Third Class
BM1/c	Boatswain's Mate First Class
BM2/c	Boatswain's Mate Second Class
BT	Boiler Tender
CEM	Chief Electrician'c Mate
CFC	Chief Fire Controlman
CM1/c	Carpenter's Mate First Class
CM2/c	Carpenter's Mate Second Class
CM3/c	Carpenter's Mate Third Class
CMM	Chief Machinist's Mate
COX	Coxswain (Also Boatswain's Mate Third Class)
CRM	Chief Radioman
CTM	Chief Torpedoman
EM1/c	Electrician's Mate First Class
EM2/c	Electrician's Mate Second Class
EM3/c	Electrician's Mate Third Class
ETM1/c	Electronic Technician's Mate First Class
ETM2/c	Electronic Technician's Mate Second Class
ETM3/c	Electronic Technician's Mate Third Class
F1/c	Fireman First Class
F2/c	Fireman Second Class
F3/c	Fireman Third Class
GM1/c	Gunner's Mate First Class
GM2/c	Gunner's Mate Second Class
GM3/c	Gunner's Mate Third Class
HA1/c	Hospitalman Apprentice (?)
MoMM1/c	Motor Machinist Mate First Class
MoMM2/c	Motor Machinist Mate Second Class
MoMM3/c	Motor Machinist Mate Third Class
MM1/c	Machinist Mate First Class
MM2/c	Machinist Mate Second Class
MM3/c	Machinist Mate Third Class
PhM1/c	Pharmacist Mate First Class
PhM2/c	Pharmacist Mate Second Class
PhM3/c	Pharmacist Mate Third Class
QM1/c	Quartermaster First Class
QM2/c	Quartermaster Second Class
QM3/c	Quartermaster Third Class
RdM1/c	Radarman First Class
RdM2/c	Radarman Second Class
RdM3/c	Radarman Third Class
RT1/c	Radio Technician First Class
RT2/c	Radio Technician Second Class
RT3/c	Radio Technician Third Class
RM1/c	Radioman First Class
RM2/c	Radioman Second Class

RM3/c	Radioman Third Class
S1/c	Seaman First Class
S2/c	Seaman Second Class
S3/c	Seaman Third Class
SC1/c	Ship's Cook First Class
SC2/c	Ship's Cook Second Class
SC3/c	Ship's Cook Third Class
SK1/c	Storekeeper First Class
SK2/c	Storekeeper Second Class
SK3/c	Storekeeper Third Class
SM1/c	Signalman First Class
SM2/c	Signalman Second Class
SM3/c	Signalman Third Class
SoM1/c	Sonarman First Class
SoM2/c	Sonarman Second Class
SoM3/c	Sonarman Third Class
ST	Sonar Technician
STM1/c	Steward's Mate First Class
STM2/c	Steward's Mate Second Class
STM3/c	Steward's Mate Third Class
TM1/c	Torpedoman First Class
TM2/c	Torpedoman Second Class
TM3/c	Torpedoman Third Class
WT1/c	Water Tender First Class
WT2/c	Water Tender Second Class
WT3/c	Water Tender Third Class
Yn1/c	Yeoman First Class (Sometimes known as 'Yeoman')
Yn2/c	Yeoman Second Class
Yn3/c	Yeoman Third Class

Officer Ranks

COMO	Comodore (Temporary rank of a commader of a group of ships.)
CDR	Commander (The rank below Captain and above Lieutenant Commander.)
CPO	Chief Petty Officer
LT	Lieutenant
LTJG	Lieutenant Junior Grade
ENS	Ensign
WO	Warrant Officer

Ships and Aircraft

Betty (Bomber)	Japanese Medium Bomber Aircraft
Can, or 'Tin Can'	Destroyer
CAP	Combat Air Patrol (Several friendly planes flying protective cover.)
Corsair	F4U Navy/Marine Fighter Aircraft
Jill	Japanese Torpedo Bomber Aircraft
LCM	Landing Craft Mechanized
LCS	Landing Craft Support
LCVP	Landing Craft Vehicle Personnel
LSM	Landing Ship Mechanized
Val	Japanese Navy Dive Bomber Aircraft
Zeke	Japanese "Zero" Navy Fighter Aircraft

Appendix A

Luce Statistics

Luce was awarded five battle stars for operations identified below:

1 Star / Kurile Islands Operations:
    Masashi Wan–Kurabu–Zaki: February 4, 1944
    Matsua: June 13, 1944
    Kurabu–Zaki: June 26, 1944

1 Star / Leyte Operation:
    Leyte Landings: October 10—November 29, 1944

1 Star / Luzon Operation:
    Lingayen Gulf Landings: January 9, 1945

1 Star / Okinawa Gunto Operation:
    Assault and Occupation of Okinawa Gunto: March 26—May 4, 1945

1 Star / Manila Bay–Bicol Operations:
    Zambales—Subic Bay: January 29 – 30, 1945

List of Commanding Officers

Commander D.C. Varian, USN June 21, 1943—November 22, 1943
Commander H.A. Owens, USN November 22, 1943—February 1, 1945
Commander J.W. Waterhouse, USN February 1, 1945—May 4, 1945

Original Statistics

Length Over–all:	376' 6"
Extreme Beam:	39' 8"
Normal Displacement:	
Tons:	2700
Mean Draft:	13'
Design Speed:	35.5 knots
Design Complement:	
Officer:	9
Enlisted:	264
Armament:	
Primary:	(5) 5"/38
Secondary:	(5) 40 mm twin mounts
	(7) 20 mm
Torpedo Tubes:	(2) 21–inch quintuple

(U.S. Naval Institute)

Appendix B

Telegrams and Letters

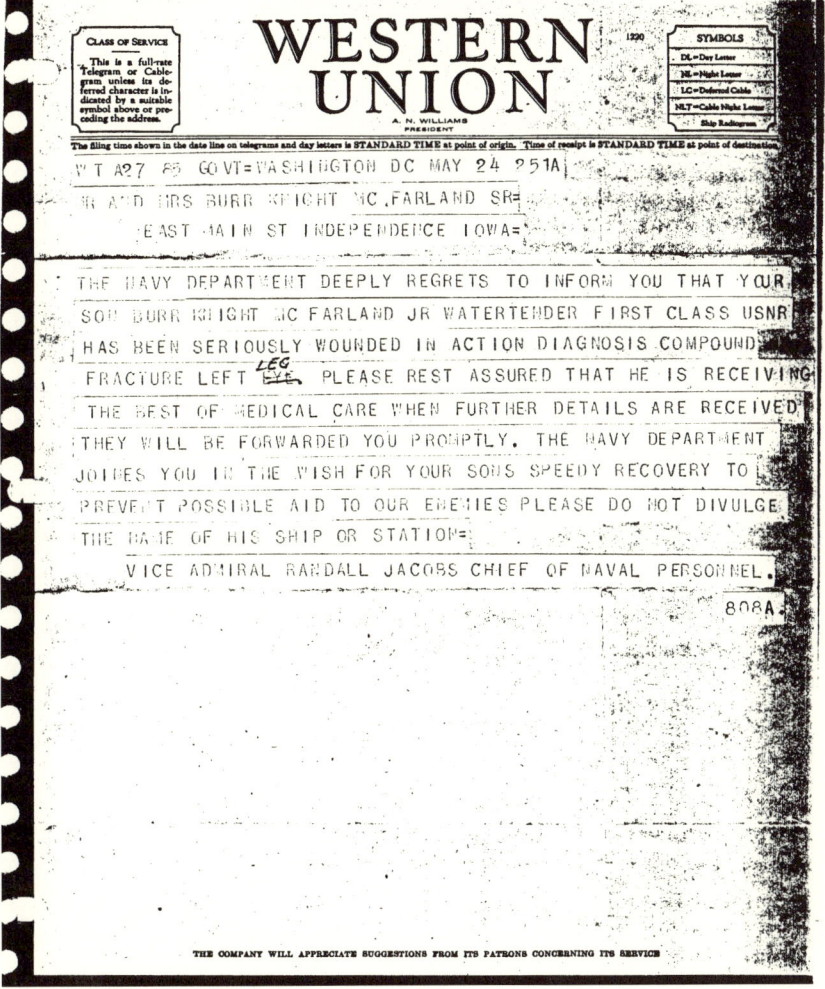

Telegram sent to Burr McFarland's parents advising them of his injuries.

```
                    WESTERN                    SYMBOLS
  CLASS OF SERVICE                             DL=Day Letter
                                               NL=Night Letter
                     UNION                     LC=Deferred Cable
                                               NLT=Cable Night Letter
                     A. N. WILLIAMS             Ship Radiogram
                       PRESIDENT
```

WU 4   114 GOVT= WASHINGTON DC JULY 14 853PM

MRS ANNE O FISCHER=
    SMITH ST PAWLING NY=

I DEEPLY REGRET TO INFORM YOU THAT CAREFUL REVIEW OF ALL FACTS AVAILABLE RELATING TO THE DISAPPEARANCE OF YOUR HUSBAND WALTER CHRISTION FISCHER CHIEF TORPEDOMANS MATE USNR PREVIOUSLY REPORTED MISSING LEADS TO THE CONCLUSION THAT THERE IS NO HOPE FOR HIS SURVIVAL AND THAT HE LOST HIS LIFE AS RESULT OF ENEMY ACTION ON 4 MAY 1945 WHILE IN THE SERVICE OF HIS COUNTRY. IF FURTHER DETAILS ARE RECEIVED THEY WILL BE FORWARDED TO YOU PROMPTLY TO PREVENT POSSIBLE AID TO OUR ENEMIES PLEASE DO NOT DIVULGE THE NAME OF HIS SHIP OR STATION UNLESS THE GENERAL CIRCUMSTANCES ARE MADE PUBLIC IN NEWS STORIES. SINCEREST SYMPATHY IS EXTENDED TO YOU IN YOUR GREAT LOSS=
        VICE ADMIRAL RANDALL JACOBS THE CHIEF OF NAVAL PERSONNEL

4 1945 935A

THE COMPANY WILL APPRECIATE SUGGESTIONS FROM ITS PATRONS CONCERNING ITS SERVICE

Typical of the telegrams sent out to families of the lost crew members of the USS Luce.

Walter C. Fischer TM½c   4/4/44

Dear Son:— Herein, you will find a copy of the U.S. Service campaign & distinguished service badges. You may compare them with your book.

Looking them over, set me to thinking. To you, they represent bravery, glamour, glory. Their wearers loom up in your youthful mind, as heroes. They have contributed, by some outstanding deed, to the great name of a still greater country. It is well so!

I have tried to analyze the many characteristics and reasons, which might help to make one a hero. My poor judgement tells me, that heroism consists of an act performed as a result of quick-thinking, desperation or carefully planned training. The results, if <u>successful</u>, are, in the opinion of a majority, heroic.

Many people, going through the life-span, doing their work unheralded, caring for others, living quietly and without public notice, never even reach the columns, much less the headlines. And yet, if one were examine their lives closely, it would be found that they are also heroes. The unknown millions of heroes,— of centuries past and to come. Often their only reward is the self satisfaction of a job "well done."

Its a tough assignment, being a "Hero," son. Once acclaimed, you are expected to live up to the name. Don't let the foregoing disturb your dreams, my boy, if you've a mind to be one. Campaign badges will long live as an incentive to the American youth (thats you), to do great deeds for the Community, the State

and the Nation. Only one thing more, don't aspire to be a hero, unless your conscience tells you that you are doing right. Don't think big of you, — Dad.

Walter C. Fischer's letter to his young son.

```
Pers-8249-mrs
```

NAVY DEPARTMENT
BUREAU OF NAVAL PERSONNEL
WASHINGTON 25, D.C.

17 July 1945

My dear Mr. Powers,

It is with the deepest sorrow that I am writing you concerning your son, Arthur Vincent Powers, who was reported missing in action following the sinking of the U.S.S. LUCE on May 4, 1945. Although officially reported as "missing", I regret to say that a very careful review of all information available has failed to reveal anything which might lead to some hope of his survival.

I know that you are anxious to hear all that I can tell you of the action in which the LUCE was sunk. Briefly, the ship had been assigned a hazardous but very important task, and was on this duty early in the morning of May 4, about thirty miles west of Okinawa, when many enemy planes were seen approaching. Although some of these planes were shot down by our aircraft, and the ship was fully ready and firing with all its guns, a Japanese plane succeeded in coming in and attacking the ship. For several minutes after the ship was hit, we continued shooting at other planes. We believed that the damage might not be fatal to the ship, but suddenly it began to go over and went down rapidly at about 8:15 a.m., carrying many of the crew with it. Other ships in the vicinity immediately came to our assistance, and picked up the survivors as quickly as possible. In view of the excellent weather conditions, it is felt certain that every survivor was picked up at this time; however, ships remained in the area, and made a thorough search, but found no additional men.

Your son's regular battle station was on a 40 Millimeter gun. Arthur's calm and efficient work under the strain of enemy action on previous occasions contributed greatly to making that gun a thoroughly dependable unit of the ship's company. We know this was the case the morning the ship was sunk. However, as this station was in the vicinity of the hit, we believe that Arthur did not have time to get away as there were no survivors from that station.

I earnestly wish that I could offer you some encouragement, but in view of the circumstances and the length of time which has passed with no report of him, I fear there can be no hope of his survival.

Nothing that I can say will in any way lighten the burden which is yours at this time, but I do hope that the knowledge of your son's splendid service and devotion to duty will give you some comfort and courage. He was a fine man and shipmate and a credit to our country. You may justly feel very proud.

With my deepest sympathy, I am

Very sincerely,

J. W. WATERHOUSE
Captain, U.S.N.

Mr. James Powers
12018 Marsden Street
Jamaica, New York

Letter to Arthur Powers' family confirming an earlier telegram advising his loss of life.

APPENDIX C
DESTROYERS LOST IN WORLD WAR II
Ultimate Sacrifice

Name	Hull	Year	Name	Hull	Year
Aaron Ward	DD-483	1943	Luce	DD-522	1945
Abner Read	DD-526	1944	Maddox	DD-622	1943
Barry	DD-248, APD-29	1945	Mahan	DD-364	1944
Barton	DD-599	1942	Manneri L. Abele	DD-733	1945
Beatty	DD-460	1943	McKean	DD-90, APD-5	1943
Benham	DD-397	1942	Meredith	DD-434	1942
Blue	DD-387	1943	Meredith	DD-726	1944
Borie	DD-215	1943	Monoghan	DD-354	1944
Bristol	DD-453	1943	Monssen	DD-436	1942
Brownson	DD-518	1943	Montgomery	DD-121, DM-17	1944
Buck	DD-420	1943	Morrison	DD-560	1945
Bush	DD-529	1945	Noa	DD-343, APD-24	1944
Callaghan	DD-792	1945	O'Brien	DD-415	1942
Chevalier	DD-451	1943	Palmer	DD-161, DMS-5	1945
Calhoun	DD-801	1945	Parrott	DD-218	1944
Colhoun	DD-85, APD-2	1942	Peary	DD-226	1942
Cooper	DD-695	1944	Perkins	DD-377	1943
Corry	DD-463	1944	Perry	DD-340, DMS-17	1944
Cushing	DD-376	1942	Pillsbury, all hands lost	DD-227	1942
DeHaven	DD-469	1943	Pope	DD-225	1942
Dickerson	DD-157, APD-21	1945	Porter	DD-356	1942
Drewler	DD-741	1945	Preston	DD-379	1942
Duncan	DD-485	1942	Pringle	DD-477	1945
Edsall, all hands lost	DD-219	1942	Reid	DD-369	1944
Emmons	DD-457, DMS-22	1945	Reuben James	DD-245	1941
Gamble	DD-123, DM-15	1945	Rowan	DD-405	1943
Glennon	DD-620	1944	Sims	DD-409	1942
Gregory	DD-82, APD-3	1942	Spence	DD-512	1944
Gwin	DD-433	1943	Stewart	DD-224	1942
Halligan	DD-584	1945	Strong	DD-467	1943
Hammann	DD-412	1942	Sturtevani	DD-240	1942
Henley	DD-391	1943	Thornton	DD-270, AVD-11	1945
Hoel	DD-533	1944	Truxiun	DD-229	1942
Hovey	DD-208, DMS-11	1945	Tucker	DD-374	1942
Hull	DD-350	1944	Turner	DD-648	1944
Ingraham	DD-444	1942	Twiggs	DD-591	1945
Jacob Jones	DD-130	1942	Walke	DD-416	1942
Jarvis, all hands lost	DD-393	1942	Ward	DD-139, APD-16	1944
Johnston	DD-557	1944	Warrington	DD-388	1944
Laffey	DD-459	1942	Wasmuth	DD-388, DMS-15	1942
Landsdale	DD-426	1944	William D. Porter	DD-579	1945
Leary	DD-158	1943	Worden	DD-352	1943
Little	DD-79, APD-4	1943			
Little	DD-803	1945	Total: 88		
Long	DD-209, DMS-12	1945			
Longshaw	DD-559	1945			

APPENDIX D
USS LUCE CASUALTY LIST
Killed In Action

BIXLER, Allen Hugh, MM2/c .... Killed at Midships repair party.
Body not recovered.
CLUKEY, Daniel A., SC3/c .... Multiple injuries extreme - body transferred to VII Division Cemetery through Graves Registration Service.
CUCUIREAN, John M., F1/c .... Killed at 20mm #3. Body not recovered.
DEGNER, Virgil G., BKR2/c .... Killed at 20mm #6. Body not recovered.
DELAPP, Wesley, S1/c .... Killed at 40mm #4. Body not recovered.
DEMENCHUK, Henry Martin, F1/c .... Body identified in water. Not recovered.
DUFFY, Bernard Edward, CEM .... Killed at midships repair party.
Body not recovered.
FOULKS, Glenn, MM3/c .... Killed at midships repair party.
Body not recovered.
LYNCH, Thomas Lee, S1/c .... Killed in 5" #5. Body not recovered.
MASON, Richard G., EM3/c .... Wound fragment chest with massive hemorrhage. Forward repair. Died in wardroom.
Body not recovered.
McMILLEN, James D., S1/c .... Service No. 765 25 97. Multiple injuries extreme body. Transferred to VII Division Cemetery through Graves Registration Service.
NEWLON, Calvin E., S1/c .... Service No. 755 75 75. Multiple injuries extreme body. Transferred to VII Division Cemetery through Graves Registration Service.
O'NEILL, William A., WT3/c .... Killed by high pressure air compressor in after fireroom. Body not recovered.
PALMER, John A., HA1/c .... Killed at midships repair party.
Body not recovered.
PERKINS, James R., EM1/c .... Killed at forward repair party.
Body not recovered.
ROBINSON, Charles B., SK3/c .... Multiple injuries extreme. In 5" #3. Died aboard rescue ship LCS 84. Body transferred to U.S.S. Crescent City (APA21).
ROEDER, Delbert W., S1/c .... Killed in 5" #5. Body not recovered.
SCHANCK, David LeRoy, GM2/c .... Killed in 5" #5. Body not recovered.
STANLEY, Christian E., RM3/c .... Died aboard rescue ship LCS 84 of multiple injuries extreme. Body transferred to VII Division Cemetery through Graves Registration Service.

Missing In Action

APPICELLI, James P., CMM .... After engine room
APPLEBY, David L., CMM .... After repair party
BEEBE, Robert C., S1/c .... #4 Handling room
BELKNAP, Robert M., MM2/c .... After engine room
BRAUN, Othmer P., S1/c .... 40mm #3

BROPHY, John Joseph, FC1/c .... I.C. Room
BROWN, Robert I., RM3/c .... #3 5"
BROWN, Willie Jr., StM2/c .... Apparently uninjured. Seen on forecastle.
                                                                                        Would not abandon ship.
BUNCE, George L., TM3/c .... Starboard "K" gun
BURBANK, George H., S1/c .... #3 Handling room
CARLSON, Robert N., S1/c .... 40mm #5
CARSLEY, Norman W., S2/c .... ? Aft 5"
CASPER, Vernon E., F1/c .... After repair party
CASTLE, Vernon, S1/c .... #3 Handling room
CEBULA, Stanley J., GM3/c .... Apparently uninjured. Would not abandon ship.
CIMBALO, Michael, S1/c .... Injured on ship
CLARK, Thomas Lee, S1/c .... #3 Handling room
COLQUITT, Herbert, S1/c .... I.C. Room
CONKLIN, John, S1/c .... #4 Handling room
COX, Bobby Jr., S1/c .... Magazine
CUSHING, Lawrence, S1/c .... #4 Magazine
DARR, William A., S1/c .... #3 5"
DASSAN, Louis A., S1/c .... 40mm #3
DELILIPPIS, Nicholas, WT3/c .... Apparently uninjured. Would not abandon ship.
DODGE, Parker Bryce, MM2/c .... After engine room
DOLAN, John Michael, S1/c .... #4 5"
DYLINGOWSKI, Robert Joseph, S1/c .... 40mm #5
EHRKY, Everett O., F1/c .... 40mm #5. Clipping room
ELLINGSON, Lloyd S., S1/c .... 40mm #5
EHRART, Charles, F1/c .... #3 Magazine
FIELDS, Francis C., SSML3/c .... #5 5"
FISCHER, Walter C., CTM .... Apparently uninjured. Seen giving first aid.
FOOR, Roy H., S1/c .... #5 Handling room
FRATELLO, Frank (N), FC3/c .... I.C. Room
FREEMAN, Morris G., F1/c .... Out of after fireroom
FRIEDMAN, Sidney, F1/c .... #4 5" Handling room
GAREFFA, Bruno J., MM3/c .... After engine room
GLEDHILL, Ralph B. Jr., F1/c .... #4 5" Handling room
GOULD, Ewin, MM3/c .... After engine room
GRAFF, George E., WT2/c .... After repair party
GREATHOUSE, Thomas J., Cox .... #3 5"
HARRELL, Clyde William, TM3/c .... Port "K' Gun
HELDER, Willis R., Cox .... #3 5"
HIGGINS, Robert J., GM2/c .... 40mm #5
HILL, John M., MM2/c .... Chest injury wardroom
HOLT, David L., F1/c .... After repair party
HULINA, Thomas, S1/c .... 20mm #1
IVERSON, Raymond K., F1/c .... Unconscious or dead amidships.
JACKSON, Frank L., RdM3/c .... C.I.C.
JONES, Robert, StM2/c .... #1 Magazine
KARR, Lester Parry, BM1/c .... #3 5"
KECK, Urstle Cletus, S1/c .... Fantail depth charge
KEWER, Charles H., S1/c .... 20mm #3
KIDWELL, Vaudie W., MM3/c .... 20mm #1
KIRTS, Elmer Boyd, DGM .... #4 5"
KRUPA, Michael Marion, MaM3/c .... 20mm #3

LANGE, Floyd R., S1/c .... 20mm #1
LAURENCE, Wilfred E., S1/c .... #4 Magazine
LENTZ, William E., FC3/c .... I.C. Room
MACDONALD, Fred H., CM3/c .... 20mm #4
MACHACEK, Frank, S1/c .... #4 Magazine
MALABY, Ira Bertram, RdM2/c .... C.I.C.
MALINOWSKI, Francis A., BM2/c .... #5 5"
MALONE, John Joseph, TM2/c .... Torpedo tube #2
MATWIZCK, Leo Peter, EM2/c .... I.C. Room
McALLISTER, Hugh W. Jr., Cox .... #4 5"
McANINCH, Verian, S1/c .... 40mm #5
McGUIGAN, James Thomas, TM1/c .... Torpedo tube #2
McKAY, Dale, S1/c .... #4 5"
McKINNEY, Albert J., S1/c .... 40mm #5 Clipping room
McKENZIE, William J., QM3/c .... #3 5"
McRAE, Marion Verl, S1/c .... #1 Magazine
MERGEL, Lloyd, E., S1/c .... After repair party
METCALF, Eulus E., F1/c .... #1 Magazine
MILES, Donald Robert, S1/c ....#4 Handling room
MIMS, Ernest, StM1/c .... Apparently minor injuries. Seen alive in water.
MIXON, Joseph, S1/c .... #4 Handling room
MOE, Lealand M., EM2/c .... After engine room
MORGEL, Frank, S1/c .... After 20mm's
MURRAY, Lawrence E., SK1/c .... #3 Magazine
MURGATROYD, William George, PhM1/c .... After repair
NAPOLI, Anthony, SF1/c .... After repair
NASNER, John Peter, MM2/c .... After engine room
PERNA, Anthony Thomas, CM2/c .... After repair
POWERS, Arthur E., S1/c .... 40mm #5
PRAMICK, Stephen J., RdM3/c .... C.I.C.
RADELL, Thomas William, EM2/c .... After engine room
RACH, Harold W., S1/c .... #4 Magazine
RAMSEY, Phillip Calvin, F1/c .... #4 Handling room
RECHKEMMER, John B., F1/c .... After engine room
REDDINGTON, Thomas Francis, FC3/c .... I.C. room
ROLLER, Samuel M., S1/c .... #1 Magazine
RUNDQUIST, Vincent A., S1/c .... #4 Magazine
SCRANTON, Jack Victor, Y2/c .... #4 Handling room
SEHL, Eugene D., F1/c .... #3 Magazine
SHATTUCK, Robert L., SoM3c .... #5 40mm Director
SHELBY, Leroy, S1/c .... 40mm #5
SHERMAN, Robert H., F1/c .... #3 Magazine
SMITH, Robert M., SC3/c .... 40 mm #3 clipping room
SON, Pren Laverne, Cox .... 20mm #1
STEWART, Robert E., GM3/c .... #5 Handling room
STITT, Clarence J., S1/c .... Apparently uninjured. Would not abandon ship.
STOWE, Lawrence L., S1/c .... #1 Magazine
STUDER, Michael Joseph, BM1/c .... #4 5"
SWEENEY, Wilfred Patrick, SC2/c .... #3 5"
TEATER, Robert E., S1/c .... #4 Magazine
THOMPSON, Robert W., S1/c .... #5 5"
THOMPSON, Wilkie E., S1/c .... 40mm #5 clipping room

THURLOW, Maynard, S1/c(TM)	40mm #5 clipping room
TIBBS, Charles A., Cox	#3 5"
TIER, George M., MM1/c	After engine room
TREBINO, Francis G., MM3/c	#3 Handling room
TREMBACH, John Peter, S1/c	20mm #5
VAHEY, John Albert, FC3/c	I.C. Room
VALL, Harold, S1/c	#2 Magazine
WANNOWSKY, Max, RT1/c	Apparently uninjured. Would not abandon ship.
WICKENS, John Reed, MM1/c	After repair
WIERS, Arthur, S1/c	#3 Handling room
WINDNAGLE, Robert I., EM3/c	After engine room
WIRE, Oliver Paul, GM2/c	#3 5"
ZEISNER, Herbert L., S2/c	40mm #3
ZWICK, Paul J., MM2/c	After engine room. Seen dead on deck.

Officers	*Location*
HOPLEY, Thomas (N), Lieut.(jg)	C.I.C.
HUTCHINSON, John H., Lieut.	C.I.C.
MacDONALD, Richard, Ensign	I.C. Room
MURRAY, Robert, Lieut.(jg) (Temporary duty fighter director)	C.I.C.
PEARCE, Robert Lincoln, Ensign (Temporary duty fighter director)	C.I.C.
SHRECK, Morris L., Ensign	After repair
WATERS, Hoyett A., Machinist	Seen dead by one CPO on starboard quarterdeck.
WINTER, Paul Anson, Lieut.(jg)	I.C. Room

Wounded In Action

Diagnosis/Prognosis/Disposition

ADAMS, Arthur W., S1/c	Fracture - simple pelvis/favorable/USS *Mercy*
BALLANTINE, B2/c	Burns - Head, arms, trunk/serious/USS *Mercy*
BILLE, Joseph J., RT2/c	Blast concussion water, abdomen/favorable/USS *Mercy*
BORACK, John F., Rkr3/c	Blast concussion water, abdomen/serious/USS *Mercy*
BOULEY, Charles R., PhM3/c	Blast concussion water, abdomen/favorable/USS *Mercy*
BROWN, Robert F., F1/c	Blast concussion water, abdomen/favorable/USS *Mercy*
BUCKNER, Robert I., TM2/c	Blast concussion water, abdomen/favorable/USS *Mercy*
BURLINGAME, Richard, WT1/c	Burns-entire body/serious/USS *Mercy*
CARPENTER, Ernest L., WT2/c	Burns-face, arms/favorable/USS *Mercy*
CHARRON, Richard A., Gm3/c	Burns-head, arms, trunk/serious/USS *Mercy*
CLARK, Jasper L., GM2/c	Blast concussion water, abdomen/favorable/USS *Mercy*
CLARK, Harry E., S1/c	Fracture-compound r. leg/serious/USS *Mercy*
COLECOM, Richard A., MM3/c	Blast concussion water, abdomen/favorable/USS *Mercy*
COLEMAN, Russel P., S1/c	Burns-head, arms, trunk/serious/USS *Mercy*
DeFRANK, Anthony, WT3/c	Burns-head, arms, trunk/serious/USS *Mercy*
DOWNS, Vernon Carrol, S2/c	Blast concussion water, abdomen/serious/USS *Mercy*
ELDER, Lawrence A., QM3/c	Wound, fragment r. leg/favorable/Unknown
FINDLEY, James Elmer, S1/c	Blast concussion water, abdomen/favorable/USS *Mercy*
FOLAND, Norman, MoMM2/c	Wound, fragment both legs/favorable/USS *Mercy*
GOLOSINSKI, Alex J., MM2/c	Wound, fragment both legs/favorable/USS *Mercy*
HALL, Lewis Buell, S1/c	Burns-head, arms/serious/USS *Mercy*
HALL, Louis Phillip, S1/c	Blast, abdomen/favorable/USS *Mercy*
HOLT, Raymond D., S1/c	/favorable/USS *Mercy*
HILES, Orville L., S1/c	Burns-face, arms, legs/favorable/USS *Mercy*
HOPPE, Floyd G., M1/c	Blast concussion water, abdomen/favorable/USS *Karnes*

HUBBARD, Melvin E., TM1/c .... Wound, fragment left arm/favorable/USS *Mercy*
HUMPHREY, Grover D., S1/c .... Blast concussion water, abdomen/favorable/USS *Mercy*
JACOBS, Alexander, S1/c .... Burns-head, arms, trunk/serious/USS *Mercy*
JOHNSON, C.R., Cox .... Blast concussion water, abdomen/serious/USS *Mercy*
KEIFER, Charles K., S1/c .... Fracture compound-r. arm & leg/favorable/USS *Mercy*
LAKE, John Charles, S1/c .... Burns-head, arms, trunk/serious/USS *Mercy*
LAWTON, Wayne J., RT1/c .... Blast concussion, abdomen/serious/Unknown
LeBRUN, Richard, SM3/c .... Fracture compound, l. leg/serious/USS *Mercy*
LEONE, Joseph P., S1/c .... Blast concussion/favorable/USS *Mercy*
LIETZ, William V., TM2/c .... Wound fragment, r. leg/favorable/USS *Mercy*
MARCHITELLI, Anthony A., GM3/c .... Wound in groin & neck/favorable/USS *Mercy*
MASSARO, Ralph M., S1/c .... Blast concussion water, abdomen/favorable/USS *Mercy*
MANTZ, Henry, S2/c .... Blast abdomen/favorable/USS *Mercy*
McEACHERN, Allen Charles, SoM1/c ... Blast concussion, abdomen/serious (died)/USS *Mercy*
McFARLAND, Burr Knight, WT1/c .... Fracture compound, l. leg/serious/USS *Mercy*
MEDERIOS, Manuel, F1/c .... Burns-head, arms/serious/USS *Mercy*
MONTIGNEY, Ralph B., S1/c .... Burns-face/favorable/USS *Mercy*
OLSEN, Cyril Theodore, F2/c .... Fracture compound, both legs/favorable/USS *Mercy*
PHILLIPS, Freeman, S1/c .... Blast concussion, shrapnel wounds/serious/USS *Mercy*
PHILLIPS, James Clemit, SC1/c .... Wounds fragment, both legs/favorable/USS *Mercy*
RAMOZ, Israel Alvarez, S1/c .... Fracture, simple ribs/favorable/USS *Mercy*
SCHNEIDER, Richard, MM1/c .... Blast abdomen/favorable/USS *Mercy*
SLATER, Raymond W., S1/c .... Blast abdomen/favorable/USS *Mercy*
STRAND, Thomas Eddison, B3/c .... Blast abdomen/serious/USS *Lauderdale*
TENNANT, Floyd B., S2/c .... Burns-head, face, trunk/serious/USS *Mercy*
TORONTO, Michael Vincent, MM3/c .... Blast abdomen/serious/USS *Karnes*
UCIC, Louis J., CCS .... Blast abdomen/serious/USS *Mercy*
WALLACE, Paul LaVerne, S1/c .... Burns-head, face, trunk/serious/USS *Mercy*
WATSON, Conrad, S2/c .... Blast concussion, abdomen/serious/USS *Lauderdale*
WEICE, Shirley, MM2/c .... Blast concussion, abdomen/serious/USS *Mercy*
WELLS, Rudolph Riley, S2/c .... Blast concussion, abdomen/favorable/USS *Mercy*
YOUNG, Joseph, S1/c .... Blast concussion, abdomen/favorable/USS *Karnes*

Minor wounded not requiring hospitalization. Treated aboard U.S.S. Lauderdale (APA179) and returned to duty.

Name Rate-Service No. *Diagnosis/Remarks*
BENARD, George, S1/c-807 29 71 .... Blast concussion water, abdomen/Rest
BERNIER, Roger F., F1/c-822 96 60 .... Blast concussion water, abdomen/Rx: aspirin
BERTHIAUME, Lionel, S1/c-806 75 04 .... Wound, fragment r. leg/Rx: Tet. Bstr. dressing
BLANCK, Thomas G., Y1/c-626 02 32 .... Wound, fragment l. leg/Rx: Tet. Bstr. dressing
CONARD, Wilbern E., S1/c-829 43 99 .... Blast concussion water, abdomen/Melena - Rx: rest
DOAUST, Arthur E., SM2/c-801 54 00 .... Wound, fragment l. leg/Rx: Tet. Bstr. dressing
DELLAVENTURA, James, WT3/c-645 35 79 .... Blast concussion water, abdomen/Rest
DERAGNON, Eugene L., S1/c-573 19 30 .... Burns, flesh, eyes & lids/Rx: Min. oil
FOTIE, William R., RM3/c-628 81 10 .... Blast concussion water, abdomen/Rest
FRITZ, Ira J., S2/c-829 91 30 .... Blast concussion water, abdomen/Rest
GORY, James M., WT3/c-721 95 93 .... Blast concussion water, abdomen/Rest
GRANGER, Andrew A., St3/c-274 43 44 .... Blast concussion water, abdomen/Rest
GRAUL, George V., WT2/c-202 00 33 .... Cunjunctivitis, fuel oil/Rx: Dressing

INTERLANDE, Alexander, S1/c-825 15 36 .... Wound, fragment leg/Rx: Dressing
JACKSON, Joe H., SF3/c-615 55 27 .... Wound, fragment back & leg/
　　　　　　　　　　　　　　　　　　　　　　　　　　　　　　Rx: Removed USS *Karnes* Dressing
MAXWELL, James R., S2/c-565 68 00 .... Wound, fragment back/Rx: Dressing
MECKEL, Robert H., S1/c-923 00 33 .... Abrasions face & leg
MILLER, Peter F., S1/c-564 19 88 .... Blast concussion/Rest
MURZYCKI, Frank J., RdM3/c-801 50 86 .... Blast concussion water, abdomen/Melena - rest
NYHOLT, Martin J., FC2/c-726 12 07 .... Conjunctivitis fuel oil/Cleansing
PIZANOWSKI, Walter T., S1/c-810 79 36 .... Concussion; l. leg
PRICE, Helmut T., S1/c-883 16 55 .... Blast concussion water, abdomen/
　　　　　　　　　　　　　　　　　　　　　　　　　　　　　　Observation in sick bay 2 days.
ROANE, William T., BM2/c-266 23 26 .... Blast concussion water, abdomen/Rest
THOMAS, Willie Bee, Ck2/c-269 16 75 .... Blast concussion water, abdomen/Rest
VANNESS, Clarence J., MM2/c-300 98 12 .... Conjunctivitis, fuel oil/Cleansing
WYNNE, Frank J., S1/c-708 47 24 .... Blast concussion water, abdomen/Rest
YOUNG, Walter G., EM1/c-295 97 04 .... Burns, blast eyes/Mineral oil
ZEIGMAN, Leonard A., WT1/c-311 28 64 ... Burns, second degree hands/Rx: Tet. Bstr. dressing
ZODL, Robert J., Cox-646 57 14 .... Wound, fragment scalp/Rx: dressing

Officers

HEMPSTEAD, Emerson P., Lt.-196 982 .... Abrasion l. arm/Rx: dressing
HEUCK, Kenneth, Lt.-161 206 .... Wound, fragment l. mid-finger/Rx: dressing - sulfadiagine
LIES, Mark J., Lt.(jg)-227 201 .... Contusion l. eye
MEDLIN, Tandy S., Lt.-214 357 .... Blast concussion water, abdomen/
　　　　　　　　　　　　　　　　　　　　　　　　　　　　　　Melena - 2 days rest in sick bay
RUNNESTRAND, Maurice N., Lt.(jg)-187 488 .... Blast concussion water, abdomen/
　　　　　　　　　　　　　　　　　　　　　　　　　　　　　　Melena - 2 days rest in sick bay
SNYDER, Harry E., Lt.(jg)-283 195 .... Blast concussion water, abdomen/
　　　　　　　　　　　　　　　　　　　　　　　　　　　　　　Melena - 2 days rest in sick bay
SCUDDER, Frank E., Ensign-373 800 .... Sprain, back/Rest 2 days in sick bay
WATERHOUSE, Jacob W., Comdr.-62529 .... Blast concussion water, abdomen/Melena - rest

Summary

	Officers	Men	Total
Killed in action		19	19
Wounded in action		57	57
Missing in action	8	122	130
Total Major Casualties	8	198	206
Minor wounded	8	29	37
Total all casualties	16	227	243
Uninjured survivors	7	85	92
Total complement	23	312	335

Appendix E

About The Author

Ron (Ronald C.) Surels, although serving time in the US Air Force during the Korean War, has a family Naval tradition going back to the early days of our country. He has traveled in Europe and the central Pacific and has visited several World War II battle sites. He has been a minister for some fifteen years, including time spent on the island of Kwajalein in the Marshall Islands as a chaplain. He has been an educator, helping to start several Christian schools. Holding a Ph.D., he also does some college teaching. His favorite hobby is reading and researching American military history. Married with three grown children, Ron lives with his wife Lynne in rural New Hampshire.

The crewman shown standing guard in the back picture of the dust jacket is believed to be SC3/c Daniel A. Clukey as identified by relatives.

BIBLIOGRAPHY

Blanton, Earl, Boston To Jacksonville: 41,000 Miles By Sea. Seaford, Virginia: Goose Creek Publications, 1991.

_____ , Dictionary Of American Naval Fighting Ships, Vol. IV. Washington, D.C.: Navy Department, 1969.

Morison, Samuel Eliot, The Two-Ocean War. Boston Mass.: Little, Brown and Company, 1963.

Naval Historical Center, War Diary USS *Luce* DD 522, January 1944 - February 1945. Washington, D.C.

Nimitz, Admiral Chester W. and Potter, E.B., The Great Sea War. Englewood Cliffs, New Jersey: Prentice Hall, Inc., 1960.

_____ , War Diary and Action Reports-USS *Luce*, DD 522. Washington, D.C.: Operational Archives Branch, Naval Historical Center, Washington Navy Yard.

Periodical:
Pinkowski, Edward, "The *Lady Luce*." Our Navy, Mid-December, 1946, 60-61.

Tapes and Letters:
All original tape recordings and letters upon which this book is based are in the possession of the author. Having been accepted as Navy history, copies of the tapes and book are filed with the Operational Archives Branch of the Naval Historical Center, Washington Navy Yard, Washington, D.C.

INDEX

Those listed in the casualty list do not appear in this index.
The casualty list is in Appendix D on page 198.

A

Aaron Ward 101
Abbruzzese, Robert 112
Adak 20, 23, 24, 28, 30, 31, 32, 33, 36,
48, 49, 51, 52, 53, 54, 55, 61, 63, 64, 65
Ageton, Arthur 69, 72, 74
Alabama 181
Allen, Donald B 4, 56, 59, 89, 95, 183
Alshain 75
Alton, Bert D .. 20, 23, 31, 39, 53, 59, 64, 183
Appalachian 84
Appicelli, James 150, 176
Appicelli, Margaret 176
Attu 2, 31, 39, 41, 42, 48, 49,
50, 51, 52, 54, 56, 58
Austin 53

B

Badger 12, 39, 43, 53, 54, 74, 81, 88, 188
Ballantine, Peter 168
Baxter 99
Beausoliel, Armond 4, 137, 138
Beaver 22, 23, 24
Bering Sea 23, 31, 33, 43, 63
Bernier, Roger 54, 146
Berthiaume, Lionel 103
Bille, Joseph J 64, 112, 117, 147,
153, 158, 170, 171, 183
Biscayne 94
Bixler, Allen 176
Blanck, Thomas G 103, 109, 114, 116,
118, 127, 140, 159, 183
Blanton, Earl 118, 121, 129, 130,
168, 183, 205
Blondin, Robert 128, 150
Borgen Bay 77
Bouley, Charles R 131
Brandt, Helen 175, 181
Bremerton 15, 21
Brockhoff, Donald 29, 183
Brown, Willie Jr 155
Burlingame, Richard A 54, 168, 183
Burns, Romaine 176
Burns, William 16, 17, 31, 106, 176, 183

C

Carpenter, Ernest 135, 149, 156, 157,
158, 164, 184
Carpenter, John 140, 141, 145, 158, 184
Casco Bay 11
Case 88, 89

Cathey, Milton L 82, 184
Cavalier 75
Clark, Harry 17
Coleman, Russell 152, 159, 162
Corsairs 110, 127, 159, 160, 165

D

Doaust, Arthur 161
Day, John 54
DeFlorio, Joan 181
DeFrank, Anthony Jr 157, 184
Degner, Virgil 52, 62, 124, 130, 133
Delaney, Marilyn 181
DESRON 49 ..... 39, 56, 61, 63, 65, 78, 79, 95
Doherty 53
Downs, Betty 123
Downs, Vernon C 123, 128, 184
Dutch Harbor 25, 26, 27, 28, 31,
36, 55, 56, 169

E

El Dorado 94
Emond, Omer 85, 96, 103, 115, 116, 119,
127, 152, 159, 162, 184
Eniwetok Atoll 70
Enterprise 15
Erbin 161
Estes 94

F

Fischer, Walter C 106, 133, 137, 144, 174
Flaum, Maryann 44, 143
Flaum, Richard F 44, 107, 109, 120,
142, 143, 184
Fletcher, Frank J 51, 52
Foland, Norman 112, 114, 123, 124, 130,
134, 154, 173, 177, 181, 184
Fotie, Fern 178
Fotie, William 11, 30, 37, 39, 47, 52, 55,
64, 71, 72, 76, 83, 85, 99, 132, 133, 144,
152, 163, 164, 171, 173, 178, 179, 180, 184
Foulks, Glen 132
Fratello, Frank 117
Freeman, Hershel 140, 141, 184

G

Gallipoli, Lorraine 175, 180, 181
Gallipoli, Marilyn 181
Gareffa, Bruno 136, 138, 148
Gory, James M 54, 184
Graul, George V 141, 158
Great Sitkin Island 49, 59, 60

Greco, Leo 14, 54, 116, 121, 131, 145, 153, 185
Guantanamo 5, 8

H

Hagan, G.T. 54
Hall, Lewis 152, 163
Hammerhead Hank's 56
Harrison, Robert 6, 7, 13, 24, 26, 27, 33, 35, 53, 57, 86, 131, 132, 149, 156, 159, 163, 173, 178, 185
Hempstead, Emerson 144, 176
Heon, Michael 131, 146, 185
Heuck, Ken 124
Hiles, Orville 55, 60, 70, 73, 75, 84, 98, 106, 133, 145, 152, 164, 170, 179, 180, 185
Hill, John M 135, 136
Honolulu 74
Hopley, Thomas 146
Hubbard, Melvin 136, 148
Huss, Joseph Jr 112, 149, 176
Hutchinson, John 108, 146, 147

I

Interlande, Alexander 152, 153, 163
Intrepid 11
Iowa 71
Isherwood 39, 61

J

Jacobs, Alexander 168
Japanese Aviators 98
Johnson, Waino 49, 65, 83, 97, 116, 118, 185
Jones, Bob 156
Jones, Clifford C 4, 5, 8, 51, 80, 95, 103, 104, 108, 109, 111, 112, 114, 120, 124, 128, 147, 157, 158, 160, 171, 185

K

Karama–Retto 165
Karnes 170, 171, 173
Keck, Urstle 12, 120
Kidd 179, 180
Kimberly 39, 43
Kiska 55
Kuluk Bay 49
Kurabu Zaki 41, 43, 46, 192
Kurile Islands 39, 51, 57, 192

L

Lake, John C 103
Lauderdale 170, 173
Lawton, Wayne 24, 152
LCS.... 117, 118, 121, 129, 151, 163, 166, 183
LeBlond, Joe 62
LeBrun, Richard 120, 123, 125, 131, 134, 153, 154, 162, 168, 169, 170

Leyte 62, 70, 73, 74, 75, 77, 83, 84, 85, 89, 94, 192
Lietz, William V 5, 36, 45, 79, 99, 109, 110, 115, 118, 120, 125, 130, 185
Lingayen 78, 79, 80, 192
Long 75
LSM 129, 151, 168
Lynch, Thomas 23, 24, 41, 44, 49, 185

M

Malinowski, Francis 134
Malinowski, Francis Jr 177
Malone, John J 110, 111, 137
Manus 70, 75, 77, 171, 183
Marchitelli, Anthony 115, 116, 118, 121, 137, 148, 151, 155, 159, 168, 186
Markab 20, 21, 22
Marks, Kenny 114
Martin, Anthony F 178, 186
Mason, R.G. 136
Massacre Bay 39, 48, 49, 50, 54
Matisak, Thomas 4, 95, 111, 112, 146, 156, 159, 160, 163, 180, 181, 186
Matsua 57, 192
McCormick, John 161
McEachern, Allen 170
McFarland, Burr 22, 65, 78, 84, 132, 144, 145, 150, 153, 169, 179, 185
McGuigan, James 110, 111, 130, 131
McGuigan, Joseph 35, 89, 118, 131, 157, 160, 180, 186
McKay, D. 133
Medeiros, Manuel 146, 162, 186
Mercy 168, 169, 170, 179
Miller, Russell 5
Mims, Ernest 157
Mindanao 64, 83, 183
mine field 42, 43
Missouri 71
Moll, Derry O 22, 114, 133, 141, 142, 154, 161, 186
Morrison 161, 179
Moyer, Robert F 15, 16, 44, 80, 105, 109, 113, 117, 125, 127, 152, 186
Murgatroyd, William C 27
Murzycki, John F 146

N

Napoli, Anthony 8, 9
New Guinea 2, 68, 75, 76, 77, 78
New Jersey 71
Nyholt, Martin J 25, 28, 31, 41, 44, 45, 46, 50, 57, 58, 59, 63, 80, 100, 107, 108, 113, 115, 117, 125, 126, 127, 142, 152, 159, 165, 184, 186

O

Okhotsk Sea 50, 51
Olsen, Cyril T 120, 125, 134, 179

O'Neill, William 135
Oro Bay 75, 76
Otomaye Wan 46, 47
Owens, Hinton A 17, 18, 43, 51, 54,
60, 65, 80, 88, 187, 192

P

Palmer 75
Panama 2, 13, 14
Panama Canal 2, 13
Paramushiro 39, 41, 43, 48, 50, 51, 58, 63
Parkerson, Tom 59, 62, 65, 69, 72, 83, 86,
97, 99, 149, 157, 165, 178, 187
Pearl Harbor 2, 15, 16, 17, 23, 32,
68, 69, 88, 89
Perdue, Gerald 132, 187
Phillips, Freeman 7, 15, 32, 33, 34,
35, 36, 43, 53, 54, 58, 70, 71, 73, 74, 76,
79, 81, 82, 85, 86, 89, 98, 99, 101, 102,
110, 111, 112, 116, 119, 120, 123, 125,
127, 131, 140, 145, 155, 156, 157,
159, 160, 164, 168, 187
Phillips, James C 4, 6, 11, 13, 15, 18,
22, 26, 27, 28, 30, 34, 52, 58, 62, 65,
71, 73, 77, 81, 99, 108, 110, 112,
119, 122, 124, 125, 130, 133, 134,
137, 153, 154, 162, 177, 179, 181, 187
Picking 21, 39, 62
Pierce, Alvah N 4, 5, 22, 94
Point Bolo 107, 151, 182
Porter 39, 60
Powers, Arthur 49, 99, 157, 175, 180, 181
Powers, Harold 176
Powers, James 180
Powers, Joseph 175, 180
Pramick, Stephen 99, 180
Preble 75
President Hayes 75
prisoner 97, 98, 99, 100, 129
PT boats 57, 58

R

Raleigh 39
Rechkemmer, John 78, 79, 150
Replogle, Arthur S 78, 84, 85, 126, 140,
149, 156, 157, 159, 160, 187
Rhule, Len 109
Richmond 23, 26, 39, 47, 52
Ries, James 117
Roberts, Clifford A 45, 57, 80, 187
Rogers, M.L. 63, 86, 87, 88

S

San Diego 13, 14, 15, 144, 178, 179
San Francisco 63, 64, 65, 68, 97, 170, 172
Sand Bay 34, 49, 60, 61
Scanlon, Ethel 180, 181
Schneider, Richard 136, 156

Scudder, Frank E 94, 147, 155, 159,
170, 173, 188
Seadler Harbor 70, 74, 77, 78
Shaffner, Dr. Louis 9, 36, 48, 52, 61,
84, 105, 135, 136, 144, 148,
155, 156, 163, 171, 188
shark 160, 161, 169
Sitkin Bay 61
Snyder, Harry E 24, 150, 153, 188
Son, Pren 87, 88
Spitting Incident 62
Sproston 23, 39, 53
Squaws Along The Yukon 54
Stanley, Christian E 152, 163
Stanley, Robert E 112, 114, 115, 116, 118,
146, 155, 171, 173, 188
Stembel 75
Sturm, Kenneth ... 7, 110, 130, 131, 156, 188
Sweeper's Cove 48, 54, 63
Sweeten, Donald 57, 188

T

Tacloban 85, 86
Tennessee 76
Thurban 75
Topor, Joe 159
Tremback, John 120
Trinidad 11, 12

V

Valery Checkhov 31, 34
Van Uitert, LeGrand G 98, 188
Vanness, Clarence J 14, 37, 132, 143, 188
Varian, Donald C 3, 4, 5, 14, 17, 18,
188, 192

W

Wallace, Paul L 108, 121, 136, 148,
149, 163, 179, 189
Wannowsky, Max 149, 156
War Hawk 83
Waterhouse, Jacob 88, 89, 102,
104, 108, 112, 113, 114, 126,
139, 149, 161, 189, 192
Welsh, John R 4, 17, 60, 64, 69, 70, 72,
83, 85, 89, 96, 97, 104, 114, 116,
119, 127, 128, 139, 152, 155, 163, 189
White, Cracus J 44
Whitney, Art 54, 125, 170, 189
Wickes 39
Wiley 162
Wisniewski, Joe 36, 48

Y

Young 39, 53

Z

Zwick, Paul 125